THE BLUES
A VISUAL HISTORY

THE BLUES

A VISUAL HISTORY

★ 100 YEARS OF MUSIC THAT CHANGED THE WORLD ★

MIKE EVANS

CONSULTING EDITOR ROBERT GORDON

STERLING

STERLING
New York

An Imprint of Sterling Publishing
387 Park Avenue South
New York, NY 10016

Editorial director Will Steeds
Senior editor Laura Ward
Project manager Alison Candlin
Book and cover design Paul Palmer-Edwards, Grade Design, London
Copy editor Kristi Hein
Picture research Sally Claxton
Profile illustrations Robert Littleford
Index Christine Shuttleworth
Reproduction Pixel Colour Imaging Ltd

ISBN 978-1-4549-1253-8

Distributed in Canada by Sterling Publishing c/o Canadian Manda Group, 165 Dufferin Street, Toronto, Ontario, Canada M6K 3H6

For information about custom editions, special sales, and premium and corporate purchases,
please contact Sterling Special Sales at 800-805-5489 or specialsales@sterlingpublishing.com.

Manufactured in China

2 4 6 8 10 9 7 5 3 1

CONTENTS

FOREWORD

I was eight years old when my father and uncle started Chess Records. With artists like Muddy Waters, Howlin' Wolf, Sonny Boy Williamson, and Little Walter Jacobs, Chess soon became the epicenter of blues in Chicago. As I grew older I realized that not only were these great artists amazing musicians that were creating a world changing beat that would inspire the birth of rock and roll, they were also poets. Aside from making you dance and tap your feet, the words of many early blues songs were street poetry. They described the life experiences of the nearly two million black people that had come up from the south to the northern cities—Chicago, Detroit, St Louis—to have a better life.

The blues grew to become a great American art form that has influenced gospel, jazz, soul, R&B, and hip-hop music, but most importantly the blues became the foundation of rock and roll ... truly the music that most changed the world. The great blues songwriter and musician Willie Dixon summed it up perfectly when he said, "The blues are the roots and the other musics are the fruits. Without the roots you have no fruits so it's better keeping the roots alive because it means better fruits from now on."

The history of the blues is traced in the pages that follow in many words and a multitude of pictures. It will take you on a journey from the humble beginnings of the blues over a century ago, to the performers of today, who are constantly breaking new ground while carrying on the traditions of the blues.

Marshall Chess

Marshall Chess

OPPOSITE:
Marshall Chess, son and nephew of Chess Records founders Leonard and Phil Chess, pictured at his desk during the 1970s.

CHESS
RECORD CORP.

Arc Music
8393

Vocal
B.M.I.

GOT MY MOJO WORKING
(M. Morganfield)
MUDDY WATERS
1652
MANUFACTURED BY CHESS RECORDS CORP., CHICAGO, ILL.

INTRODUCTION

As a teenager in 1950s Britain, the first blues I was aware of was promoted as a branch of American folk music, which was enjoying a new-found popularity at the time. Josh White and Big Bill Broonzy were the most prominent blues artists in the UK, playing concerts from early in the decade. They were venerated by earnest young men and women seeking "authentic" music in contrast to the perceived vulgarity of commercial pop music—and burgeoning rock 'n' roll in particular.

Like thousands of others, my own interest was prompted not as a zealous folk enthusiast, but by the hugely popular "skiffle" records of Lonnie Donegan that introduced a generation to the folksongs of Lead Belly and Woody Guthrie, as well as the blues of Leroy Carr and others. In response to this new interest, the record companies—as in America's simultaneous folk revival—began issuing the work of hundreds of blues musicians that had previously only seen the light of day in America, on single-disc shellac 78s going as far back as the 1920s.

Suddenly a treasure trove of blues from every era was opening up, and it soon became apparent that the background of many of these singers and musicians wasn't necessarily in the cotton fields of the Deep South—which the mythology of the folk revival had had us believe—but as often in the neon-lit clublands of the big cities. In America, rhythm and blues had emerged over the previous decade or so, with its honking saxophones and electric guitars having much in common with its precocious offspring rock 'n' roll, which perhaps explained the anathema it aroused in so-called blues purists.

By the early 1960s, R&B was the hip religion, with the likes of Muddy Waters, John Lee Hooker, and Ray Charles its high priests. And in the words of Keith Richards, we had the "tablets of stone"—the basic articles of faith, etched in shiny black vinyl.

Since then the influence of the blues has been felt in every aspect of contemporary music, from soul to hip-hop, alternative rock to straight pop. But that is nothing new. From the beginning of the 20th century, the blues—music that originated exclusively in the poorest section of American society, the black communities of the rural South—has infiltrated and inspired jazz, swing, country, and almost every other area of popular music, leaving its indelible mark on the soundtrack of our times.

The fortunes of blues musicians have ebbed and flowed over the decades, from obscurity to celebrity (and sometimes back again), through revivals and renaissance, at the mercy of the vagaries of commerce and fashion. Our book traces their story, and the story of their music, with the aid of historical record, visual documentation, and the words of the blues men and women themselves.

Today the blues is a vibrant genre in its own right, while continuing to inform the broader musical landscape at every level, but what is the key to its longevity and seemingly universal application? There's the fundamental melancholy sound of the blues of course, the sheer emotional impact that tugs at your soul, that's impossible to explain in just a straightforward technical description of flatted notes and so on—as Louis Armstrong famously said about jazz "If you have to ask what it is, you'll never know." The same is true of the blues.

But despite its seeming simplicity, at its most basic a music that can be created with a single-string instrument or even an improvised jug, the blues—uniquely born out of the African-American experience, with its roots in the dark days of slavery—has managed to touch the sensibilities of humanity around the globe. As the music of the artists in these pages testifies, along with countless more too numerous to mention, the world would be a lesser place without it.

Mike Evans

POLITICAL MAP OF THE UNITED STATES.

DESIGNED TO EXHIBIT
THE COMPARATIVE AREA OF THE FREE AND SLAVE STATES,
AND THE TERRITORY OPEN TO SLAVERY OR FREEDOM BY THE REPEAL OF THE MISSOURI COMPROMISE.
With a Comparison of the Principal Statistics of the Free and Slave States, from the Census of 1850.

NEW YORK: Published by WM. C. REYNOLDS, No. 195 Broadway, and J. C. JONES, No. 1 Pine Street.

PLANTATION SONGS

ELI SHEPPERD

ROOTS OF THE BLUES

Blues music has its roots in Africa, in the sounds that traveled the slave ships and that evolved during the black peoples' struggle in America. The roots of the blues reach deep into the age of slavery in the United States and into the years that immediately followed, the Emancipation. Beginning in the seventeenth century and extending well into the nineteenth century, the unaccompanied vocal music and call-and-response singing that slaves brought from West Africa meshed with a variety of other elements—including European church music, popular minstrel songs, and ragtime music—to create this new sound that came to be known as the blues.

Not surprisingly, given the reason for the slave trade, the vocal music ancestry of Black America is firmly rooted in the workplace. It was no accident that the call-and-response format of traditional African agricultural songs persisted in the fields and levee camps across the Deep South, and—as the burgeoning black population gradually converted to Christianity—in the churches, which often offered the only respite from toil.

The hundreds of thousands of Africans transported to the United States as slaves came from an almost exclusively oral culture, and once in bondage, they were given little encouragement or opportunity to learn to read and write. Indeed, illiteracy was endemic among generations of black Americans in the South, up to the middle of the twentieth century. As a consequence, slaves themselves left no written record of any African-American songs that evolved before the abolition of slavery in 1865; the earliest formal collection of any kind, *Slave Songs of the United States*, was published in 1867. The first publication of African-American folk music of any kind, it featured spirituals (and a few secular songs) transcribed by three Northern abolitionists, William Francis Allen, Lucy McKim Garrison, and Charles Pickard Ware.

Many of the earliest pre-Emancipation songs were thought to have their origins in Africa, at first as a reminder of home, and for later generations as a bonding factor, strengthened by their use to help lighten their shared labor in the fields. The first slaves were encouraged to use drums to keep up the rhythm and pace of their work, but this was later banned when their overseers feared the slaves might use the instruments to secretly communicate and incite rebellion. With drums forbidden, the slaves developed work songs or chants, with the leader of a slave group calling the chant and the rest repeating the phrase or answering in response.

Similarly, the early instrumentation of the blues had its roots in African music making. The banjo was key in the music's genesis, although by the time of the first rural blues recordings of the 1920s it had been supplanted by the guitar. Various instruments of West African origin, such as the *kora*, have a skin head and strings and are primitive ancestors of the banjo. Likewise, the African drum tradition represented a rhythmic element in black American music from its earliest days. And in the twenty-first century the diddley bow can still be found played in the rural South. This homemade instrument of Ghanaian origin features one string stretched across a board; the pitch is changed by moving a slide.

OPPOSITE, TOP LEFT:
Five generations of a slave family on Smith's Plantation in Beaufort, South Carolina.

OPPOSITE, TOP RIGHT:
An example of a home-made "diddley bow," an instrument still found in the rural South.

OPPOSITE, BOTTOM RIGHT:
From the archives of the Library of Congress, an African American known as "Happy John" playing the banjo, photographed c.1897.

OPPOSITE, BOTTOM LEFT:
William Francis Allen (far left) who tirelessly campaigned for the abolition of slavery, pictured with his family.

WHAT IS THE BLUES?

On a purely technical level, the most common form of vocal blues is the twelve-bar verse with the first two of three lines repeated. For instrumentalists, a basic three chords move from the tonic chord to the subdominant and on to the dominant, ending on the tonic (in the key of F this is F–Bflat–C–F). Other common blues chord progressions include eight-bar (as in Leroy Carr's "How Long Blues"), and sixteen-bar (Willie Dixon's "Hoochie Coochie Man"). Melodically the blues is always characterized by the flatted 3rd, 5th, and 7th of the major scale, the so-called "blue notes." But the blues has always been much more than just notes on a page or the number of lines in a verse. The place of the music in the cultural history of black America is crucial, and, as in all great art, the emotional resonance of the blues is far more significant than its formal structure.

" The blues came from the man farthest down. The blues came from nothingness, from want, from desire. And when a man sang or played the blues, a small part of the want was satisfied from the music. The blues go back to slavery, to longing. My father, who was a preacher, used to cry every time he heard someone sing 'I'll See You On Judgement Day.' When I asked him why, he said 'That's the song they sang when your uncle was sold into slavery in Arkansas. He wouldn't let his masters beat him, so they got rid of him the way they would a mule.' "
W.C. HANDY

" You know there's only one blues though. That's the regular twelve-bar pattern and then you interpret over that. Just write new words or improvise different and you've got a new blues. Now, you take a piece like 'St. Louis Blues.' That's a pretty tune and it has kind of a bluesy tone, but that's not the blues. You can't dress up the blues. The only blues is the kind that I sing and the kind that Jimmy Rushing sings and Basie plays. I'm not saying that 'St Louis Blues' isn't fine music, you understand. But it just isn't blues. "
T-BONE WALKER

" See, my blues is not as easy to play as some people think they are. 'Cause here, this is it. I may have thirteen beats in some song, and the average man, he not used to that kind of thing. He got to follow me, not himself, because I make the blues different. Do that change thing when I change, just the way I feel, that's the way it went. I mean, you take that song 'Just To Be With You.' Now

that's a good blues tune, and I made it just the way I felt, sometimes I play thirteen, sometimes I play fourteen beats. And I got just about as good time in the blues as anyone. "
MUDDY WATERS

" Maybe our forefathers couldn't keep their language together when they were taken away, but this—the blues—was a language we invented to let people know that we had something to say. And we've been saying it pretty strongly ever since. "
B.B. KING, Lagos University, Nigeria, 1973

" The Northern honky-tonk blues is a blues you can dance to; the Southern down-home blues, that is the blues that tells of the trouble you had, of the troubles the player heard, of the troubles about people they love and hate. All the blues have a meaning of problems, like 'I left my baby and my baby left me.' The blues have come a long way, if you go back to our people coming from Africa. Blues is here today, and blues is here to stay, you know what I'm sayin'? "
LYNWOOD PERRY, guitar mentor to Taj Mahal

" And now, at this time we would like to do something that we're sure that each and everybody can understand, and that's the blues ... *everybody* can understand the blues! "
RAY CHARLES, Newport Jazz Festival, July 5, 1958

ABOVE:
A street scene in Atlanta, Georgia in 1864, with a storefront clearly identified as an establishment dealing in slave auctions.

ABOVE RIGHT:
House servants, probably man and wife, pictured in 1907 in the dining room of Bulloch Hall, the scene of the marriage of President Theodore Roosevelt's parents. Domestic workers were usually drawn from the slave population before the Emancipation, and many—like their fellow laborers in the fields—retained their role for years afterwards.

King Cotton

The slave trade was driven by a huge demand for agricultural labor. In the United States, vast plantations were established across the South, growing sugar cane, tobacco, and the crop that came to dominate the economy—cotton. This in turn drove an Atlantic trade that shipped slaves from Africa to America, and bales of harvested cotton to Europe—in particular to the "dark satanic mills" of Lancashire, in the industrial northwest of England, where the textile trade was centered.

From Virginia in the east, down through North and South Carolina, Georgia, and Alabama, throughout the Mississippi Delta, and to Texas in the west, the cotton industry was by far the biggest employer of slaves, and by the 1820s over half the population of the South consisted of human beings "owned" by their white masters.

Contrary to popular impressions, not all the Southern plantations were vast estates with hundreds of workers; many were small, some employing fewer than a dozen slaves. But the expanding number of plantations added up to a huge black population—by the middle of the nineteenth century well over half of the three-quarters of a million people in Mississippi were born into slavery.

Work in the cotton fields was arduous, especially under the searing summer sun when the crops had to be weeded or chopped. And planting, weeding, and picking the cotton was just a part of the work on the plantations; other crops were tended and livestock raised, too. The men also worked as blacksmiths, carpenters, and general laborers; and the women as house servants—cooking and cleaning for the plantation owner and his family.

Far worse than the work itself was the cruel discipline usually meted out by the slave owners—or their hired "drivers" or overseers. The slightest transgression, or even mere slacking, was answered with a lashing or worse. The whip could be applied without sanction by any white person on any black, be they young or old, innocent or guilty. And a slave who escaped and was recaptured faced a far worse fate—hunting dogs, the gun, or even the lynch mob.

15

"THE FATHER OF THE BLUES"

Though not a blues musician himself, the composer W. C. Handy was responsible for bringing the blues form into popular songwriting, as well as penning a number of classic blues songs well-loved by singers, musicians, and listeners ever since.

William Christopher Handy was born in Florence, Alabama, on November 16, 1873. The son of a church minister, he began playing the cornet during his childhood and by his late teens had decided on a musical career. In 1893 he performed with his own quartet at the Chicago World's Fair, a huge event that attracted many leading musicians, including the ragtime pianist Scott Joplin. After the fair, Handy took to the road as a jobbing musician, working with an outfit called Mahara's Minstrels and eventually leading the troupe, which toured extensively—even playing as far afield as Cuba.

In 1902 he fronted a band in Clarksdale, Mississippi, the Knights of Pythias, something of a cross between a marching band and a dance orchestra. And it was while he was based in the South that he began to pick up on local rural music played by unschooled players on simple guitars and banjos—it was his first introduction to what he termed a "primitive" form of music, and it would change his life forever.

In 1909 Handy and his band relocated to Memphis, where they based themselves in the Beale Street area, the hub of the city's thriving music and entertainment scene. By then Handy was also beginning to establish himself as something of a songwriter as well as a bandleader and musician.

The first song that led to Handy's being hailed as the "Father of the Blues" was "Memphis Blues," published by Handy's own Memphis-based company in October 1912 and sometimes claimed to be the first vocal blues to be written down and published—although that accolade actually belongs to "Dallas Blues" by Hart Wand, a fiddler and bandleader from Oklahoma City, whose song was published over six months before the Handy composition, in March 1912.

"Memphis Blues" had its origin in a campaign song that Handy had written for a candidate in the mayoral elections in Memphis, in 1909. Then entitled "Mr Crump"—the successful candidate was Edward Crump, later to be known as "Boss" Crump, who effectively ruled the city for the next three decades, even when he was not holding office—the song was amended and retitled "Memphis Blues" when Handy published it in 1912.

The song introduced a style of the blues to many American households for the very first time—thus its frequent citation as the "first" blues song. Handy followed with other compositions that became jazz classics, including, most famously, "St. Louis Blues," in 1914, and in 1916, "Beale Street Blues." Significantly, it would be several years before any blues numbers were actually released on record, by which time the idiom had been adopted enthusiastically by the jazz outfits and singers—including Mamie Smith and Bessie Smith—whose "bluesy" style was becoming a craze across America.

Handy continued to publish music through the 1920s and 1930s and went on to author five books on the blues and other African-American music, including his autobiography. When he died in 1958, at the age of eighty-four, more than 25,000 people attended his funeral in Harlem's Abyssinian Baptist Church. Over 150,000 more gathered in the nearby streets to pay their respects to the man who first added the blues to the language of popular music worldwide.

OPPOSITE, TOP LEFT:
A vintage album of W.C. Handy songs, from the days before the advent of long-player records. At this time, an "album" was a collection of 78s bound together, similar in style to a photograph album. The album comprised four 78s recorded on June 25 1941, the "A" side of each single featuring vocals by the great Lena Horne.

OPPOSITE, FAR RIGHT:
The original 1917 sheet music of "Beale Street Blues." The marching band is Handy's own group, with "Handy's Concert Band" visible on the drum. The bar on the right, "PWees," was a favorite hangout of Handy, where he wrote some of his greatest songs including "St Louis Blues." The establishment never closed, and was a regular meeting place for the musical fraternity on Beale.

OPPOSITE, BOTTOM LEFT:
An early portrait of Handy as a teenage musician, taken when he was 18 or 19, in 1892.

"A lean loose-jointed Negro had commenced plunking a guitar beside me while I slept ... As he played, he pressed a knife on the strings of the guitar in a manner popularized by Hawaiian guitarists who used steel bars. The effect was unforgettable. His song too, struck me instantly—'Goin' where the Southern cross the dog.' The singer repeated the line three times, accompanying himself on the guitar with the weirdest music I had ever heard."

W. C. HANDY

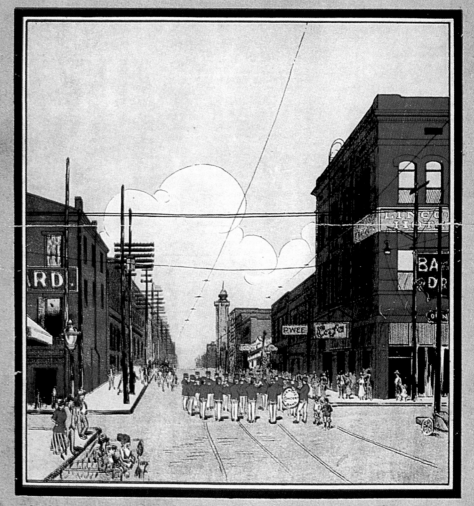

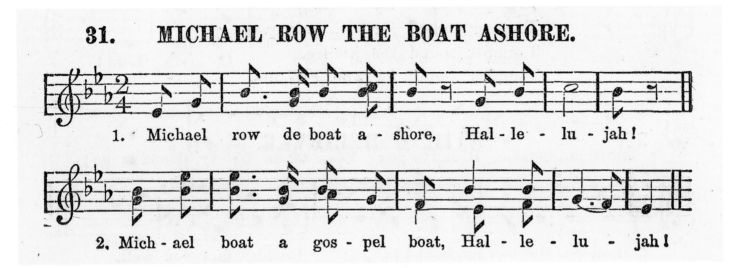

Hollers, Shouts, and Spirituals

While the collective call-and-response of early work songs would endure in the music of black churches, another musical trope that emerged from the rural South—the field holler—was equally significant in the birth of the blues. Unlike a worker on a railroad gang or other group effort, a field hand did not have to coordinate with his fellow workers. He sang at his own speed, while others echoed his often wordless call or "holler."

Similar to the field holler, and dating from the earliest days of slavery, was the ring shout, a religious ritual practiced among blacks in the West Indies and North America and almost certainly rooted in West African ceremonies. Worshippers would form a circle, moving around counterclockwise, shuffling and stamping their feet, clapping their hands, and spontaneously shouting or singing. When the slave population adopted Christianity, these rituals became a major feature in black worship across the South, and they persist today in so-called "hot gospel" prayer meetings in the more fundamentalist evangelical churches.

The widespread conversion of African slaves to Christianity began as far back as the eighteenth century, when what later became known as the Negro spiritual first evolved, rooted in the black adoption of (mainly British) Christian hymns. Most of the popular hymns were common to white Protestant churches across the South and rural America generally, and in the earliest spirituals the slave community simply voiced their own concerns and needs—hence the vision of "a better life in heaven," already common in European and colonial hymns, was a frequent theme. Although spirituals were rooted in the earlier years of slavery, those that developed during and after the Civil War took on a stronger identity as springing from the African-American experience. Songs like "Michael, Row the Boat Ashore," "Wade in the Water," "The Gospel Train," and "Swing Low, Sweet Chariot," all perpetuating the idea of salvation in the next life, became well-loved classics that have endured to the present day.

"Suddenly one raised such a sound as I had never heard before, a long musical shout rising and falling and breaking into falsetto, his voice ringing through the woods in the clear, frosty night air, like a bugle call. As he finished the melody was caught up by another, then another, and then by several in chorus."

FREDERICK LAW OLMSTED, *A Journey in the Seaboard Slave States*, 1856

After the abolition of slavery and during the Reconstruction era following the end of the Civil War in 1865, the promises of freedom and autonomy were shortlived, especially in the Deep South, where further legislation—the notorious "Jim Crow" laws—soon guaranteed that black men and women were almost as tied to their white masters (now "employers") as they had been as slaves. (Despite the undisputed success of much of the Reconstruction, these widespread segregation laws, as well as restrictions on voting rights, would not be fully reformed until the Civil Rights Act of 1964.)

Many freed slaves stayed on at the plantations out of necessity, or eked out a meager living as sharecroppers—tenants sharing the profits of their toil with landowners (usually to the sharecropper's great disadvantage). Thousands more, however, found work elsewhere, in industries such as lumber, mining, turpentine camps, and on the construction of the ever-expanding railroad—jobs that inspired a wealth of new work songs that were eventually absorbed into the broader culture of American folk music. From the story of the thirsty field worker in "Bring a Little Water, Sylvie," to the legend of the steel-driving railroad man John Henry, hundreds of songs—later collected by folklorists and preserved on record by singers such as Lead Belly—were an oral testament to the working African American, handed down from the days before the blues began.

ABOVE AND OPPOSITE, TOP RIGHT:
Extracts from spirituals.

OPPOSITE, TOP LEFT:
One of a 1996 set of commemorative stamps issued by the US Postal Service celebrating American Folk Heroes, with a bold illustration by designer David LaFleur featuring the legendary railroad worker John Henry, the subject of the famous work song. The other characters from US folklore featured in the series of four were Paul Bunyan, Mighty Casey, and Pecos Bill.

OPPOSITE BOTTOM:
From the early 1900s, a scene showing mule teams at a levee, in New Orleans, loading cotton off a railroad train.

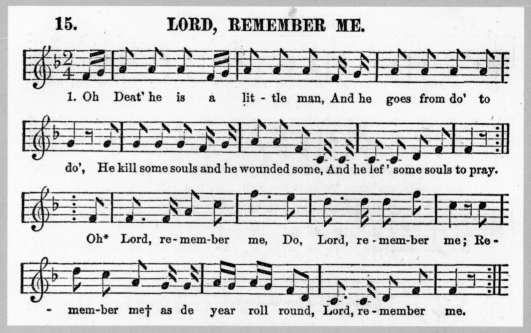

15. **LORD, REMEMBER ME.**

1. Oh Deat' he is a lit-tle man, And he goes from do' to do', He kill some souls and he wounded some, And he lef' some souls to pray.

Oh* Lord, re-mem-ber me, Do, Lord, re-mem-ber me; Re- mem-ber me† as de year roll round, Lord, re-mem-ber me.

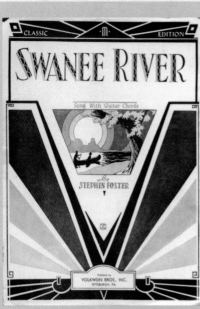

TOP LEFT:
Music for Scott Joplin's best-selling song, "Maple Leaf Rag," published at the turn of the twentieth century.

TOP RIGHT:
Born in Texas in 1868, Scott Joplin was known as "The King of Ragtime," writing forty four original ragtime pieces, a ragtime ballet, and two operas. He died in 1917, but his tune *The Entertainer* was a hit again in the 1970s when it featured in the movie *The Sting*.

BOTTOM LEFT:
The infamous "coon" song written by Ernest Hogan and published in 1895. It was originally titled "All Pimps Look Alike to Me."

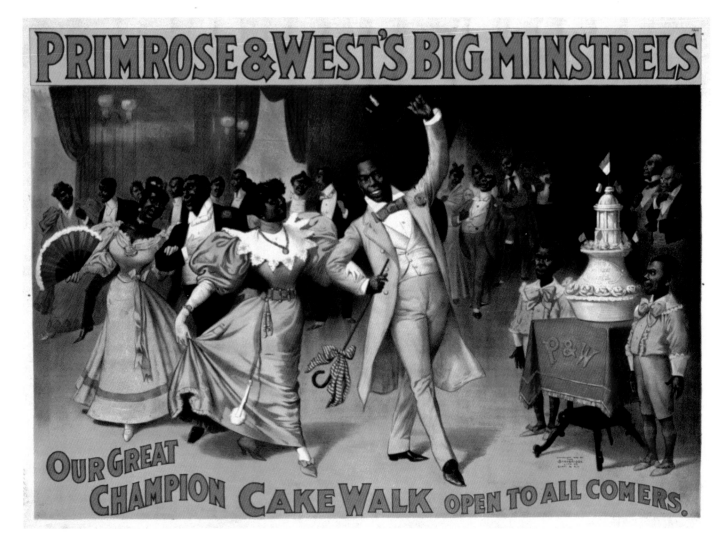

Ragtime

By the late nineteenth century many African Americans
were making music professionally, in the bars and dance
halls of the black areas of the big cities, and in touring
medicine shows, minstrel troupes, and the nationwide
circuit of vaudeville theaters. Distinct styles began to
emerge. Much as early black gospel music was initially
an adaptation of English hymns, the new sounds were
based partly on existing "white" popular music (the
sentimental songs of Stephen Foster, like "My Old
Kentucky Home" and "Old Black Joe," were particularly
favored in minstrel shows). Such was the background of
ragtime—the syncopated music that predated jazz by
a decade and was key in the popularization of black
American music generally, including the blues.

Ragtime itself was preceded by the cakewalk, a
flamboyant, strutting dance routine that had its roots in
plantation culture but became a popular novelty on the
vaudeville stage and a minor dance hall craze. The "jigs"
of the cakewalk were in turn applied by black pianists in
New Orleans' red light district of Storyville to imitate
the sounds of the city's popular marching bands—
with a syncopated beat that harked back to African
polyrhythms. Crucially, this moved the accent of the

music from the first beat favored by the brass bands to
the second beat—the offbeat (also called the afterbeat
or backbeat), which created the "swing" that would
characterize most African-American music from then on.

Initially these "rags" appeared as sheet music (as this
predated the advent of the phonograph), variously
described as "rags," "jigs," or even "marches." The first
piece to appear with ragtime in the title was "Ma Ragtime
Baby" by Fred Stone, published in 1893. The first big
ragtime hit, however, came out in 1895; written by Ernest
Hogan, "All Coons Look Alike to Me" would eventually
sell over a million copies. An African American himself,
Hogan later expressed regret for the racial slurs implicit
in the song, which triggered an unfortunate, albeit
short-lived fashion for "coon songs" full of racist images
of black people.

The positive side of Hogan's success was the ragtime
craze that followed. The style quickly spread from its
New Orleans origins, and by the end of the century was a
nationwide fad when pianist Scott Joplin published the
most celebrated rag, "Maple Leaf Rag," in 1899. And the
first ragtime song to be published with a twelve-bar blues
section, "One o' Them Things" by James Chapman and
Leroy Smith, appeared in 1904. Ragtime was intrinsically

21

linked to the earliest development of jazz, and—as in the case of influential musicians like the ragtime and jazz pianist Jelly Roll Morton, whose music straddled both camps—significantly influenced by the blues.

One musical element common to these various manifestations of African-American pre-blues music is the use of the flatted third and seventh notes in the European scale—the "blue notes" (which in later years also included the flatted fifth). Whether in the passionate delivery of a secular work song, a sacred spiritual, or a spirited ragtime tune, the blue note (sometimes merely implied by intonation rather than part of the accepted melody) was a key characteristic of African-American music, and at the core of the blues as it first evolved at the beginning of the twentieth century.

In the absence of any sound recordings in the late nineteenth century, it is impossible to pin down the earliest instance of actual blues music as we would recognize it. Some form of the blues—its simple twelve-bar song structure or variations of the same—seems to have been evident from the 1870s or so, and there were specific accounts of the blues dating from 1890 onwards, suggesting that the form had been around for some years before that.

An early reference to the blues in Texas was made in 1890 by collector Gates Thomas, who transcribed a song titled "Nobody There" that had close structural similarities to a blues melody. Thomas went on to publish other texts of blues-type songs collected from across South Texas in 1901 and 1902, including "Baby, Take a Look at Me," which was also noted by Charles Peabody, an archaeologist working in Mississippi. Peabody, after excavating a site not far from Clarksdale, in 1903 wrote about his black diggers singing various improvised songs in the blues form.

Here Come the Blues

The very first jazz musician of real repute was the New Orleans cornet player Buddy Bolden, who was playing his "Buddy Bolden Blues" before the turn of the century. Ma Rainey, one of the greatest of the classic blues singers to flourish during the 1920s, recalled how she first heard the blues in Missouri in 1902, when performing in a travelling tent show while still a teenager. And Jelly Roll Morton, in a 1938 interview with musicologist Alan Lomax for the Library of Congress, recalled that one of the first blues he heard—with the classic twelve-bar lyric of two repeated lines followed by a third concluding line—was by a female piano player in a New Orleans brothel around 1902.

From 1905 to 1908, the folklorist and song collector Howard W. Odum undertook an extensive field trip through the Mississippi Delta and Georgia. He subsequently published a large anthology of African-American folk songs, over half of which were blues, and many of which included lyrics that appeared in blues

"The name of this musician was Mamie Desdumes. Two middle fingers of her right hand had been cut off, so she played the blues with only three fingers on her right hand.

'I stood on the corner, my feet was dripping wet I stood on the corner, my feet was dripping wet, I asked each and every man I met …'

Although I had heard them previously, I guess it was Mamie first really sold me on the blues."

JELLY ROLL MORTON

songs recorded years later. Odum apparently recorded many of his finds, on primitive "cylinder" equipment, all of which, tragically, are now completely lost.

It was in 1903, while awaiting a delayed train in Tutwiler, Mississippi, that cornet player and bandleader W. C. Handy came across the blues for the first time, hearing the "weirdest music" being played by a lone guitarist. This music, and other blues he heard around the South, had a profound effect on Handy, who went on to establish himself as the leading writer and publisher of popular songs in the blues idiom.

Despite being dubbed the "Father of the Blues," Handy did not in fact compose the first published blues music. Nevertheless, his 1912 debut, "Memphis Blues," and later successes including classics like "Beale Street Blues" and "St. Louis Blues," did bring the blues form into the mainstream music market for the first time, and for that alone Handy stands as a major figure in the history of the blues and popular music.

Some claim that Hughie Cannon's 1904 version of the folk song "Frankie and Johnny," which he called "He Done Me Wrong," qualifies as the first printed example of the blues, whereas others cite Antonio Maggio's 1908 instrumental tune "I Got the Blues"—the latter was almost certainly the first to use "blues" in its title. But "Dallas Blues," by the Oklahoma musician Hart Wand, published in March 1912 and preceding Handy's song by six months, was the earliest bona fide vocal blues to appear as sheet music. In fact, Handy's October release also followed "Baby Seals Blues" by H. Franklin Seals, published in August 1912.

Blues and near-blues songs became increasingly fashionable with music publishers through the second decade of the century, coinciding with the widespread popularity of ragtime and then jazz music. At the same time, the phonograph was supplanting the piano as the prime vehicle for home musical entertainment, paving the way for the blues to appear on commercial recordings for the first time.

OPPOSITE:
Hart Wand's historic "Dallas Blues." Published in March 1912, it is widely considered the first genuine blues to be published as sheet music. One of many examples of often grotesque imagery used to depict African Americans in the promotion of "black" music.

CLASSIC BLUES

Given the music's seemingly male domination and often macho image, it is an irony of history that the very first blues stars were women— the big-voiced ladies like Mamie Smith, Ma Rainey, and Bessie Smith, who took an exuberant version of the blues onto the vaudeville stage and the touring tent show circuit—and, more importantly, into the recording studios for the first time. With a typical repertoire that also embraced ragtime tunes and other popular songs of the day, the classic blues singers were part of a uniquely American music revolution that was about to sweep the world: jazz.

The early "composed" blues by songwriters such as W. C. Handy and Hart Wand were soon absorbed into the play lists of the jazz bands proliferating across America. Jazz would soon turn into a national—and subsequently international—craze, once it took off in the form of phonograph records. Indeed, the very first jazz record ever released, by the Original Dixieland Jazz Band (ODJB), was in the blues form; "Livery Stable Blues" was recorded on February 26, 1917, and released on the Victor label just twelve days later.

The ODJB hailed from the "birthplace of jazz," New Orleans. An all-white ensemble fronted by cornet player Dominic James "Nick" LaRocca and clarinetist Larry Shields, they had cottoned on to the rising popularity of jazz in the city, emanating from the large African-American population and flourishing particularly in the bars and bordellos of the Storyville red light district.

The Jazz Connection

Jazz had been played in a recognizable form in New Orleans since the end of the nineteenth century, its leading exponents including cornet and trumpet players Freddie Keppard and Joe "King" Oliver, clarinet virtuoso Sidney Bechet, and the earliest jazz musician of note, cornetist Charles "Buddy" Bolden, who led his own band from the early 1890s. With brass band music and popular ragtime tunes among its key ingredients, jazz was also heavily influenced by the blues, which musicians picked up in the form of field hollers heard on their travels or from ex-slaves who had moved to New Orleans after the Emancipation—and, from 1912, in the form of printed sheet music. From the start, jazz was characterized by both the form and intonation of the blues, using the twelve-bar structure (or its eight-bar, sixteen-bar, and other variants) and "blue notes" (the flatted third and seventh) as the cornerstone of its basic language.

The ODJB's debut release was a huge success, and kick-started the jazz fad (or "jass" as it was often billed) that went on to identify the 1920s as the Jazz Age. Soon any jazz outfit worth its salt was making records, among them emigrants from New Orleans' black jazz fraternity who had moved north. These included King Oliver, the pianist and composer Jelly Roll Morton, and the most influential musician in jazz history, the cornet and trumpet star (and seminal vocal stylist) Louis Armstrong.

After recording as part of King Oliver's Creole Jazz Band, in December 1925 Armstrong embarked on a series of recordings with his Hot Five and Hot Seven line-ups that would change the course of musical history. The sessions, which took place in Chicago in the middle of 1928 and were released as 78 rpm singles on the OKeh label, created a template for much jazz to come. And the majority of the most famous sides were blues—among them "Potato Head Blues," "Gut Bucket Blues," "Basin Street Blues," and the recording that has since been hailed as among the most significant in jazz, "West End Blues." The sheer perfection and economy of Armstrong's phrasing during the three-minute-plus performance of this piece (not to mention his wordless scat singing) still stands as the definitive demonstration of what could be achieved within the apparent constraints of the simple twelve-bar format.

OPPOSITE, TOP LEFT:
The only known photograph of pioneering cornet player Buddy Bolden and his band, with Bolden standing second left. The other musicians were: (standing, l to r) Jimmy Johnson on double bass, Willie Cornish on valve trombone, and Frank Lewis on clarinet; and seated, Jefferson Mumford on guitar and William Warner, clarinet.

OPPOSITE RIGHT:
Sheet music for "Livery Stable Blues," featuring a caricature of an indolent black man, which is typical of much racial stereotyping at the time.

OPPOSITE BOTTOM LEFT:
The Original Dixieland Jazz Band, with (left to right) Tony Sbabaro, Eddie "Daddy" Edwards, Nick LaRocca, Larry Shields, and Henry Ragas.

"The earliest blues singers—wandering guitarists who played for pennies along the southern roads—followed no strict musical form. But as first New Orleans musicians and then others around the country began to try to play the blues on their instruments, and songwriters started to see commercial possibilities in them, an agreed-upon form was developed: stripped to the essentials, blues came to be built on just three chords most often arranged in twelve-bar sequences that somehow allowed for an infinite number of variations and were capable of expressing an infinite number of emotions."

GEOFFREY C. WARD AND KEN BURNS, *Jazz: A History of America's Music*, 2001

Another seminal jazz and blues musician and composer, Ferdinand Joseph LaMothe (professionally known as Jelly Roll Morton) was born in 1890 and spent his early years as an itinerant musician, gambler, and general hustler around the South, picking up on ragtime music and blues in just about equal measure. When in his native New Orleans, he regularly worked the brothels and bars of Storyville, and he soon developed a flair for composition. A flamboyant character and self-publicist, he later became notorious among music historians for claiming to have "invented" jazz. Nevertheless, his "Jelly Roll Blues," published in 1915, was one of the earliest, if not the first, published jazz composition—and a key example of blues being an integral part of jazz from its very beginning.

Morton moved to Chicago in the early 1920s, where both his solo recordings and those with his band, the Red Hot Peppers, were as popular and influential as Armstrong's seminal work.

Meanwhile, in New York City, pianist and composer Duke Ellington caused a sensation when his eleven-piece band began a residency at the Cotton Club in Harlem. Even in the relatively liberal North, racist attitudes were prevalent and the Cotton Club was a prime example. For its whites only audience, the club featured spectacular floorshows, often depicting black people as stereotypical savages straight from the jungle, with scantily dressed dancers accompanied by wild, rhythmic jazz; the crowds of well-to-do folk from downtown Manhattan loved it. The first band to play the club when it opened in 1923 was that of Fletcher Henderson, another key bandleader in the popularization of jazz. But when Ellington took over in 1927, his lush arrangements and hot soloists were like nothing that had come before. His sultry-sounding "jungle music," as it was dubbed, drew heavily on the blues—in fact, his first big hit, "Creole Love Call," with an evocative vocal by Adelaide Hall, was an exotic-sounding interpretation of a basic twelve-bar blues.

ABOVE:
A New Orleans street scene in the early 1900s, around the time that ragtime, and emergent jazz and blues, were making the city the prime melting pot of a new American music.

MA RAINEY

One of the first singers to bring the down-home elements of rural blues into the minstrel and vaudeville shows of the classic blues era, Ma Rainey was already a name on the tent-show circuit a decade before her debut Paramount release "Last Minute Blues" in 1923. Instant success with a string of records saw her touring as a top-of-the-bill solo artist, famous for her extravagant costumes and no-holds-barred vocals. Accompanied in the studio by leading jazz musicians as well as major blues artists, the "Mother of the Blues," as Ma Rainey became known, carried on touring through the Depression years until 1935, when she retired to her native Georgia. She died of a heart attack in 1939.

> "My audience wants to see me beautifully gowned, and I have spared no expense or pains . . . For I feel that the best is none too good for the public that pays to hear a singer."
>
> MA RAINEY

Born
Gertrude Pridgett, April 26, 1886, Columbus, Georgia

Died
December 22, 1939, Rome, Georgia

Instruments
Vocals

Recording Debut
"Last Minute Blues" / "Bo-Weavil Blues"
Recorded December 1923, Chicago, Illinois
Paramount Records

Awards
Inducted into Blues Hall of Fame, 1983
Inducted into Rock and Roll Hall of Fame (Early Influences) 1990
"See See Rider Blues" inducted into Grammy Hall of Fame, 2004

Playlist
"Bo-Weavil Blues" [1923]
"Moonshine Blues" [1923]
"Last Minute Blues" [1923]
"Jelly Bean Blues" [1924]
"See See Rider Blues" [1924]
"Soon This Morning" [1926]
"Ma Rainey's Black Bottom" [1927]
"Misery Blues" [1927]
"Blame It on the Blues" [1928]
"Leaving This Morning" [1928]

MAMIE SMITH
And Her
JAZZ HOUNDS
AND COMPANY OF 18 ENTERTAINERS
A Company of Metropolitan Stars, Many of Whom
Never Played in the South.
DO NOT MISS THIS JAZZ REVUE

COLISEUM, MARCH 21ST, 8:30 P. M.
Hear Mamie sing "Crazy Blues," "Lovin' Sam From
Alabam," "The Road is Rocky," "If You Don't Want
Me Blues."
SEE THE WONDERFUL IMPORTED GOWNS
Get Your Tickets Now
1707 Elm Street   1708 Live Oak Street
PRICES: $1.00, $1.50, $2.00   Tax Extra
Auspices—Fred Douglas Improvement League
Management O. K. Concert Bureau.

"We're telling you there's none finer or grander when it comes to warblin' mean and hot low-down ravagin' Blues, until you don't know whether your sensations is your wigglin' spine or if your spine has got the wigglin' blues."

OKeh Records' promotional copy for "The Famous Moanin' Mama," blues singer Sara Martin, c. 1923

OPPOSITE:
Written and published in 1931, "Mood Indigo" was one of Duke Ellington's many hits based solidly on the blues, in this case using the 16-bar format.

ABOVE RIGHT:
An advertisement from the *Dallas Express* for a "jazz revue" featuring Mamie Smith and Her Jazz Hounds. The paper began publishing in 1893, and with its slogan "The South's Oldest and Largest Negro Newspaper" represented the black population for over seventy years.

Musicians like Ellington, Armstrong, and Morton—and many more—were the pioneers of nothing less than a jazz revolution that transformed music across the western world. Both via the domestic phonograph record player, and in live venues ranging from "speakeasy" clubs (the prohibition of alcohol in the United States lasted from 1920 to 1933) to the ubiquitous local dance hall, jazz was the conduit through which the blues form became a staple ingredient of popular music.

It was in this musical environment that the earliest well-known blues singers made their names—often accompanied by the greatest jazz players of the day. Many honed their craft in traveling tent shows and on the vaudeville stage before being picked up by record companies eager to jump on the burgeoning jazz bandwagon. And the very first of these blues artists credited with having a record released was Mamie Smith.

"Crazy Blues"

Like many of her early blues peers, Mamie Smith was a show-biz professional—a dancer, pianist, and actress as well as a vaudeville singer, whose vocal repertoire embraced jazz and popular songs of the day as well as the blues. A fine performer with a prolific recording career, her appearance in blues history books was guaranteed when she became the first artist to make a vocal blues record—"Crazy Blues," released in 1920.

Born Mamie Robinson in 1883, she had already made a couple of pop song sides earlier in 1920 when songwriter Perry Bradford convinced OKeh Records that there was a market for earthier blues records. Bradford was thinking particularly of the huge numbers of black Americans who had migrated to the big cities of the north. Legend has it that Fred Hager, the recording manager at OKeh, defied a threatened boycott by record store managers over the release of the record. Bradford put together a band called the Jazz Hounds to back Mamie (who had become Smith when she married William Smith, a Harlem club waiter), and on August 10, 1920, they cut the landmark disc, which sold seventy-five thousand copies within a month. It was said to have sold more than a million copies in the next year, with sales eventually topping the two-million mark.

Importantly, the record's success demonstrated to other record companies that there was money to be made by aiming specific releases at the black community; this was the beginning of "race records," whereby companies devoted separate catalogs to African-American musicians and singers. In doing so they opened the door for scores of black acts hitherto ignored by the industry, including the first wave of classic female blues singers following in the wake of Mamie Smith's success.

A string of key releases swiftly followed the OKeh lead, including Lucille Hagamin's "The Jazz Me Blues" (released in November 1920), the great Ethel Waters' "Down Home Blues" (May 1921), and Trixie Smith's 1922 "Trixie's Blues" and her most famous release, "Railroad Blues," recorded in 1925 and backed by Louis Armstrong. But it was Ma Rainey, often billed as the "Mother of the Blues," who was already steeped in the blues long before she ever entered a recording studio.

JUG BAND BLUES

Considered by many as simply purveyors of "novelty" music, the jug bands that flourished in the 1920s were nevertheless an important feature of both country blues and the jazz-based classic blues scene. As its name implied, the signature sound of these "good time" outfits was the jug, which in many ways took the place of the tuba or double bass. Its distinctive low, almost guttural sound—not dissimilar to primitive blown instruments brought over from Africa during the slave trade—provided backing for a motley selection of instruments including banjo, guitar, fiddle, harmonica, clarinet, and saxophone— and at the more homemade level, the likes of the kazoo, whistle, and washboard.

As with the blues singers, it was the urban jug bands that first appeared on record, with violinist Clifford Hayes paving the way with his Old Southern Jug Band in late 1923 and 1924. From Louisville, Kentucky, their sides for Vocalion Records had all the energy of a hot jazz outfit, with some spirited jug solo breaks by Earl McDonald.

The group formed the basis for the Dixieland Jug Blowers, who with their 1926 recordings were considered the greatest of the "city" jug bands. And the classic blues singer Sara Martin cut ten sides with Hayes's basic jug band trio for the OKeh label in 1924.

Also out of Louisville came Whistler's Jug Band. Formed in 1915 by guitarist, vocalist, and nose whistle player Buford Threlkeld (who went by the stage name of Whistler), in 1924 the jazz-influenced outfit released the first of several records for the Gennett label. Further sessions in 1927, this time for OKeh, featured thirteen-year-old Rudolph Thompson (aka "Jazz Lips") on jug, with the leader living up to his nickname on nose whistle, as well as delivering some effective blues vocals including "Low Down Blues" and "Pigmeat Blues."

The Beale Street area of Memphis had long been a social center for the city's African-American population, with clubs and bars providing a wealth of employment for blues and jazz artists, when local guitarist Will Shade decided to put together a jug band. It was 1926, and Shade hoped to emulate Hayes's Jug Blowers. What developed, however, was something significantly different. The Memphis Jug

Band, as Shade called his group, was more inclined to a country blues sound, and with its infectious mix of blues, jazz, and ragtime the band attracted the attention of Victor Records' talent scout and folk/blues enthusiast Ralph Peer. Over the next seven years the Memphis Jug Band recorded nearly eighty sides for Victor, Columbia, and OKeh, while also providing backing for female Memphis blues singers Hattie Hart and the great Memphis Minnie.

Memphis was the base for various other jug bands of note, among them the South Memphis Jug Band, led by Jack Kelly, Noah Lewis and his Jug Band, and Jed Davenport's Beale Street Jug Band. But the band whose success would rival that of the Memphis Jug Band was Gus Cannon's Jug Stompers. Born in Clarksdale, Mississippi, Cannon had moved to Memphis in 1916; there he forged a musical career as a medicine show banjo player and entertainer. He first recorded in 1927 as "Banjo Joe" before assembling the Jug Stompers, who released their debut record on Victor in January 1928.

Cannon's Mississippi roots might have been one reason for his leaning towards a bluesier sound than many good-time jug bands, reinforced by the wailing harmonica of Noah Lewis. Although they ceased recording in 1930, Cannon's Jug Stompers made some fine blues-inflected recordings including "Wolf River Blues," "Minglewood Blues," and the self-penned "Walk Right In"—a million-selling hit for the Rooftop Singers in 1963, for which Cannon received not a dime in royalties.

OPPOSITE, TOP RIGHT:
Victor Records publicity material for releases by the Memphis Jug Band, including "I Whipped My Woman With a Single Tree."

OPPOSITE BOTTOM:
Gus Cannon's Jug Stompers with (left to right) Gus Cannon on banjo and his jug on an elaborate harness, Ashley Thompson on guitar, and Noah Lewis on harmonica.

OVERLEAF:
From the Florida State Archives, a group of African-American youngsters with their own jug band.

"THE DISTINCTIVENESS OF THE JUG GAVE A SPECIAL QUALITY TO THE MUSIC . . . THERE DEVELOPED WITH THE BANDS A LARGE BODY OF MUSIC SUITED TO THE JUG BANDS. USUALLY IT WAS COUNTRY DANCE MUSIC AND BREAKDOWNS, SOME OF IT RELATED TO THE SONGS OF THE OLD MINSTREL THEATRE, BUT THE GREATEST OF THE BANDS, LIKE THE MEMPHIS JUG BAND OR CANNON'S JUG STOMPERS COULD PLAY INTENSELY MOVING BLUES AS WELL."

SAMUEL CHARTERS

Ma Rainey

Striding onto the stage with her smile revealing big gold-capped teeth, a long necklace of twenty gold coins draped against her sequined dress, and an ostrich plume in one hand, Ma Rainey cut a formidable figure before she even opened her mouth to sing. When she did let loose with her strong, gravelly voice, audiences were mesmerized. Her style of singing represented a crucial link between the female-dominated urban blues initially popularized by Mamie Smith and the other blues mamas, and the down-home sound of the predominantly male country blues.

Gertrude Pridgett was born on April 26, 1886, in Columbus, Georgia. Her grandmother and both her parents were singers, and she began her career, after appearing at the age of fourteen at a local talent show, touring regularly with vaudeville and minstrel shows. This was the era when minstrel shows were not just the white-imitating-black "nigger minstrel" entertainments of popular recollection, but as often all-black concert troupes presenting music, song, and comedy with an inevitable touch of "Uncle Tom" stereotyping of their own. Gertrude's parents were minstrel performers, and in 1904 she met and married William "Pa" Rainey, a minstrel show performer and manager. The two sang and danced together, mainly performing sentimental ballads and "coon" songs, and also touring with various tent shows including the Rabbit Foot Comedy Company (the precursor to F. S. Walcott's famous Rabbit's Foot Minstrels), and Tolliver's Circus and Musical Extravaganza.

Significantly, Ma Rainey was one of the first performers to incorporate blues into minstrel and vaudeville stage shows, with her own unique mix of country blues, ragtime, and "hot" jazz. Although the details are obscured by legend, in 1912 the young Bessie Smith joined Ma Rainey in the Moses Stokes Company, and she was certainly influenced by Rainey, even if not actually coached by her as some accounts later claimed.

In December 1923, Ma Rainey signed a five-year contract with Paramount Records, which dubbed her "Mother of the Blues" and debuted her recording career with "Last Minute Blues" backed with "Bo-Weavil Blues." After nearly twenty years on the road, she had established a large fan base in the South with her sensational stage act and vocal style, and the subject matter of numbers like "Bo-Weavil," "Moonshine Blues," and "Stack O'Lee Blues" confirmed her strong country roots.

In 1924, buoyed by the increasing popularity of her records, Rainey went on tour as a solo vaudeville star, playing to both black and white audiences, and backed by the renowned bandleader and pianist Thomas Dorsey (who would become a leading gospel music composer).

Much of the touring work (which continued off and on until 1928) was promoted by the powerful Theatre Owners Booking Association. TOBA, as it was generally called, controlled a circuit of (mainly white-owned) vaudeville theaters specifically catering to African-American audiences and featuring black artists. This was at a time when virtually all entertainment venues were racially segregated, especially in the South and Southwest. Many of the performers, although obliged to

ABOVE LEFT:
A flyer for F.S. Walcott's famed Rabbit Foot Minstrels.

OPPOSITE, TOP RIGHT:
An advertisement or flyer for Ma and Pa (Billy and Gertrude) Rainey, touring "enroute" with the Rabbit's Foot company.

OPPOSITE LEFT:
The most famous photograph of Ma Rainey, resplendent with her gold teeth and glitzy finery.

OPPOSITE, BOTTOM RIGHT:
A newspaper advert for the Alabama Minstrel show, featuring "50 colored stars" which included (though unnamed here, but shown in a photograph) Ma Rainey and her Rabbit Foot Minstrels.

THOSE DIRTY BLUES

From the days of the early blue singers, traveling the vaudeville and tent show circuit across the South and elsewhere, there was a rich repertoire of racy and often sexually explicit blues songs which were made acceptable for the more genteel sections of their audience—and the burgeoning record-buying public—by the use of colorful ambiguity and double entendre. These bawdy lyrics, especially in the performances of raunchy vocalists like Ma Rainey and Lucille Bogan, often featured highly evocative imagery, thinly veiled references to the generally taboo subjects of sexual activity and genitalia. And Joe Turner's "one-eyed cat" even got past the censors in Bill Haley's cleaned-up version of "Shake, Rattle and Roll."

"We were restricted with our possibilities of promoting this song ["Good Rockin' Tonight"] into realms beyond where we had it (ie the R&B market) because it was considered filth. They had a definition in those days of the word 'rock' meaning the sex act, rather than having it known as 'a good time' as they did later."
HENRY GLOVER, King Records A&R executive

"He shakes my ashes, freezes my griddle,
Churns my butter, strokes my pillow
My man is such a handy man ...

He threads my needle, gleans my wheat,
Heats my heater, chops my meat.
My man is such a handy man"
VICTORIA SPIVEY, "My Handy Man" 1928,
written by Andy Razaf

"Organ grinder, organ grinder
Organ grinder, play that melody
Take your organ, grinder, and grind some more for me ...

Grind it north, grind it north
Grind it north, grind it east or west
But when you grind it slow, that's when I like it best"
ETHEL WATERS, "Organ Grinder Blues" 1928,
written by Clarence Williams

"Umm better find my mama soon
Umm better find my mama soon
I woke up this morning, black snake was makin' such a ruckus in my room"
BLIND LEMON JEFFERSON, "Black Snake Moan" 1927

"Now I ain't no plumber, no plumber's son
I can do your screwin' till the plumber-man comes
Cos I'm an all around man, oh I'm an all around man
I mean I'm an all around man,
I can do most anything that comes to hand

"Now I ain't no miller, no miller's son
I can do your grindin' till the miller-man comes
Cos I'm an all around man, oh I'm an all around man
I mean I'm an all around man,
I can do most anything that comes to hand"
BO CARTER, "All Around Man" 1931

"I'm like a one-eyed cat, peepin' in a seafood store
I'm like a one-eyed cat, peepin' in a seafood store
I can look at you, tell you don't love me no more"
BIG JOE TURNER, "Shake, Rattle and Roll" 1954

ABOVE LEFT:
The great Ida Cox, aka "The Sepia Mae West," photographed in the 1940s.

ABOVE RIGHT:
Ma Rainey's picture was part of a 1994 series of US postage stamps dedicated to blues and jazz singers. Others in the series included Bessie Smith, Muddy Waters, Billie Holiday, Jimmy Rushing, Robert Johnson, and Howlin' Wolf.

work the TOBA circuit for their living, felt that the organization exploited black artists—indeed, in the business TOBA was said to stand for "Tough on Black Artists." Never one to mince words, Ma Rainey famously declared that it meant "Tough on Black Asses."

Like many of the classic blues artists, Ma Rainey was noted for her down-to-earth lyrics and often bawdy songs. Indeed, probably her most popular hit was the 1927 "Ma Rainey's Black Bottom," with racy double entendres throughout:

> "All the boys in the neighborhood
> They say your black bottom is really good
> Come on and show me your black bottom
> I want to learn that dance."

By 1928 Rainey's fame had spread far and wide, with over a hundred recordings for Paramount, including many of her own compositions. Her success was as spectacular as her stage appearances; she performed and recorded with the some of the finest jazz musicians, including Louis Armstrong, Fletcher Henderson, Tommy Ladnier, and Coleman Hawkins; likewise she was also accompanied by major bluesmen from time to time, including Blind Blake and Tampa Red.

When Ma Rainey's contract with Paramount expired in 1928, the company decided not to renew it, claiming that "down-home material has gone out of fashion." The Great Depression was also starting to bite, with vaudeville declining in the wake of growth in radio, records, and the

new talkies. The Mother of the Blues continued working until 1935, when she retired to her hometown of Columbus, Georgia, and invested her hard-won earnings in two theaters, the Lyric and the Airdrome. She died of a heart attack in 1939, just as her work was attracting serious attention among blues collectors. She was inducted into the Blues Hall of Fame in 1983, and in 1994 the U.S. Postal Service issued a stamp in her honor.

All-Around Entertainers

Among the record companies quick to cash in on the precedent of Mamie Smith's success with "Crazy Blues" was Black Swan, the first label to be owned and operated by an African American, Harry Pace. Pace had been in music publishing since 1912 as a partner of W. C. Handy—the two wrote songs together—until splitting over business differences in 1921.

One the label's major signings (before they were bought out by Paramount) was Ida Cox, another graduate of the Rabbit Foot Minstrels. Born Ida Prather in Toccoa, Georgia, in 1896, she had a hard, nasal voice with a somewhat limited range. But her emotional delivery of blues and near-blues songs endeared her to audiences across the Deep South as she travelled from place to place, accompanied by her husband, the pianist Jesse Crump. Through the 1920s she often headed her own vaudeville troupe, Ida Cox and Her Raisin' Cain Company and, in the 1930s, Cox's Darktown Scandals Review. Her career stretched across the decades, right up to her death from cancer in 1967. One of the recorded highlights was

when she took part in the first legendary "Spirituals to Swing" concert staged by John Hammond at New York's Carnegie Hall in 1938, singing a soaring version of her own song "Four Day Creep."

In her heyday Ida Cox was known as both "The Sepia Mae West" and "The Uncrowned Queen of the Blues." Most of the female blues singers of the 1920s were given extravagant nicknames by tour promoters and record companies, including "Everybody's Mammy" Martha Copeland and Clara Smith "The World Champion Moaner." On account of her tall, slim figure, Ethel Waters was billed as "Sweet Mama Stringbean."

Victoria Spivey was a big fan of Ida Cox—and eager to emulate her success. In 1926, the twenty-year-old Spivey traveled from her native Texas to St. Louis, where OKeh Records were on a field trip looking for new blues acts to record. Having worked as a teenager in bars and nightclubs around Dallas—occasionally with blues guitarists, including Blind Lemon Jefferson—Spivey impressed the OKeh talent scouts, who signed her immediately. Her first release for the label was the self-composed "Black Snake Blues," followed by a string of records (she cut a disc almost once a month) over the next two years, before she moved to the RCA Victor label in 1929.

When the crunch of the Depression came, virtually ending the careers of many of her fellow blues artists, Spivey shifted gears by branching out into the new medium of sound movies, landing a part in director King

Vidor's first talking picture, the all-black *Hallelujah!* in 1929. Other musical films followed, as well as stage shows that included the hugely popular *Hellzapoppin' Revue.*

Supported by these other show business activities, Spivey was able to carry on making records. She had releases on both the Vocalion and Decca labels between 1931 and 1937, accompanied by some of the biggest names in music, including King Oliver, Louis Armstrong, pianist Clarence Williams, and the blues guitarist Lonnie Johnson.

Apart from a ten-year break starting in 1951, when she retired to lead a church choir, Victoria Spivey carried on in the recording industry up to her death in 1976. She formed her own label, Spivey Records, releasing work by major blues artists including Otis Spann, Big Joe Turner, Otis Rush, and many more. One of the label's first projects was *Three Kings and the Queen* in 1962 featuring Spivey, Big Joe Williams, Roosevelt Sykes, and her old colleague Lonnie Johnson—and a young Bob Dylan accompanying Big Joe on harmonica and backing vocals.

The first releases on the pioneering Black Swan label included light classics, spirituals, and blues, the latter producing its first big seller, "Down Home Blues" by Ethel Waters. Like Mamie Smith and many of the vaudeville singers committing blues to disc for the first time, Waters' repertoire included ballads and pop songs outside the blues genre, and it was in this capacity as an all-around singer and entertainer that she achieved her eventual worldwide fame.

ABOVE LEFT:
Sheet music for "Am I Blue," one of the songs from the 1929 movie musical *On With the Show*, which featured Ethel Waters playing herself in a mainly singing role.

ABOVE RIGHT:
Like Ethel Waters, a star of stage, screen, and radio—and of course records—Victoria Spivey was a show-biz all-rounder. But at the core of her success was her talent as a blues singer.

BESSIE SMITH

Dubbed the "Empress of the Blues," Bessie Smith was perhaps the greatest of the classic blues singers of the 1920s. She grew up in abject poverty in Chattanooga, Tennessee, singing on street corners as a child, and joining a touring tent show while still a teenager. Graduating to the vaudeville stage in 1915, she built up a big following across the South and the eastern seaboard states before making her record debut with "Down Hearted Blues" in 1923. A spectacular recording career over the next ten years included such classics as "St. Louis Blues," "Empty Bed Blues," and "Nobody Knows You When You're Down and Out," accompanied by some of the great jazz names of the era. She died after a fatal car crash in Clarksdale, Mississippi, in 1937, at the age of forty-three.

> **"She came in, she planted those two flat feet firmly on the floor, she did not shake her shoulders or snap her fingers. She just opened that great kisser and let the music come out"**

ROBERT PAUL SMITH, *Record Changer* magazine, reviewing Bessie Smith's performance at the Famous Door, NYC, February 1936

Born
Elizabeth Smith, April 15, 1894, Chattanooga, Tennessee

Died
September 26, 1937, Clarksdale, Mississippi

Instruments
Vocals

Recording Debut
"Down Hearted Blues" / "Gulf Coast Blues"
Recorded February 16, 1923, New York City
Columbia Records

Awards
Inducted into Blues Hall of Fame, 1980
Grammy Lifetime Achievement Award, 1989
Inducted into Rock and Roll Hall of Fame (Early
   Influences), 1989

Playlist
"Down Hearted Blues" [1923]
"Tain't Nobody's Business If I Do" [1923]
"St Louis Blues" [1925]
"Yellow Dog Blues" [1925]
"Careless Love" [1925]
"Jazzbo Brown From Memphis Town" [1926]
"Empty Bed Blues" [1928]
"Nobody Knows You When You're Down
   And Out" [1929]
"Black Mountain Blues" [1930]
"Gimme A Pigfoot (And a Bottle of Beer)" [1933]

By 1925 Waters was playing New York's smart Plantation Club on Broadway, and in 1933 she had a huge hit with the original version of the standard "Stormy Weather." She went on to become one of the most well-known and respected names in African-American culture, both on the Broadway stage and as an actress on the silver screen; in 1949 she was nominated for an Oscar for her supporting role in the controversial race relations drama *Pinky*. Waters died in 1977 at the age of eighty.

Bertha "Chippie" Hill worked with Ethel Waters as a dancer in 1919, at just fourteen years of age. She went on to work with Ma Rainey in the Rabbit Foot Minstrels before branching out with her own song and dance act on the TOBA black vaudeville circuit. She moved to Chicago in the mid-1920s, singing with King Oliver's band and signing with OKeh Records, with whom she made a series of sensational recordings with Louis Armstrong starting in November 1925; the sides, including "Low Land Blues," "Kid Man Blues," and "Trouble in Mind," are prime examples of 1920s female blues with classic jazz accompaniment.

Chippie Hill's credentials also included work with other blues artists, such as Lonnie Johnson in 1927, Tampa Red the following year, and the pianist-singer Leroy Carr in 1929. Though the Depression hit hard, she was back in the mid-1940s singing with the great pianist Lovie Austin and her Blues Serenaders. Getting her career back on track, Hill worked with the legendary

pianist James P. Johnson and veteran trombonist Kid Ory—and even sang at a jazz festival in Paris—before being tragically struck and killed in a New York hit-and-run accident in 1950.

During an amazing seventy-year career, Alberta Hunter performed in every kind of venue, from Chicago dives (where her pianist was shot dead on stage during a gangster brawl) to the high-class nightclubs and theaters of Europe. First recording with Black Swan in 1921, she moved to Paramount (who took over the ailing black-owned company) in 1922 when she became the first African-American singer to be backed by a white band with the Original Memphis Five supporting her on "Tain't Nobody's Business If I Do," "If You Want to Keep Your Daddy Home" and "Bleeding Hearted Blues."

After a prolific spell also recording for Gennett, OKeh, Victor, and Columbia, Hunter had moved to Europe by 1928, where she starred opposite singer Paul Robeson in the first London production of the Jerome Kern and Oscar Hammerstein musical *Show Boat*. She was a big hit in Paris, and she toured throughout Europe in the 1930s, as well as in Russia and the Middle East. She enjoyed huge success through World War II (when she entertained US troops around the world), quit music at the age of fifty-nine to take up nursing, and then resumed with a comeback career in 1977 at the age of eighty-two, performing (and recording blues albums) regularly until her death in 1984.

ABOVE LEFT:
Mamie Smith and her Jazz Hounds in a wonderfully posed publicity shot from the mid-1920s.

ABOVE RIGHT:
Music for "Bleeding Hearted Blues," written by Lovie Austin and recorded by Alberta Hunter.

ABOVE LEFT AND RIGHT: The great Bessie Smith. The evocative photo portrait of a melancholy Bessie was taken on February 3, 1936, by the eminent photographer Carl Van Vechten, well-known for his patronage of artists, writers, and performers associated with the Harlem Renaissance.

Unlike most of her blues-singing contemporaries of the 1920s vaudeville scene, who relied on "composed" blues by the likes of W. C. Handy, Perry Bradford, and Clarence Williams, Alberta Hunter also wrote material of her own. One of her songs, which she penned with pianist Lovie Austin (a prolific blues pianist who also recorded with Ma Rainey, Ethel Waters, and Ida Cox), was "Down Hearted Blues." A moderate success for Hunter, the song made history—selling over two million copies in total— when covered by Bessie Smith as her debut single.

The Empress

As soon as Bessie Smith's records started selling well, Columbia Records nicknamed their new star "Queen of the Blues," but the title was amended to "Empress of the Blues," as the big-voiced singer from Chattanooga emerged as the greatest of all the female blues voices of the classic era.

Smith (born Elizabeth Smith in 1894) began performing as a child, busking on street corners as singer and dancer with her brother Andrew on guitar, to help bring money into their poverty-stricken household—both parents had died by the time Bessie was nine, as well as another brother. The two, along with four siblings, were brought up by their older sister Viola, until the oldest boy Clarence ran away from home in 1904 to join a traveling troupe of performers, the Moses Stokes Company, as a comedian and dancer. When the company visited Chattanooga in 1912, Clarence arranged for Bessie to audition for them, and she was hired immediately— primarily as a dancer, as there was already an established singer in the troupe, Ma Rainey. The two became good friends, and although it is open to conjecture whether Rainey actually tutored Bessie, the older singer's influence must have certainly rubbed off on her.

Bessie stayed with the Stokes troupe until 1915, when she joined the TOBA vaudeville circuit as a singer, and she gradually built up her own following across the South and along the eastern seaboard. She was already an established name among black audiences by the time Mamie Smith (no relation) released the ground-breaking "Crazy Blues" in 1920. Determined to follow her namesake on phonograph records, Bessie auditioned for the same label, OKeh, but to no avail. Further rejection from record companies followed before she finally cut her first sides for Columbia on February 15, 1923. The sessions, which continued the following day, produced her first release—the cover of Alberta Hunter's "Down Hearted Blues," coupled with "Gulf Coast Blues" by pianist Clarence Williams.

It was the start of an amazing ten-year recording career, with the single selling a quarter of a million copies in its first year, followed by a string of hits in the newly established "race records" market. In fact, Columbia's first release on their "race" catalog was Bessie Smith's "Cemetery Blues," in September 1923.

RACE RECORDS

When the African-American songwriter Perry Bradford convinced the OKeh record company that there was a market for releases by black artists aimed directly at the black community, he set in motion the precedent of "race" music, which was adopted by most of the major American labels through the 1920s and 30s.

Following the success of Mamie Smith's "Crazy Blues" (which he had persuaded the company to record), in 1921 OKeh took Bradford's advice and began strenuously promoting black music to the black audience, initially under the banner of "Colored" records in their new "Colored Catalogue." They had already used the term "race" in an advertisement in the African-American newspaper *Chicago Defender* in October 1920, referring to Mamie Smith as "Our Race Artist," and in 1922 the label was advertising its "Race phonograph stars" and "Race records" in the paper.

By 1923 OKeh had released forty discs by black artists—six jazz instrumentals, eleven religious records, and twenty-three blues recordings—all promoted almost exclusively to the African-American market. The other major labels were quick to take notice, and Paramount, Victor, Columbia, Vocalion, and the rest soon had established their own race music operations, sending talent scouts on field trips to sign up musicians and singers for their burgeoning jazz, gospel, and blues lists.

It should be noted that although the term "race" may seem derogatory today, at the time it was preferred to "colored" or "Negro" by African Americans, especially in the more progressive urban North. The *Chicago Defender*, for instance, frequently used "race man" and "race woman" to refer to individual members of the black community, and as an adjective, "race" was symbolic of racial pride and solidarity, much as "black" would become used in the 1960s. A conscious effort by OKeh not to offend its newfound customer base was probably behind the label's switch from "colored" in the first place.

There was a boom in record sales generally through the mid-1920s. In 1926 total sales reached $128 million (a figure not met again until after Word War II), and over six million discs were sold in the race market alone. The number of race records released peaked in 1928, when over five hundred hit the stores in that one year, and over 20 percent of the major Victor label's output was from its race catalog.

Inevitably, some white record producers and marketing men began to realize that there was a market for black music among white audiences too, and gradually, through the Depression-hit 1930s and into the 1940s, the companies dropped their black-only marketing strategy. Nevertheless, the music industry bible, *Billboard* magazine, was still publishing a "Race Records" chart in the post-war years (a follow-on from the "Harlem Hit Parade" that it had run from 1942) until 1949, when it was renamed the "Rhythm and Blues" chart at the instigation of one of their journalists, Jerry Wexler.

OPPOSITE LEFT:
A newspaper advert for Columbia's race records catalog of stars including Ethel Waters, Clara Smith, and Bessie Smith—all recordings made "without Scratch"!

OPPOSITE, TOP RIGHT:
The 10-inch paper covers that came with 78rpm singles were ideal for record company advertising, usually listing the latest releases—here spotlighting new music from Brunswick's race catalog.

OPPOSITE, BOTTOM RIGHT:
News article in the African-American newspaper the *Chicago Defender*, reporting Mamie Smith's 1920 recording debut, with two songs published by W.C. Handy's company Pace & Handy, a short while before she released the first-ever blues record "Crazy Blues."

"You know, it has been a big thing, (using terms) from 'colored' to 'Negro' to 'black' to 'African-American.' And back then, the word 'race,' used as an adjective, always had a great deal of esteem attached to it. Because, back in the day, when you called a man a 'race man,' that was a man who lived, exuded and swore by his essential Negritude. Back in Harlem, they would say, 'That man is a race man to the bricks'—meaning from the top of his head to the ground."

JERRY WEXLER

OVERLEAF:
From the late 1920s, the cover illustration for an OKeh Records catalog.

PACE & HANDY

Announcement was made this week by the General Phonograph company, makers of the famous Okeh record, of the first release of a phonograph record made by a colored girl. Miss Mamie Smith, a Harlem young lady, has recorded for the Okeh two numbers published by Broadway's large race publishing house, Pace & Handy Music company, Inc. The two songs are "That Thing Called Love" and "You Can't Keep a Good Man Down," which appear on Okeh record No. 4113. This unusual event was secured only through the influence of Pace & Handy Music Company, who in two years on Broadway have taken their place among the largest and oldest publishers in America.

Lovers of music everywhere, and those who desire to help in any advance of the Race should be sure to buy this record as encouragement to the manufacturers for their liberal policy and to encourage other manufacturers who may not believe that the Race will buy records sung by its own singers.

The Columbia Phonograph company has issued an announcement that Aug. 28 to Sept. 3 will be observed as Marion Harris week by its thousands of dealers throughout the world. One of the first numbers recorded by Miss Harris when she contracted with the Columbia was Pace & Handy's "St. Louis Blues." This song is being featured throughout the country by special window displays and other forms of advertising. Notwithstanding this number has been recorded on every phonograph program, it bids fair to create a sensation as a vocal number by this famous comedienne.

It is a notable fact that the only country-wide weeks set aside by the Columbia have been in honor of compositions or recordings by W. C. Handy. The first of these occasions was when "Handy orchestra week" was universally observed in honor of the release of records made for the Columbia by Handy's orchestra. The second celebration of Marion Harris week features "St. Louis Blues," one of Mr. Handy's best known compositions and a classic of which the country never seems to tire.

"THERE'S FOURTEEN MILLION NEGROES IN OUR GREAT COUNTRY, AND THEY WILL BUY RECORDS IF RECORDED BY ONE OF THEIR OWN, BECAUSE WE ARE THE ONLY FOLKS THAT CAN SING AND INTERPRET HOT JAZZ SONGS JUST OFF THE GRIDDLE CORRECTLY."

PERRY BRADFORD

"...just this side of voluptuous, buxom and massive, but stately too, shapely as an hourglass, with a high-voltage magnet for a personality"

MEZZ MEZZROW, musician, recalling Bessie Smith

A plethora of classics followed her debut, including "Tain't Nobody's Business If I Do" later in 1923; "St. Louis Blues" in 1925 with Louis Armstrong, already regarded as one of the finest records of the era; "Yellow Dog Blues," with a band including Fletcher Henderson and Coleman Hawkins (1925); the archetypal Bessie Smith song "Empty Bed Blues" in 1928; and the following year's magnificent Depression-era anthem penned by songwriter Jimmy Cox, "Nobody Knows You When You're Down and Out":

"Once I lived the life of a millionaire, spendin' my
        money I didn't care
I carried my friends out for a good time, buying bootleg
        liquor, champagne and wine
When I begin to fall so low, I didn't have a friend and no
        place to go
So if I ever get my hand on a dollar again, I'm gonna
        hold on to it 'til that eagle grins."

And in 1929 she also made her only film appearance, a two-reel short entitled *St. Louis Blues*, following the theme of the W. C. Handy song with an extravagant backing that included James P. Johnson on piano, a string section, members of the Fletcher Henderson band, and an angelic-sounding choir.

Despite the slump in vaudeville after 1930, Bessie carried on working solidly. The classic blues style, however, had fallen out of fashion and, as record sales were decreasing generally, Columbia decided to drop her from its roster in 1931. Then, in 1933, she was once again in the studio, now under the auspices of John Hammond for OKeh (which Columbia had taken over in 1925).

This time, sensing the changes in music around her, Bessie attempted something more akin to the swing-era sound, which was then only in its infancy but which was about to become as big a trend as hot jazz had been during the 1920s.

The Hammond recordings in New York were not—at Bessie's specific request—a blues session, although the producer himself later confessed he preferred her earlier material. All four songs—"Do Your Duty," "Gimme a Pigfoot (and a Bottle of Beer)," "Down in the Dumps," and "Take Me for a Buggy Ride"—were written by Leola and Wesley Wilson, a husband-and-wife vaudeville team with long-standing credentials in the record business. But to this day these studio performances stand among Bessie Smith's finest. Three days later, an eighteen-year-old newcomer who idolized Bessie Smith came into the very same studio to record with the same lineup of musicians—her name was Billie Holiday.

Bessie Smith continued to draw big crowds across the South, and was also spending more time in the hub of modern music, New York City. But her ambition to make her mark as a regular jazz singer, playing famous Manhattan venues such as Connie's Inn off Broadway and the Apollo Theater in Harlem, was tragically cut short on September 26, 1937 when she was involved in a car accident on the road between Memphis, Tennessee, and Clarksdale, Mississippi.

She was traveling with her lover, Richard Morgan, who was driving, when their fast-moving Packard hit the rear end of a truck and rolled over, crushing Bessie's left arm and ribs. A doctor who was in a following car drew up and tended to the injured singer, while his companion called for an ambulance from a nearby house. When Bessie was finally admitted to hospital it was too late; she died of her injuries later that morning.

Some accounts implied that her death could have been avoided had she not first been refused admission to an all-white hospital in Clarksdale, but this has been proven false—she was taken straight to the G. T. Thomas Hospital, which was for black patients, where her condition proved too critical for the surgeons to save her.

Bessie Smith's funeral was held in Philadelphia—the city where she had lived for some time—on October 4, 1937. The day before, an estimated ten thousand people, mainly from the city's black community, filed past her coffin. But her grave remained unmarked until 1970, when a tombstone was erected, paid for by Juanita Green (who had worked for Bessie as a maid) and the blues-rock vocalist Janis Joplin.

OPPOSITE:
A long shot facing east from 8th Avenue along West 125th Street (now also known as Martin Luther King Jr Boulevard) in Harlem during the 1930s, with the Apollo Theater prominently visible on the left. When it opened in 1914 the Apollo was a whites-only venue, but after closing briefly in the early 1930s it reopened in 1934, catering primarily for black patrons. It became a prime center for African-American entertainment, and has been a launch pad for hundreds of jazz, blues, and soul artists over the years. It was the home of the nationally syndicated TV variety show *Showtime at the Apollo*, which ran for over a thousand episodes between 1987 and 2008.

> **"I will turn back my mattress and let you oil my springs,
> I want you to grind me daddy till the bells do ring,
> Ooh daddy, want you to shave 'em dry,
> Oh pray God daddy, shave 'em baby won't you try?"**
>
> LUCILLE BOGAN, "Shave 'Em Dry"

The Blue Blues

Many of the songs made famous by the classic blues singers of the 1920s can be considered risqué in their treatment of sexual themes, full of the double entendre that made numbers like Bessie Smith's "Empty Bed Blues" notorious in their day:

"Bought me a coffee grinder that's the best one
    I could find
Bought me a coffee grinder that's the best one
    I could find
Oh, he could grind my coffee, 'cause he had a
    brand new grind ..."

But for sheer outrageousness, no singer matched Lucille Bogan. Her explicit lyrics often addressed taboo themes like prostitution, adultery, and lesbianism, and social issues including alcoholism, drug addiction, and marital abuse. Raised in Birmingham, Alabama, Bogan (née Anderson) first recorded some vaudeville songs for OKeh in New York in 1923 before cutting "Pawn Shop Blues" later that year in Atlanta, Georgia—one of the first black blues singers to have recorded outside of NYC

or Chicago. But the records didn't sell particularly well, and Lucille didn't enter a studio again until 1927, when she made her first hit, "Sweet Petunia," for Paramount. Nevertheless, her experience of tough juke joints and dance halls around the South during the intervening four years gave her plenty of source material for self-penned songs, which by 1930 concentrated almost exclusively on the seedier—and sexual—side of life.

Songs like "Tricks Ain't Walkin' No More" and "Sloppy Drunk Blues" established her reputation for the scandalous, and from 1933 to 1935 she recorded over one hundred songs, mostly under the pseudonym of Bessie Jackson. These included some of her biggest successes, often with titles that gave away the bawdy nature of the songs—such as "My Georgia Grind" and "Mr. Screw Worm in Trouble." And in 1935 she recorded the song for which she is most famous, "Shave 'Em Dry," with lyrics so shocking that she actually recorded two versions: one for the general record-buying public, and an unexpurgated version with hard-core language that would startle most listeners even today.

ABOVE LEFT:
The only known photograph of the queen of the risqué blues, Lucille Bogan.

LEROY CARR

Hugely influential among generations of blues artists, Leroy Carr pioneered the archetype of the laid-back, piano-playing blues crooner, leading the way toward a more urban-oriented style of blues. With his long-time accompanist Scrapper Blackwell on guitar, from 1928 he forged a series of blues classics in songs like "When the Sun Goes Down," "Mean Mistreater Mama," and their most famous release, "How Long, How Long Blues." A major star in the blues firmament of the early 1930s, his career was cut short in 1935 when he died of kidney failure at the age of thirty.

> **"He came to fame towards the end of the 'classic blues' era, which had been typified by female singers with their origins in the vaudeville tradition, and who—like their rural, male counterparts—usually chose to tackle a song at full vocal tilt. Carr brought a more contemplative attitude to his material."**
>
> **JOHN COLLIS**, CD notes *Leroy Carr: American Blues Legend*

Born
Leroy Carr, March 27, 1905, Nashville, Tennessee

Died
April 29, 1935, Indianapolis, Indiana

Instruments
Piano, Vocals

Recording Debut
"How Long, How Long Blues" / "My Own Lonesome Blues"
Recorded June 19, 1928, Indianapolis, Indiana
Vocalion Records

Awards
Inducted into Blues Hall of Fame, 1982
"How Long, How Long Blues" inducted into Grammy Hall of Fame, 2012

Playlist
"How Long, How Long Blues" [1928]
"Midnight Hour Blues" [1932]
"Mean Mistreater Mama" [1934]
"Blues Before Sunrise" [1934]
"Shady Lane Blues" [1934]
"When the Sun Goes Down" [1935]

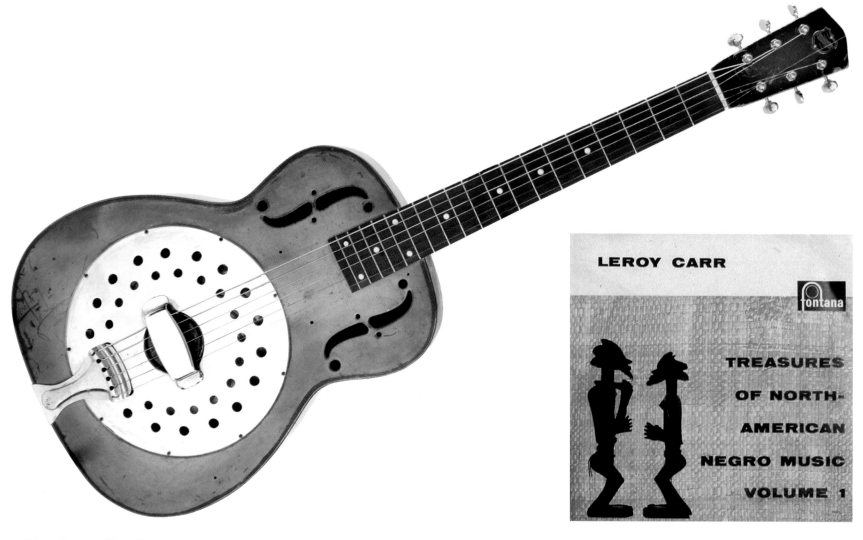

How Long, How Long

Less strident in delivery than his female counterparts—or indeed, than the guitar-picking country bluesmen who began to appear on record from the mid-1920s—piano player and vocalist Leroy Carr represented a more restrained form of blues. Briefly a bootlegger when Prohibition was at its height, he quit the illegal alcohol business to become a full-time musician, and from 1928, with his regular guitarist partner Francis "Scrapper" Blackwell, he made some of the most influential recordings in the history of the blues.

The Nashville-born Carr met up with Blackwell in Indianapolis, where his parents had moved when he was still a child. The two began to perform together, and in 1928 Vocalion Records producer Mayo Williams recognized the potential of the duo, with Carr's elegant vocals and rolling piano perfectly matched by Scrapper's measured picking style.

Their debut release on the Vocalion label turned out to be their biggest triumph: "How Long, How Long Blues" was a national hit in 1928, and became an instant eight-bar blues classic, covered by innumerable artists ever since. There followed a string of big sellers for the pair, including seminal songs that have become blues standards, such as "(In the Evening) When the Sun Goes Down," "Blues Before Sunrise," and "Midnight Hour Blues."

Despite his success, Leroy Carr fell victim to the alcoholism that had plagued him since his days of bootlegging moonshine liquor, and he died of kidney disease in 1935, aged just thirty. Scrapper Blackwell all but retired after Leroy's death, until reappearing on the music scene during the 1950s; in October 1962 he was shot dead in an alley mugging, a few months short of his sixtieth birthday.

Leroy Carr's laid-back vocal style had a huge influence on artists as diverse as Nat King Cole, T-Bone Walker, and Ray Charles, while his evocative self-penned songs have been covered by Robert Johnson, Big Bill Broonzy, Eric Clapton, and many, many others.

The classic blues period lasted into the early 1930s, when record sales of all types of music plummeted with the onset of the Depression. By this time blues generally had become an established element in the catalogs of all the major record companies, with the more traditional rural blues artists now vying for popularity—particularly in the African-American "race records" market—with their big city, jazz-oriented counterparts.

ABOVE LEFT:
A National Resonator guitar, typical of that played by generations of blues musicians including Leroy Carr's accompanist Scrapper Blackwell.

ABOVE RIGHT:
A 1958 UK extended play record on the Fontana label, which featured four classic 1930s tracks by Leroy Carr: "Midnight Hour Blues," "Gone Mother Blues," "Mean Mistreater Mama," and "Blues Before Sunrise."

OPPOSITE:
A photography studio portrait of Leroy Carr with his longtime musical partner, guitarist Scrapper Blackwell.

DOCKERY FARMS
EST. 1895 BY
WILL DOCKERY 1865-1936
JOE RICE DOCKERY
1906-1982

BACK COUNTRY BLUES

Paramoun
ELECTRICALLY RECORDED
12909-B
High Water Everywhere
Part II
(Patton)
Charley Patton
Vocal
Guitar Ac
L60
THE NEW YORK RECORDING LABORATORIES - PORT WASHINGTON, WIS. TRADE

BROWNIE McGHEE
SONNY TERRY

Gennett
11862
524
5459-B
STOVE PIPE BLUES
(Williams)
Daddy Stove Pipe
Vocal with Guitar & Harmonica
DIVISION OF
THE STARR PIANO CO.
RICHMOND
IND.

COUNTRY BLUES

The acoustic guitar styles that characterized much of the basis of the blues evolved in a multitude of forms across the Southern states of America. Most closely associated with the term "country blues" were the Mississippi Delta slide guitar players like Robert Johnson, his mentor Son House, and Elmore James—although the latter became better known as a founding influence in Chicago electric blues. But country blues extended from the East Coast "Piedmont" blues of Blind Willie McTell and Brownie McGhee, to the Texas blues crafted by the likes of Blind Lemon Jefferson and Lightnin' Hopkins, with a diversity of regional variations in between. After being "rediscovered" via the pioneering field recordings made by John and Alan Lomax and others, many country players enjoyed a new lease of life during the folk and blues revivals of the 1950s and 60s.

It didn't take long, with the classic blues boom in full swing by the mid-1920s, for the big record companies to seek out the rural bluesmen (and they *were* mostly men) who were as popular in the South as the female vaudeville entertainers. The majority accompanied themselves on guitar, and they were often itinerant musicians who had built up a reputation with the rural public before being "discovered" by the record makers on their field trips to the South and elsewhere.

The earliest of these rural blues artists to make records was Sylvester Weaver, who released two instrumental sides on the OKeh label in October 1923, "Guitar Blues" and "Guitar Rag." They were the very first country blues to appear on disc, and also the first featuring the slide guitar style that would become one of the key trademarks of country blues from then on. Over the following couple of years the first of the country blues vocalists likewise released records, beginning in 1924 with Ed Andrews, Daddy Stovepipe, and Papa Charlie Jackson, and then in early 1926 with the debut releases by one of the music's true pioneers, Blind Lemon Jefferson.

Into the field

Studio recording was still a relatively primitive affair, so it was a fairly straightforward exercise for record companies like OKeh and Paramount to sometimes cut records on the road during field trips—and far easier than arranging for an artist to make the long journey to Chicago or New York, the main centers of the recording industry. An engineer would set up a temporary studio in a hired hotel room or empty shop premises, and a label talent scout—often on the lookout for gospel and hillbilly performers, as well as blues musicians—would be on hand to supervise the session. Each recording was restricted to the three-minute maximum running time of a 78-rpm ten-inch disc, so several different artists might be recorded in a single day.

It was during such a trip to Atlanta, Georgia, in March 1924 that history was made, when an OKeh Records team came across Ed Andrews busking on the street. In the first-ever field recording of a vocal country blues artist, Andrews cut just two tracks—"Barrelhouse Blues"

and "Time Ain't Gonna Make Me Stay"—the latter was subsequently promoted as the A-side on the record. Billed in OKeh's race records publicity material alongside singles by Sara Martin, among others, the June release was an inauspicious introduction of country blues to the record-buying public. Andrews' delivery sounded rough-and-ready, and his guitar technique was basic, to say the least. He never made any more recordings, and there is no further mention of him anywhere in the annals of the blues.

Recording just a couple of months after Ed Andrews, and reckoned to have been the earliest-born blues artist to record, Johnny Watson—best known as Daddy Stovepipe—was born in Mobile, Alabama, in 1867. He was a professional musician before the turn of the century, playing guitar with a Mexican mariachi band, then worked as an all-around entertainer in the famous Rabbit Foot Minstrels. By the early 1920s he had moved to Chicago, where he played as a guitar-harmonica one-man band on the South Side's Maxwell Street. It was here he acquired the name Daddy Stovepipe, after the trademark top hat he always wore, and it was here he was spotted by Gennett, cutting his first sides, "Sundown Blues" and "Stove Pipe Blues," in Richmond, Virginia (surprisingly not Chicago), on May 10, 1924. By then he was fifty-seven years old and almost certainly the first blues harmonica player to appear on record. Watson went on to make various records as Stovepipe, including some memorable jug band–style sides with his wife, Mississippi Sarah, in the early 1930s. After World War II he was back busking in Chicago, and at the grand old age of ninety-three he cut four sides for the compilation album *Blues from Maxwell Street*. He died three years later, in 1963.

OPPOSITE LEFT:
Chicago's bustling Maxwell Street located on the South Side, which—by the end of the 1920s—had become the heart of the African-American community in the city.

OPPOSITE RIGHT:
From the Library of Congress, "Retrospection," a study of an old African American leaning on his banjo, taken in Savannah, Georgia, in 1902.

"Right where blues songs were born is where Ed. Andrews was singing 'em and playing 'em when the special OKeh Recording Expedition discovered him. Why, man alive, he was just scattering happiness all around, wherever he appeared. And now, on his first OKeh records, "Time Ain't Gonna Make Me Stay," this boy is certainly up-holding his good reputation."

OKeh Records advertising copy for Ed Andrews' "Time Ain't Gonna Make Me Stay"

The first commercially successful records by a self-accompanied country blues singer were made in August 1924 by Papa Charlie Jackson. Like Daddy Stovepipe, Papa Charlie busked frequently in Chicago's Maxwell Street, and he also played clubs around the city. Accompanying himself on banjo, Jackson cut his debut, "Papa's Lawdy Lawdy Blues" and "Airy Man Blues," for the Paramount label, and the following month made his most famous recording, "Salty Dog Blues." Papa Charlie's specialty was the six-string banjo, tuned like a guitar, on which he was something of a maestro, also appearing on various jazz recordings and accompanying classic blues singers including Ida Cox and Ma Rainey. A link between country blues and urban jazz styles, Jackson—who died at age forty-eight in 1938—had a sophisticated approach to playing that defies exact classification. His music featured straight blues playing, a little ragtime here and there, and a certain amount of "hokum"—spicy pop songs full of sexual innuendo, which he helped pioneer with his 1925 hit "Shake That Thing."

Ed Andrews, Stovepipe, and Papa Charlie differed widely in the kind of music they made, but with their debut releases all three signaled the record companies' new strategy to delve into rural America for the "real" blues, having realized there was a big market for it among African Americans across the country. And in 1925, on a field trip to Dallas, Texas, Paramount Records discovered the first country blues player to achieve an audience nationwide: a blind street singer by the name of Lemon Henry Jefferson.

Blind Lemon

Lemon was one of seven children born to Alec and Carlissy Banks Jefferson, poor sharecroppers in Freestone County, East Texas. Facts about his exact birth date are hazy, but a census record uncovered in the 1990s puts it at September 24, 1893. Much detail of his life has vanished into obscurity, with only two known photographs of him in existence, but it's generally presumed he was blind from birth.

How Jefferson began playing music as a youngster is also unclear, but he must have picked up on the bluesmen traveling around the area and taught himself guitar. By his late teens he was playing and singing in various East Texas towns including Waco, Buffalo, and Dallas, where he settled for some time. In Dallas he met and befriended Huddie Leadbetter, later to become world famous, known as Lead Belly. The two teamed up together for a short while, with the younger Jefferson an early influence on Lead Belly's guitar playing.

ABOVE LEFT AND RIGHT: Another early blues artist of whom there is only one photograph known to be in existence, Blind Lemon Jefferson's image appeared on much of his publicity material almost as a branding logo.

BLIND LEMON JEFFERSON

Born blind in East Texas, Blind Lemon Jefferson was the classic itinerant blues musician playing on street corners for a living. The first of the great country bluesmen to cut records, his unique single-string sound marked him as something special when Paramount Records came seeking new talent in Dallas in 1925. He recorded nearly a hundred sides over the next three years, with resounding success, becoming the first big star of country blues—he could even afford to employ a chauffeur. Unlike most of the early country blues players, Jefferson wrote much of his own material—songs that have since been covered by numerous artists including B. B. King, the Grateful Dead, and Bob Dylan.

"Blind Lemon was a medium-size brownskin who kept himself neatly dressed. He was erect in posture, and his speech was lovely and direct to the word. He had no glasses when I first saw him. A young man who was very attentive to him acted as his guide. Although he was supposed to be completely blind, I still believe he could see a little bit. If he couldn't, he darn sure could feel his way 'round—the old wolf!"

VICTORIA SPIVEY

Born
Lemon Henry Jefferson, September 24, 1893, Couchman, Freestone County, Texas

Died
December 19, 1929, Chicago, Illinois

Instruments
Vocals, Guitar

Recording Debut
"I Want to Be Like Jesus in My Heart" / "All I Want Is That Pure Religion" [as Deacon L. J. Bates]
Recorded December 1925 or January 1926, Chicago, Illinois, Paramount Records

Awards
Inducted into Blues Hall of Fame 1980

Playlist
"Long Lonesome Blues" [1926]
"Rabbit Foot Blues" [1926]
"Black Horse Blues" [1926]
"Matchbox Blues" [1927]
"Black Snake Moan" [1927]
"See That My Grave Is Kept Clean" [1927]

"Blind Lemon," as he became known, was a regular at the corner of Elm Street and Central Avenue in Dallas. Soon he was striking out on the road as a travelling blues musician—though his broad repertoire embraced spirituals and folk tunes as well—playing in the Mississippi Delta, Memphis, and even further afield.

In 1925 a Dallas record store proprietor (many such retailers acted as part-time talent scouts for the record companies) made a demo disc of Jefferson and sent it to Mayo "Ink" Williams, the pioneering African-American blues producer, at Paramount Records in Chicago. Not long afterward, Williams had Blind Lemon travel north to the Windy City for his first recording sessions.

Initially he cut two gospel numbers—"I Want to Be Like Jesus in My Heart" and "All I Want Is That Pure Religion"—under the pseudonym of Deacon L.J. Bates, but he was back in the studios again three months later, in March 1926, to record some blues under his own name. His first release from the four-song session, "Booster Blues" backed with "Dry Southern Blues," was the start of a prolific though short recording career, in which he cut nearly a hundred sides between 1926 and 1929.

Those releases, whose huge success made Blind Lemon Jefferson the first great star of country blues, changed the

history of the music. With his unique combination of eerie high-pitched vocals and highly skilled guitar playing, there was a sound to Jefferson's records that identified them on first listen. His self-penned compositions and weirdly individualistic delivery—"uncommercial" many would have said—established the idea of blues players as musical personalities in their own right, not just interpreters of attractive or catchy songs.

Blind Lemon died in Chicago in December 1929, probably from a heart attack, though rumors—from him being poisoned by a jealous lover to attacked by a dog—abounded for years. As with his birth, there was no official record of his passing nor a death certificate.

"The Masked Marvel"

Along with Blind Lemon Jefferson, Charley Patton is widely considered the most important of the early country blues players, and among the first of the great bluesmen to come out of the Mississippi Delta. Although he was around forty when he cut his first records in 1929, he had been a consummate performer since his teen years and was already hugely influential on other emerging blues players, including Robert Johnson, Howlin' Wolf, and John Lee Hooker.

ABOVE LEFT:
The image of Charley Patton staring straight at the camera is also an only-known picture, believed to be taken in 1929 when it appeared as a full-length portrait on the front of a 1930 "blues calendar" published by Paramount Records.

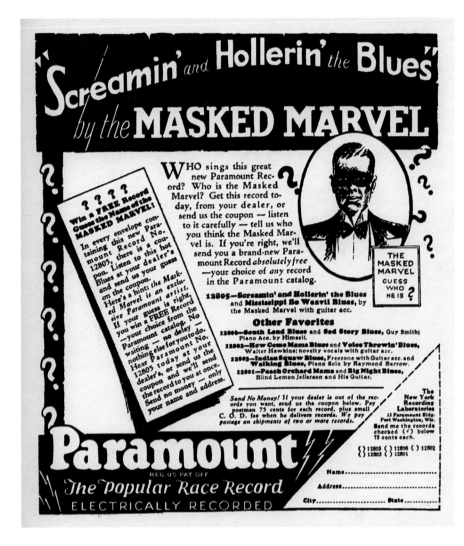

ABOVE RIGHT:
Entry form for the "Masked Marvel" contest. The initial pressing run of 10,000 copies of "Screamin' and Hollerin' the Blues" were released under the pseudonym "The Masked Marvel," with the contest formally announced in the *Chicago Defender* on September 7, 1929. The numbers of winners is not known, but sales of the single must have exceeded the first 10,000 as later pressings appeared credited as Charley Patton on the label.

As with many country bluesmen of the era, Patton's exact birth date is hard to pin down. Biographer John Fahey estimates him to have been "about twenty-one" when he married his second wife in 1908 (putting his birth date at 1887–88), while the University of Memphis musicologist Dr. David Evans states he was "almost certainly born in 1891." What we do know is that Patton was born into a family of sharecroppers near the town of Edwards, in central Mississippi. His light complexion gave rise to various conjectures as to his racial origins— he was always considered African American, but in fact was a mix of black, white, and Native American Cherokee.

In 1900 his family moved a hundred miles north to the enormous ten-thousand-acre Will Dockery Plantation in the Delta region, and it was there that Patton was first mesmerized by the playing of guitarist Henry Sloan. Sloan played a very early form of the blues, and as the young Patton latched on to him, following him from gig to gig, Sloan gave him his first, and probably only, guitar tuition. By the time he was nineteen or twenty, Charley had developed a solid style of his own, performing and writing his first songs, including "Down the Dirt Road Blues" and the number that would become his theme song, "Pony Blues."

In his early twenties Patton began playing regularly with guitarist Willie Brown, who would also feature on many of his later records. His playing began to influence others around him in the Dockery area, including the influential guitarist and vocalist Tommy Johnson, whose repertoire included "Pony Blues." And around 1914, Charley was also playing alongside members of the Chatmon family, who (with guitarist Walter Vinson) would become famous as the Mississippi Sheiks.

Into the mid-1920s, Patton traveled far and wide across the Delta, west to Arkansas, south to Louisiana, and north to the hub city of Memphis. As a live performer—he was still two or three years away from recording—his influence was being felt by the likes of Howlin' Wolf (who recalled seeing him play outdoors near Dockery Plantation in 1926), an entranced John Lee Hooker, and a young Robert Johnson—who followed Charley to gigs, just as the latter had, himself, stalked Henry Sloan some twenty years earlier.

After being heard by a Mississippi music store owner, Patton cut his first sides for Paramount on June 14, 1929, in Richmond, Indiana. Those initial eighteen songs included his debut release, "Pony Blues" and "Banty Rooster Blues," which immediately cemented his

THE LEGEND OF THE CROSSROADS

One of the most enduring myths surrounding the Delta blues—and one that still attracts fans and pilgrims generation after generation—is the Faust-like legend of how Robert Johnson sold his soul to the Devil at a lonely crossroads at midnight, in exchange for his phenomenal talent as a guitarist.

The legend in the Delta was that if a bluesman waited at a crossroads on a dark moonless night, Satan himself would appear and offer to tune his guitar—at a price. The myth attached itself to Johnson by way of explaining the astounding progress he made on the instrument between 1930 and 1932, a transformation noted by his contemporary Son House. It was seemingly further substantiated by the singer's self-penned material, in songs like "Me and the Devil," "Preachin' Blues (Up Jumped the Devil)," "Hell Hound on My Trail," and of course "Cross Road Blues."

"I went to the crossroads, fell down on my knees,
I went to the crossroads, fell down on my knees,
Asked the Lord above, Have mercy,
Now save poor Bob, if you please."
"Cross Road Blues"

The enduring power of the crossroads legend, which has fascinated generations of blues fans, was confirmed with the 1986 movie *Crossroads*, a comedy-drama in which a young white guitar player teams up with an old African-American musician on a quest to uncover the truth of the Robert Johnson story. After various adventures the pair end up at a deserted Mississippi crossroads, where indeed the Devil appears, with the film ending in a spectacular guitar duel. The movie featured a blues soundtrack by Ry Cooder and Steve Vai on guitars, and Sonny Terry on harmonica.

And exactly where was the mysterious crossing? Legend pinpoints the junction of Highway 61 and Highway 49 near Clarksdale, Mississippi, but as the point where those two "roads" now intersect is over half a mile from its original position in the 1930s, there is no longer an actual crossroads where an aspiring blues player might hope to convene with the Devil some dark and lonely night.

OPPOSITE:
A typically deserted crossroads – exactly the kind of landscape where Robert Johnson made his mythical pact with the Devil.

FULL-RANGE RECORDING

Vocalion

with Guitar

Blues Singing
(DAL 398)

ME AND THE DEVIL BLUES
-Johnson-

ROBERT JOHNSON

04108 A

"He [Robert Johnson] told me about going to the crossroads. Matter of fact he spoke that he went to the crossroads, and I didn't know exactly at the time what he mean, and what he'd done. But from then on, when I go to the country I went to the crossroads . . . maybe [Robert] did talk about the crossroads just to frighten people—he said he went down to the crossroads and went down on his knees and met a man, but I never met a man! Robert was a big bullshitter."

DAVID "HONEYBOY" EDWARDS

reputation with a broader public. For the third release from the session, "Screamin' and Hollerin' the Blues," backed by "Mississippi Boweavil Blues," Paramount hit on an audacious marketing gimmick. Instead of crediting Charley Patton, the artist's name on the label was given as "The Masked Marvel." Every copy of the 78 came with a coupon on which listeners could guess who the singer was; those who submitted a correct entry won a free record from the Paramount catalog.

The Masked Marvel publicity stunt illustrated how the blues was now regarded as a commercial proposition, part of the pop music of the day. And indeed, Charley Patton acted the pop star, famous for his flamboyant showmanship—playing the guitar behind his head, behind his back, and between his knees. But equally stunning was the imagery he brought to his self-penned songs, full of the local color of the South in numbers like "Green River Blues," "Down the Dirt Road Blues," and his celebrated account of the 1927 Mississippi floods, "High Water Everywhere."

Another twenty-eight recordings followed five months later; then, in 1930, a third session was arranged with Patton's old colleague Willie Brown, pianist Louise Johnson, and his common-law wife Bertha Lee contributing vocals on some tracks. The great bluesman Son House was also involved.

Charley Patton played extensively across the South, where his popularity was at a high; he performed every year in Chicago, and appeared in New York City in the year of his death, 1934. He died of a heart disorder just two months after his final recording session.

Delta blues

As the blues evolved across the rural South in the earliest part of the twentieth century, regional variations had naturally developed, and, given the slower communications of that era, many styles had time to establish their own character, little influenced by what might be happening just a hundred miles away. All that was to change with the proliferation of the phonograph and radio, but by the time blues musicians were making records in the mid-1920s, various modes and techniques had already emerged as distinct genres in their own right—including Delta blues, historically the best-known and most influential style of country blues.

Life in the Delta region of Mississippi—the flat flood plain between the Mississippi and Yazoo rivers in the northwest of the state—was hard, especially if you were black. Most post-Emancipation work for African Americans was still as a laborer in the cotton fields, or as struggling to make a living as a sharecropper. Local blues was played on the cheapest and most portable instruments, often homemade in the first instance, and most prominently guitars; and most of the bluesmen were also singers rather than just instrumentalists.

The guitar technique that came to prevail in Delta blues was essentially as accompaniment to vocals, and often characterized by the fluid sound of "bottleneck" playing, which originally employed the neck of a bottle (soon replaced by metal "bottlenecks" manufactured for the purpose) to slide up and down the frets of the instrument, creating a continuous shift in pitch and a keening, "worried" sound.

ABOVE:
From 1961, a Gibson J-45. The classic guitar, which has been used by blues musicians for decades, was first manufactured in 1942. Nicknamed "The Workhorse," it has become one of the best-selling acoustic guitars of all time.

CHARLEY PATTON

One of the all-time greats and a true originator of the country blues, and the first of the recorded seminal Delta bluesmen, Charley Patton was an inspiration to musicians like John Lee Hooker and Robert Johnson before he had even walked into a recording studio. While still in his teens, Patton was writing his own material and perfecting a unique guitar style that has been emulated by generations since. By the time he made his first records for Paramount in 1929, he was already something of a celebrity across the southern states where he performed, and studio success only enhanced his fame. Numbers like his signature "Pony Blues" have been covered by innumerable artists and are now standards of the genre, while his evocations of life in the Deep South stand as a chronicle of a world now lost forever.

> "Charley Patton's appeal to us is on an emotional level more than any other, and it is a profound appeal. His evocations of hard times, loneliness, traveling, rural landscapes and natural disasters, religious faith, sexual politics and emotional turmoil reach close to our hearts."
> DICK SPOTSWOOD

Born
Charles Patton, April 1891, Edwards, Hinds County, Mississippi

Died
April 28, 1934, Indianola, Mississippi

Instruments
Vocals, Guitar

Recording Debut
"Pony Blues" / "Banty Rooster Blues"
Recorded June 14, 1929, Richmond, Indiana
Paramount Records

Awards
Inducted into Blues Hall of Fame 1980

Playlist
"Pony Blues" [1929]
"Down the Dirt Road Blues" [1929]
"Screamin' and Hollerin' the Blues" [1929]
"Green River Blues" [1929]
"High Water Everywhere" [1929]
"A Spoonful Blues" [1929]
"Pea Vine Blues" [1929]
"All Night Long Blues" [1930]
"Stone Pony Blues" [1934]
"34 Blues" [1934]

OPPOSITE:
A close-up detail of a bottleneck player in action with his resonator guitar, with a manufactured steel "bottleneck".

TOP AND BOTTOM LEFT:
The rent parties, where bluesmen like Sleepy John Estes often found work, were sometimes more than just word-of-mouth affairs, with elaborate flyers and invitations printed to attract "customers" for the money-raising event.

ABOVE RIGHT:
Homemade instruments fashioned from domestic items, of the kind often found in the rural South, including horns, a washboard, and a rudimentary drum.

When the record company scouts started to journey down South, flushed with the success of their initial blues releases and eager to find fresh material for their new Race Records catalogs, the Delta was fertile ground for their recording trips. Although Charley Patton was one of the earliest of the great Delta players to cut records, he certainly wasn't the first. That honor is generally accorded to Freddie Spruell, a Chicago-based singer-guitarist who nevertheless played in the characteristic Delta style. He recorded "Milk Cow Blues" for OKeh Records in June 1926, and the single was credited to "Papa Freddie."

Sleepy John Estes

Highly influential as an early Delta-style player, though born and raised outside the Delta region in West Tennessee, was Sleepy John Estes. He was born in 1899, and by age twenty he was playing around Brownsville, Tennessee, with two regular accompanists—Hammie Nixon on harmonica and guitarist Yank Rachel—who would work with him on and off for the next fifty years.

Sleepy John made his first recordings in Memphis in September 1929, at a session set up for Victor Records by Ralph Peer, one of the pioneers of field recordings. In 1931 he moved to Chicago with Hammie Nixon, where he played "rent" parties (where residents would throw open their house and sell booze to help to pay the rent) and on street corners. He had one of the most distinctive voices in early blues; his strong vocals conveyed the power of his evocative lyrics, which addressed personal issues, life on the land ("Working Man Blues"), and even local politicians ("Lawyer Clarke Blues").

After going blind in 1949, Estes slid into poverty and obscurity. But he later became another conspicuous example of an old Delta bluesman being "rediscovered" during the 1960s folk-blues revival. He appeared at the Newport Folk Festival in 1964 and toured Europe and Japan throughout the 1970s.

As a songwriter, Sleepy John's legacy is formidable, with artists covering his songs ranging from Muddy Waters to Led Zeppelin and Johnny Winter. He died as a result of a stroke, in June 1977.

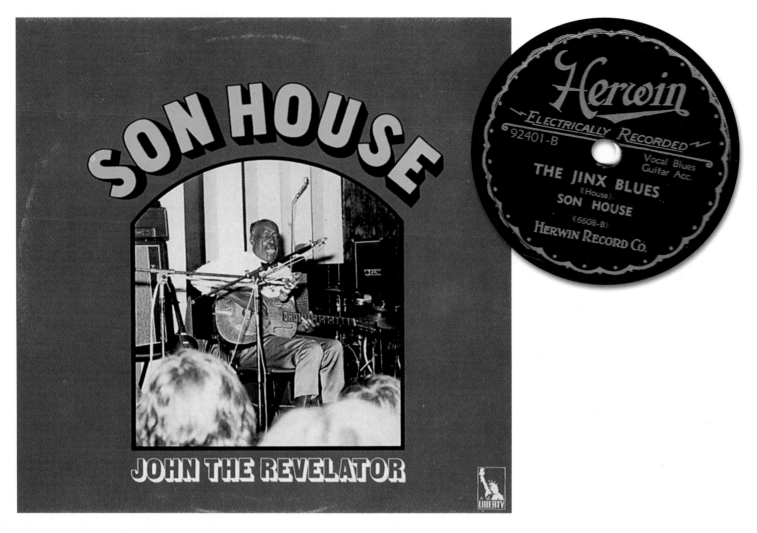

Son House

When Charley Patton traveled to Grafton, Wisconsin, in 1930 for his third session for Paramount, he was accompanied by his wife Bertha Lee, regular sideman Willie Brown, pianist Louise Johnson, and an extraordinary singer-guitarist who was pivotal in the development of Delta blues: Son House. An ex-Baptist preacher, Eddie James House brought to the blues all the intensity of a hot gospel sermon—one of his classic songs was called "Preachin' the Blues"—and he would be a key influence on Robert Johnson, Muddy Waters, and the subsequent history of the blues.

Born in 1902, "Son" House grew up on a plantation near Clarksdale, Mississippi, and was preaching in church by his mid-teens. In his mid-twenties he taught himself to play guitar. God-fearing folk saw this as the result of a conversion from the music of the Lord to the music of the Devil; according to House's own recollections, his immediate inspiration was hearing bottleneck-style guitar for the first time, played by Willie Wilson.

He bought a guitar from a musician named Frank Hoskins, took lessons from his friend James McCoy, and within a very short time was playing the blues himself. House started playing at rent parties and local get-togethers. From all accounts, though details are sketchy,

Son House's development as a musician was remarkable, and he was soon in demand around the Clarksdale area. His career seemed cut short however, when during a brawl in a juke joint in 1928, he shot and killed a man (allegedly in self-defense). He was sentenced to fifteen years in the notorious Mississippi State Penitentiary at Parchman Farm. After a judge re-examined his case in 1929 House was released from prison, and he went to live in Lula, Mississippi, where he met up with Charley Patton. The two men soon became firm friends, and when Patton had a recording date for Paramount in Grafton Wisconsin in 1930, he took Son House with him, convincing Paramount they should record him too.

Four records—eight songs—were released from the sessions, but none sold particularly well. Son House remained just a local attraction, playing dance halls and juke joints around the Delta through the 1930s, usually accompanied by Willie Brown, until his next recordings in 1941 for Alan Lomax and the Library of Congress. He disappeared into obscurity again after moving to New York, only to be rediscovered during the 1960s blues revival. But it was during his days as a traveling musician in the early 1930s that Son House made a crucial impact on those around him—most importantly on the most celebrated of all the Delta bluesmen, Robert Johnson.

ABOVE LEFT:
Released after his "rediscovery," a 1970 album by Son House *John The Revelator* recorded live at the 100 Club in London in the summer of that year. The veteran bluesman finally retired just four years later, and died in Detroit, Michigan, in 1988.

WORKING MAN BLUES

The blues has its roots in the rural workplace of plantation labor and sharecroppers. Most of the early exponents of country blues were indeed "sons of the soil," while after the diaspora north and west, many doubled a musical life with the bread-winning occupations open to blacks across America, from railroad workers to barbers, and hotel porters to chauffeurs for the rich. And, as in Skip James' "Hard Times Killing Floor Blues," it wasn't just the work that was chronicled—in this case the "killing floor" of the slaughterhouse—but the hard times that persisted outside its blood-spattered doors in the teeth of the Great Depression.

" Now, they oughta cut out so many trucks and tractors, white folks, you oughta work more mules and men Now, you oughta cut out so many trucks and tractors, white folks, you oughta work more mules and men Then you know that would make, whoo boy, money get thick again ... "
SLEEPY JOHN ESTES, "Working Man Blues," 1941

" Oh I started out young. They handed me a cotton sack when I was about eight years old. Give me a little small one, tell me to fill it up. Really that never was my speed, I never did like the farm but I was out there, with my grandmother, didn't want to get away from around her too far. Them older people like my grandmother, they didn't think you could make it in no kind of city. They think if you get in the city—starvation. But they were living in starvation on the planatation.
    I went to school but they didn't give you too much schooling because just as soon as you was big enough, you get to working in the fields. I guess I was a big boy for my age, but I was just a boy and they put me working right alongside the men. I handled the plow, chopped cotton, did all of them things. "
MUDDY WATERS

" You see a white face there and he don't look like the people you've been seeing around, you think he's a cop or FBI or something suspicious. A lot of people was doing a lot of undercover stuff then. "
JIMMIE ROGERS

" Robert Johnson was playing with Son House and Willie Brown the first time I seen him. Out from Robinsonville, a big plantation called Flowers, a big house all painted white. They had a big quarters—most people who worked on the plantation had houses built up around the barn, that's the quarters. He was playing a juke house in the quarters. "
HONEYBOY EDWARDS

" I worked there [in Memphis] as an usher ... seatin' people in the New Daisy Theater for about two, three dollars a week. You could live on that: a nickel would get you almost two loaves of bread. You could just about get along on that, it was good. You had five bucks, you had a lotta money. "
JOHN LEE HOOKER

" ... there was a lot of guitar playing in the neighborhood, like in the barbershops. Barbers were always guitar players. In the slack time between haircuts, they'd sit up in the chair and work out their little parts. They were good with their hands, so they were good with the guitar. A lot of times, the guitar player is the barber for the band on the road. "
TAJ MAHAL

" You know that people They are drifting from door to door But they can't find no heaven. I don't care where they go. "
SKIP JAMES, "Hard Times Killing Floor Blues," 1931

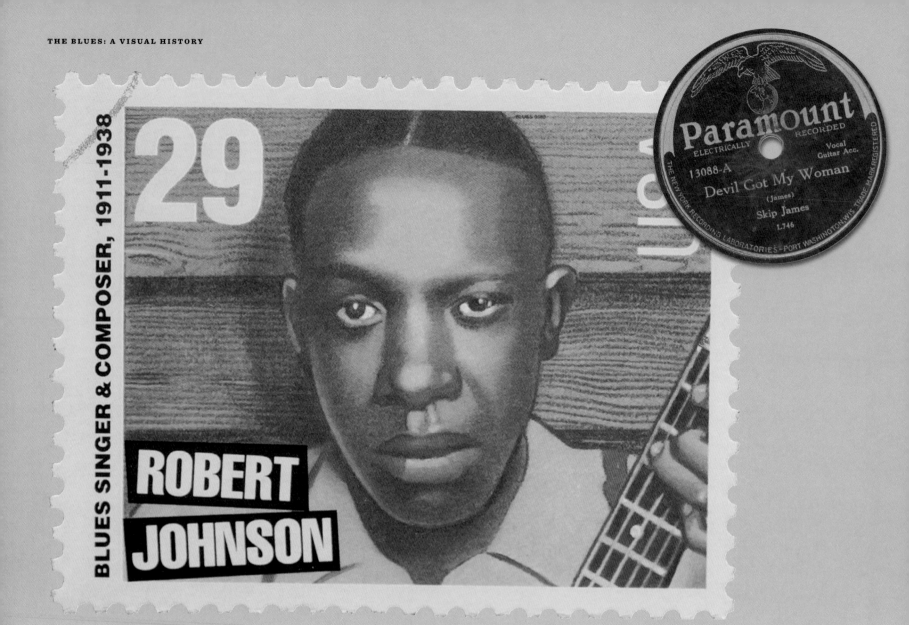

BLUES SINGER & COMPOSER, 1911-1938

29

ROBERT JOHNSON

Paramount
ELECTRICALLY RECORDED
Vocal Guitar Acc.
13088-A
Devil Got My Woman
(James)
Skip James
L746

"King of the Delta Blues Singers"

With a powerful, almost other-worldly voice that cuts through the surface noise of primitive 78s, deeply emotional lyrics, and an innovative instrumental style that would inspire generations of guitarists to come, the sheer impact of Robert Johnson's music is impossible to overstate. In a year or so he went from being a below-average musician to someone who impressed the very best of the established Delta blues players.

Robert Leroy Johnson was born in Hazelhurst, Mississippi, in 1911, and moved with his family to Memphis in 1914, before settling back in the Delta four years later. It was there, in the town of Robinsonville, that as a teenager Johnson began playing harmonica and hanging around the local blues scene. As his confidence and ability grew, he would follow guitarist Willie Brown to gigs, often sitting in with him on his performances—and also with Brown's sometime partner Charley Patton when he hit town.

In 1930 Son House, newly released from his stretch at Parchman Farm, had settled in Robinsonville.

"Robert was tall, brownskin, skinny, had one bad eye. He looked out of one of his eyes; one eye looked like it had a cataract—in that bad eye. At that time he was playing on a Sears-Roebuck 'Stella' guitar. Yeah, he was good."

DAVID "HONEYBOY" EDWARDS

He began playing regularly with Willie Brown, and the young Johnson was entranced by his guitar style, so much so that he abandoned his harmonica in favor of a guitar. He would watch and listen to the two older men every chance he got, absorbing their sound—especially that of Son House, who recalled that at the time Johnson's playing was nothing better than "a racket."

Johnson left Robinsonville in 1931 for his home town of Hazelhurst, where he got married and also fell under the influence of a local guitarist, Ike Zinnerman. Over the next year or so he practiced his guitar technique, learning much of his new material from phonograph records.

ABOVE LEFT AND RIGHT:
Skip James' 1931 record "Devil Got My Woman" was later adapted by Robert Johnson as "Hell Hound on My Trail," using the same minor tuning which gave James' guitar style its dark, atmospheric sound. Rediscovered in the 1960s, James died in 1969, having influenced generations of musicians.

ABOVE LEFT:
The album that reawakened interest in the music of Robert Johnson in 1961, *King of the Delta Blues Singers*, with its original cover painting by Burt Goldblatt.

ABOVE RIGHT:
The Gunter Hotel in San Antonio, Texas, where Robert Johnson's first recording sessions took place in November 1936.

When he returned to Robinsonville and played for Willie Brown and Son House, the pair couldn't believe what they were hearing: how had Johnson improved so much in so short a time?

Much of Johnson's new material was clearly derived from records by the likes of Skip James, Kokomo Arnold, and Leroy Carr, but his dazzling technique put most other blues musicians in the shade. He began to travel the South extensively, his reputation growing as he worked the blues circuit of speakeasies, levee camps, and juke joints. And he played to the crowd, delivering not just blues, but also hillbilly numbers and pop songs—like many of the most successful traveling blues performers, he made his money by giving audiences what they wanted.

In 1936, Robert Johnson decided it was time he made some records of his own, and he sought out record store owner H. C. Speir in Jackson, Mississippi. Acting as a talent broker for most of the big record companies, Speir has since been credited as "the godfather of Delta Blues," without whom some of the great blues players would simply never have recorded. Speir heard Johnson and immediately put him in touch with the American Recording Corporation (ARC), who arranged a session to take place in San Antonio, Texas, on November 23, 1936.

The recordings made over four days produced sixteen songs, including Johnson's debut 78 "Terraplane Blues" and "Kind Hearted Woman Blues." The record, on the Vocalion label, was a small-scale local hit, selling around five thousand copies, but didn't change Johnson's lifestyle by any means. He was still playing the same venues as always when he attended another recording session, this time in Dallas, in 1937. In addition to the sheer dynamic of his performances on record, it was significant that Johnson tailored the songs perfectly to the three-minute limitation of a 78-rpm disc, a discipline often overlooked by his blues-playing contemporaries.

Over the two recording sessions, Robert Johnson recorded a total of just twenty-nine songs, and most were never released in his lifetime—on August 16, 1938, he died in Greenwood, Mississippi, at the age of twenty-seven. The circumstances of his death are still shrouded in a certain amount of mystery, but the most accepted of various accounts is that he was poisoned by a jealous lover—or, possibly, the jealous husband of a lover.

Tragically, the work of Robert Johnson would not reach an audience any wider than specialist blues collectors until 1961, when an LP collection of his recordings appeared under the title *King of the Delta Blues Singers*. Aptly named, the album sparked worldwide interest in the man who posthumously influenced a generation of musicians, including Ry Cooder, Bob Dylan, Eric Clapton, the Rolling Stones, and countless more.

One of Robert Johnson's key inspirations in terms of songwriting was Skip James, whose "Devil Got My

THE FIELD RECORDINGS OF JOHN AND ALAN LOMAX

Among various collectors and folklorists responsible for the preservation of the early country blues—and other forms of American rural folk music—the most famous were John A. Lomax and his son Alan Lomax, who, through their field recordings for the American Library of Congress and other institutions, recorded literally thousands of hours of folk music, much of it authentic blues which would otherwise have been lost forever. Field recording was not simply the preserve of the Lomaxes, of course—record companies sent teams of talent spotters rushing to the rural South following the success of the first classic blues singers, and other musicologists, like the African Americans Zora Hurston and John Wesley Work, recorded and archived traditional folk music.

From the early 1920s, folklorist Robert W. Gordon had been recording folk music from various rural communities across the United States, on behalf of the Library of Congress. In 1928 the Library established the Archive of American Folk Song, and John Lomax, researching his *Anthology of American Ballads and Folk Songs*, offered to go on an extended field trip at his own expense if the Library would fund his equipment. In June 1933, with his son Alan Lomax, he set off on the first of many important field trips across the South.

Using a state-of-the art aluminum disk recorder installed in the trunk of their Ford sedan, the father-and-son team made hundreds of recordings over the next eighteen months in plantations, lumber camps, juke joints, churches, and especially prisons—or more precisely, the notorious prison farms that supplied cheap labor courtesy of the racially biased legal system in the Southern states.

It was in one such establishment, the Louisiana State Penitentiary at Angola, that the Lomaxes encountered a twelve-string guitar player by the name of Huddie Ledbetter—to be better known as Lead Belly (or Leadbelly). After being released for good behavior, the singer was employed by John Lomax as an assistant for the recording sessions. He was launched into the public spotlight in December of 1934, when he began performing during Lomax's lecture tour, and he went on to be one of the most celebrated exponents of traditional folk-blues. Another penal colony that the Lomaxes' attention made famous was Parchman Farm in Mississippi, described by Alan Lomax in his book *The Land Where the Blues Began*. He noted how the work songs the prisoners chanted in their daily toil related directly to the days before the blues and to slavery itself.

Interrupted only by World War II, the Lomaxes continued their field trips until John's death, aged eighty, in 1948. By then, along with other zealous academics and song collectors, they had contributed enormously to the widespread rediscovery of the old blues, bringing to the world's attention the work of Sleepy John Estes, Son House, Muddy Waters, and many other seminal artists. After his father's death, Alan Lomax carried on their work, recording other key blues musicians including Big Bill Broonzy, Sonny Boy Williamson, and Memphis Slim.

OPPOSITE LEFT:
John Lomax during a field trip in Alabama in 1940, meeting a local called Uncle Rich Brown.

OPPOSITE, TOP RIGHT:
John Lomax (left) on board a boat during a recording expedition to the Bahamas in the summer of 1935.

OPPOSITE, BOTTOM RIGHT:
Prisoners on Parchman Farm, Mississippi, recording for Alan Lomax in 1959.

"I had to face that here were the people that everyone else regarded as the dregs of society, dangerous human beings, brutalized, and from them came the music which I thought was the finest thing I'd ever hear coming out of my country . . . These people were poetic and musical, and they had something terribly important to say."

ALAN LOMAX, recalling Parchman Farm

Woman" and "32-20 Blues" both were later adapted by Johnson. Another "discovery" of H. C. Speir, in 1931 James made several important recordings for Paramount, each usually distinguished by his falsetto vocals and subtle guitar style, then drifted into obscurity during the Depression—only to be rediscovered, like so many others, during the folk-blues revival in the 1960s.

Another key name in Delta blues, Big Joe Williams is remembered as much for his song legacy as his own fine recordings, particularly "Crawlin' King Snake"—a number more usually associated with John Lee Hooker, which Big Joe recorded in 1941—and his 1935 blues hit "Baby Please Don't Go," which many have covered since and was a best seller for Van Morrison with his group Them in 1964.

Booker T. Washington White, or "Bukka" White as he was known, first recorded for Victor in 1930. He had left his native Mississippi for Chicago, where he worked as a street musician playing gospel songs, only to return to the Delta, inspired by Charley Patton to play the blues. Only two of his fourteen Victor sides were released at the time; the next session he recorded was for John Lomax in 1939, while he was serving time at Parchman Farm.

Yet another bluesman who would have died in obscurity were it not for the folk revival that came twenty years later, Bukka White's few recordings—including some sensational 1940 sides with Washboard Sam—now stand as classics in the genre.

No thorough account of the legacy of Delta bluesmen can neglect to mention Arthur "Big Boy" Crudup. Born in 1905, he first made a name for himself around Clarksdale, Mississippi, before moving north to Chicago. In the late 1940s he recorded for a variety of labels, helping spearhead the evolution of the Delta style when he toured with Sonny Boy Williamson II and Elmore James—both Delta blues players who were better known as pioneers of amplified "Chicago" blues. Outside the world of blues music, however, Crudup is best known as a songwriter, having composed two of Elvis Presley's key early records—his 1954 debut disc "That's All Right" and the 1956 single "My Baby Left Me."

The move to Chicago by a number of important Delta bluesmen—as well as Williamson and Elmore James, these included Muddy Waters, Howlin' Wolf, and Johnny Shines (who had toured with Robert Johnson in 1935)—was crucial in the 1950s, in the eventual change from country-based acoustic blues to electric blues. But as noted earlier, country blues wasn't restricted to the Delta style; it manifested itself elsewhere in various regions of the United States.

ABOVE LEFT:
Bukka White, whose "Fixin' To Die Blues" helped his rediscovery during the 1960s folk boom after it was covered by Bob Dylan on his eponymous 1962 debut album.

ABOVE RIGHT:
A famed accompanist to Bukka White among others, Washboard Sam (real name Robert Brown) was a big name in his own right on the 1930s Chicago blues scene. He retired from music in 1949 to become a police officer, and made a brief comeback in the early 1960s before his death from heart disease in 1966.

OPPOSITE:
Arthur "Big Boy" Crudup. Despite his songs being covered by Elvis Presley and dozens of other artists, Crudup—like most veteran blues musicians "rediscovered" in the 1950s and 60s—received hardly any of the royalties he should have earned.

ROBERT JOHNSON

Without doubt the most influential of all Delta Blues musicians, Robert Johnson, with a legacy of fewer than thirty recordings, created a template for the music that still applies today. Following in the footsteps (literally) of blues pioneers Charley Patton and Son House, he honed a personal style that combined a spectacular guitar technique with starkly evocative vocals. Many of his original songs were indeed derivative of previous blues records he had picked up on, but what came through in Johnson's music was like nothing ever heard before, a potent combination of music and singing that laid bare the emotion behind the lyrics. The blues, and the popular music it would revolutionize decades later, would never be the same.

"Robert Johnson is little, very little more than a name on aging index cards and a few dusty master records in the files of a phonograph company that no longer exists. A country blues singer from the Mississippi Delta that brought forth Son House, Charley Patton, Bukka White, Muddy Waters, and John Lee Hooker, Robert Johnson appeared and disappeared, in much the same way as a sheet of newspaper twisting and twirling down a dark and windy midnight street."

Original liner notes, *Robert Johnson: King of the Delta Blues Singers*

Born
Robert Leroy Johnson, May 8, 1911, Hazlehurst, Mississippi

Died
August 16, 1938, Greenwood, Mississippi

Instruments
Vocals, Guitar

Recording Debut
"Terraplane Blues" and "Kind Hearted Woman Blues"
Recorded November 23, 1936, San Antonio, Texas
Vocalion Records

Awards
Inducted into Blues Hall of Fame, 1980

Playlist
"Terraplane Blues" [1937]
"32-20 Blues" [1937]
"Crossroad Blues" [1937]
"I Believe I'll Dust My Broom" [1937]
"Sweet Home Chicago" [1937]
"Hell Hound on My Trail" [1937]
"Me and the Devil Blues" [1938]
"Preachin' Blues" [1939]

Like many of his contemporary bluesmen, Blind Blake often appeared on record as accompanist to other front men. The record by "Banjo Joe" was actually the debut release of Gus Cannon, of jug band fame. The picture of Blake, the only one known to exist, was taken in around 1927.

Piedmont blues

While Delta blues were developing along the Mississippi River in the south, out on the east coast another form of the music was taking shape: Piedmont blues. The finger-picking guitar technique, which involves a syncopated approach similar to ragtime, was named after the Piedmont plateau area stretching down from Richmond, Virginia, to Atlanta, Georgia, where many of its leading exponents were based.

Among them, the blind itinerant musicians Blind Blake, Blind Willie McTell, and Blind Boy Fuller all helped establish the style, while singer-guitarists like Josh White, Brownie McGhee, and Rev. Gary Davis (aka Blind Gary Davis) came to greater prominence during the folk-blues revival of the 1950s. The style went on to inspire many younger musicians including Ry Cooder, Eric Bibb, and Doc Watson.

Blind Blake

To be black and blind in the American South in the 1920s and 1930s meant, in most cases, that your prospects were, to put it mildly, desperate. It was not surprising, therefore, that many in such seemingly hopeless circumstances took to playing guitar, learning some songs, and hitting the road as busking entertainers on the streets of Southern cities.

That was the path taken by Blind Blake, a traveling musician born Arthur Blake in Newport News, Virginia, in 1896. Little is known about his life, outside of a remarkable recording career that established him as an originator of the "fingerstyle" ragtime guitar central to Piedmont blues.

A spectacular performer, Blake first recorded under his own name for Paramount Records in Chicago, cutting his debut release "West Coast Blues" and "Early Morning Blues" in August 1926. Between then and Paramount's demise in 1932 he was the label's best-selling artist and the most frequently recorded in their race records catalog. He cut some eighty sides for them as a solo performer, as well as appearing on many sessions for other artists including Ma Rainey, Gus Cannon, and Ida Cox.

Because Blind Blake mixed his blues with ballads and other popular song styles, there has always been discussion as to whether he can be classed as a pure blues performer. But on the evidence of his many blues recordings, and his instrumental prowess as a pioneer of the Piedmont ragtime style, he must be recognized as one of the prime voices in country blues.

Blind Willie McTell

Born in 1898, William Samuel McTell—Blind Willie McTell—was raised first in Thompson and later in Statesboro, both in Georgia. Willie ran away from home in his early teens and began playing on street corners and in traveling medicine shows. After a spell at a school for the blind in Macon, Georgia, he was back roaming the East Coast by the mid-1920s, playing the streets and town squares, and in October 1927 recorded four sides for Victor Records.

His sweet-sounding tenor voice lacked the hard-edged quality of many bluesmen, and it came across particularly effectively on record—especially with his syncopated technique on the twelve-string guitar, which he used because of its bigger sound. A year later he laid down some more songs for Victor, among them his all-time classic "Statesboro Blues." Like many itinerant musicians, McTell took opportunities as they presented themselves, so when a rival company offered to record him, he simply adopted a pseudonym to avoid contractual problems. Some key recordings he cut for Columbia, for instance, were released under the name of Blind Sammie; his other aliases included Georgia Bill, Pig & Whistle Red, and Hot Shot Willie.

Becoming a fixture on the streets of Atlanta, McTell released numerous records through the 1930s for Victor, Vocalion, Columbia, OKeh, and Decca, and although none were hugely successful at the time, his output under various names was prolific. In 1940 John Lomax recorded him for the Library of Congress archive, and in 1949 McTell cut some sides for the Atlantic and Regal labels. He carried on playing, still based on the sidewalks of Atlanta, until his death from a stroke in 1959—just before the 1960s blues revival, for which he was a major inspiration.

Blind Boy Fuller

Despite making records over only a six-year span, Blind Boy Fuller was arguably the most popular of the original Piedmont blues players. Born Fulton Allen in Wadesboro, North Carolina in 1907, he learned to play the guitar as a child. In his mid-teens, while working as a laborer and with no immediate plans to embark on a musical career, he began to lose his eyesight. Doctors attributed it to ulcers behind his eyes; other accounts blamed an ex-girlfriend who threw corrosive lye water in his face. Whatever the cause, by 1928 he was totally blind and had turned to playing as a street musician to earn a living.

Absorbing the records of musicians like Blind Blake, he soon developed a virtuoso guitar technique of his own, honed to perfection through constant appearances at house parties, on street corners, and outside the huge tobacco warehouses and factories in Durham, North Carolina. It was in Durham, in 1935, that talent scout J. B. Long secured Allen a recording session for ARC in New York. After the thirteen-song session, which also included guitarist Blind Gary Davis and washboard player Bull City Red (both had traveled with Allen from Durham), Long decided to rename Allen "Blind Boy Fuller" to promote his debut single—a stunning version of the traditional "Rag, Mama Rag," backed with "I'm a Rattlesnake Daddy."

Fuller made more than 130 recordings during the next six years, spanning various genres including ragtime, folk, pop, and solid blues—all complemented by a formidable finger-picking style on his trademark National resonator guitar. His records—including iconic classics "Get Your Yas Yas Out" (later adapted by the Rolling Stones as "Get Yer Ya-Yas Out") and "Step It Up and Go"—proved to be hugely popular with African-American (and later, white) record buyers.

Blind Boy Fuller made his final recordings in June 1940. He was already beset by acute kidney problems—probably brought on by his prodigious drinking—which finally led to his death eight months later, at just thirty-three years of age.

ABOVE:
"Razor Ball," one of the Columbia discs that Blind Willie McTell made under the pseudonym of Blind Sammie; it was the 'B' side of "Talkin To Myself," both recorded in Atlanta, Georgia on April 17, 1930.

OPPOSITE LEFT:
A very 1920s-style advertisement for Hohner harmonicas and accordions. German-based Hohner was—and still is—the world's leading brand name in harmonicas, and much favored by blues players of the instrument.

OPPOSITE, TOP RIGHT:
When bluesmen like Blind Willie McTell made a record, usually the first thing the record company would do was get them into a local photography studio for a publicity shot.

OPPOSITE, BOTTOM RIGHT:
Blind Boy Fuller, also looking somewhat out of place in the genteel setting of the photographers' studio.

LEFT:
Lightnin' Hopkins during the 1960s. *Rolling Stone* magazine put Hopkins at number 71 in their list of 100 greatest guitarists of all time.

Texas blues

Just as Delta blues and Piedmont blues often found
their fullest expression outside the regions where they
originated, gradually evolving away from their country
roots, so Texas blues, born in the Southwest, made its
mark most prominently as part of "big city" electric
blues in the postwar years of the 1940s, in the work of
formidable musicians like T-Bone Walker, Albert Collins,
and the rhythm and blues singer Big Mama Thornton.

The roots of Texas blues, however, go back to the early
days of recorded blues and the work of Blind Lemon
Jefferson. Typically, from the start the Texas sound had
more of a jazz feel to it, with single-string improvised
guitar licks used as the punctuation for vocals, a device
largely pioneered by Jefferson. And it was a direct
protégé of Blind Lemon who formed the link between
acoustic Texas blues and its amplified successors:
Sam "Lightnin'" Hopkins.

Lightnin' Hopkins

Hopkins was born in Centerville, Texas, in 1912. He
picked up guitar at a very early age with a "cigar box"
instrument his elder brother taught him to play, and his
interest in the blues was consummated at the age of eight
when he heard Blind Lemon Jefferson performing at a
local picnic. A couple of years later he dropped out of
school and began playing small-time gigs around Texas,
often as a duo with his cousin, the country blues singer-
guitarist Texas Alexander. He also accompanied Blind

Lemon from time to time at informal church events,
with the master allegedly insisting no one could back
him except Hopkins.

He continued playing with Alexander until the mid-
1930s, when he was sentenced (for an offense now
unknown) to a stretch in the Houston County Prison
Farm. On his release, he rejoined his cousin playing juke
joints and such, and the two attempted to break into the
Houston music scene, but to no avail—Hopkins still
had to rely on manual laboring jobs to make a living.

It was in Houston in 1946, when he was actually
performing on the street, that Hopkins was spotted
by a scout from the Los Angeles-based label Aladdin.
A session was arranged for November, at which the
guitarist recorded twelve tracks with pianist Wilson
Smith, including his debut single "Katie Mae Blues."
Aladdin decided to nickname Hopkins "Lightnin'" and
Smith "Thunder," with the disc released as "Thunder
and Lightnin'"

The record was a big hit in the Southwest, and as
Lightnin' Hopkins he went on to record more sides for
Aladdin in 1947, followed by sessions for Gold Star in
Houston. He was highly prolific, recording for more than
twenty labels and releasing up to a thousand songs during
his career. His biggest hits started in 1948 with the
success of "Shotgun Blues" in the national R&B charts,
a powerful evocation of Texas blues of a previous era.
More big sellers followed, including "Tim Moore's Farm"
and "T-Model Blues" in 1949, and "Give Me Central 209"
and "Coffee Blues" in 1952.

Though he was initially fazed by the onset of electric
blues, Lightnin' made some amazing electric sides for
the Herald label, including the blistering "Lightnin's
Boogie" and "Hopkins' Sky Hop." Whatever the mode,
Hopkins' sheer dexterity made complex improvisations
seem deceptively simple, and his talent in coming up with
spontaneous lyrics to fit a given occasion was the mark
of the true blues poet.

Like many of his contemporaries, Lightnin' Hopkins
was caught up in the renaissance of folk blues, recording
for Folkways Records in 1959, and appearing with Joan
Baez and Pete Seeger at Carnegie Hall in 1960. It was the
start of a new life for his career, taking him around the
world to appear at music festivals through the 1960s and
'70s. He died of cancer in 1982, just six weeks shy of his
seventieth birthday; the *New York Times* obituary called
him "one of the great country blues singers, and perhaps
the greatest single influence on rock guitar players."

THE GREAT MIGRATION

At the beginning of the twentieth century—the era when the blues began—the vast majority of African Americans lived in the rural South, but by the start of the economic Depression in 1929, nearly two million had moved to the industrial cities of the North and Midwest. This was the first wave of what became known as the Great Migration. The second wave began during World War II and lasted until 1970, by which time another five million black Americans had sought a better life away from the rigors of agricultural toil in the former slave states. But it was the first migration that had the biggest impact on the history of the blues and on black American culture generally.

Despite the optimism following the abolition of slavery, most facets of white supremacy were reinstated in the Southern States after the Reconstruction period ended in 1876. These "Jim Crow" segregation policies were made the law of the land. Work on the plantations was as grueling as ever, with only rock-bottom wages in return. The good intentions of the sharecropping alternative were quickly manipulated, and field hands gained little in financial security. When the boll weevil epidemic of 1898 wiped out crops across the region, the numbers of African Americans emigrating from the South began increasing, year by year.

With the onset of World War I in 1914, and the consequent diminishing numbers of European immigrants that had supplied workers to the factories, there was suddenly a shortage of labor in the industrial centers of the North, Midwest, and West. Industry was as busy as ever, meeting war production demands, so recruiting drives aimed at black workers in the South began in earnest. Appeals for laborers, as advertisements and editorial pieces, appeared in black newspapers like the widely read *Chicago*

Defender. By 1920 more than a million African Americans had left the South, mainly by train or bus, some by the riverboats that plied their way up the Mississippi, and a few in automobiles or even horse-drawn wagons.

The *Chicago Defender* was particularly active in encouraging the mass movement of Southern black workers and their families. Throughout its long history (the paper was founded in 1905 and is still published today) the *Defender*, with its motto "Race Prejudice Must Be Destroyed," has championed the African American cause. Decades before the Civil Rights movement it was a campaigning voice against the Jim Crow laws of the South.

In 1917 the paper launched what it called its "Great Northern Drive," likening the migration to the biblical exodus from Egypt, with Chicago cast as a new Promised Land. In its vigorous endorsement of life in the North—especially Chicago—the *Defender* ran numerous editorials and reports about the prospects for black Americans in the "Windy City," contrasted with often lurid accounts of the worst aspects of life in Dixieland, including beatings, lynchings, and so on.

OPPOSITE:
A superb color picture from the Library of Congress, showing sharecroppers chopping cotton on their rented land near White Plains, Georgia, in 1941.

"There was no leader, there was no one person who set the date who said, 'On this date, people will leave the South' They left on their own accord for as many reasons as there are people who left. They made a choice that they were not going to live under the system into which they were born anymore and in some ways, it was the first step that the nation's servant class ever took without asking."

ISABEL WILKERSON, *The Warmth of Other Suns: The Epic Story of America's Great Migration*

"I were in a place called Marigold Mississippi. And you know they had a restaurant in there and in back they had a peephole ... And you could imagine what they were doing back there. They were reading the *Chicago Defender*, and they had a lookout man on the door with a peephole. If a white man come into the restaurant, they'd stick the *Defender* into the stove, burn it up, and start playing checkers. That's the way they had to smuggle the *Defender* down there. That's what they really call a bad negro, a negro that had the nerve to smuggle the *Defender* down in the state of Mississippi ...."

BIG BILL BROONZY

In addition to its news features, and the advertisements for jobs in the North, through the 1920s the *Defender* also carried literally hundreds of ads for jazz and blues records. Ironically, although the paper's editorial line was strongly critical of conditions for African Americans in the South, many of the blues titles from the "race records" catalogs seemed to represent a romanticized view of "back home" aimed at the recently-settled migrants. Not that the burgeoning black populace of the Northern cities were anxious to return to the land of cotton, but the songs tapped into a natural nostalgia for the places they had left behind. Among scores of such records, Ethel Waters released the "Down Home Blues," Clara Smith sang her "Down South Blues," there was Bessie Smith with "Gulf Coast Blues," Papa Charlie Jackson was "Alabama Bound," while Bertha "Chippie" Hill extolled the virtues of her "Georgia Man."

Outside of factory work, where conditions were hard and often dangerous, most jobs for the newly arrived black population were menial "service" occupations such as kitchen hand, cleaner, doorman, and railroad porter. Even in the more relaxed North, the only establishments run entirely by African Americans were those where any kind of racial integration was deemed out of the question—barber shops, hairdressing salons, and funeral parlors.

In 1925 African-American railroad porters made history, when they formed the first black-led labor union, the Brotherhood of Sleeping Car Porters. But arguably of equal importance was their role in the migration itself, by the nature of their job providing a link between life in the industrialized North and rural South. The Pullman porters became ad hoc distributors of the *Defender*, which had few official outlets in the South, and on their return journeys northward would bring back copies of local newspapers and magazines which were a great source of stories for *Defender* journalists to develop.

The porters also played a crucial role in the distribution of blues records, with most releases emanating from Chicago and New York, servicing a Southern audience that otherwise might have been missed by the music companies' official sales network. In many respects the porters were a living source of communication between African Americans in the South and the diaspora of fellow blacks across the country.

The immediate effect of the migration on African-American music was twofold. Musicians and singers were attracted by the greater opportunities in the North, and much of the (mainly black) blues audience that had been concentrated in the South dispersed across the country, with new black ghettos springing up in the big cities. Places like Chicago's South Side, and Central Avenue in Los Angeles, joined Harlem in New York City as the urban nerve centers for every aspect of black culture—including, in its various manifestations, the blues.

Blind Willie Johnson

Back in the era of Blind Lemon Jefferson, the other seminal voice of early Texas blues—Blind Willie Johnson—was not strictly a blues performer, in that his repertoire consisted almost exclusively of gospel songs. But his powerful, haunting narratives were delivered in a blues musical context (unlike most sacred music at the time), and, crucially, he was one of the founding fathers and greatest exponents of the bottleneck guitar style.

Born at the very beginning of the twentieth century (most accounts estimate his birth year as 1902) just south of Waco, Texas, Willie Johnson was blinded when he was about seven years old, in a domestic fracas involving his stepmother hurling a bottle of lye water, aimed at his father. Before the accident he had already expressed the wish to be a preacher, and as he improved on the cigar-box guitar his father had fashioned for him, he put his blues-drenched technique to the service of the Lord, fashioning gospel songs and spirituals out of the "Devil's music" of the blues.

He became a Baptist minister and took his evangelizing music onto the streets of Waco and neighboring cities including Dallas. His deliberately rough vocal delivery served to emphasize the passion of his singing, accompanied by an almost unearthly bottleneck guitar sound—which he actually created with a pocket knife.

In December 1927, Columbia Records brought Johnson into the studio, where he recorded six songs, among them some of his most memorable sides, including "Nobody's Fault But Mine" and his most famous performance (a virtually wordless evocation of the crucifixion of Christ)

"Blind Willie Johnson had great dexterity, because he could play all of these sparking little melody lines. He had fabulous syncopation; he could keep his thumb going really strong. He's *so good*—I mean, he's just so good! Beyond being a guitar player, I think the guy is one of these interplanetary world musicians . . ."

RY COODER

"Dark Was the Night—Cold Was the Ground", which Ry Cooder used as inspiration for his soundtrack for the 1984 movie *Paris Texas*. In all, he cut just thirty sides for Columbia, between then and April 1930, also including "John the Revelator" and his rumination on the Titanic disaster, "God Moves on the Water."

Blind Willie Johnson continued to perform on the streets of Texas cities, including Beaumont, where he settled in the 1940s. It was there he died from pneumonia in 1947, after his house had burned down and, with nowhere else to go, he slept rough for a week in the water-soaked ashes.

The ultimate honor to Blind Willie Johnson's memory came in 1977 when NASA launched the *Voyager I* space probe. Now hurtling through deep space after its thirty-six-year journey to the edge of the solar system, the craft contains a gold-plated disc that includes sounds of life on Earth, including Mozart, Beethoven, Louis Armstrong, Chuck Berry, and Blind Willie's recording of "Dark Was the Night—Cold Was the Ground."

ABOVE LEFT:
Another itinerant blind singer, Blind Willie Johnson applied his stark bottleneck style to his own brand of gospel music—and became a Columbia Records "race" recording star in the process.

ABOVE RIGHT:
The gold-plated NASA disc that includes the haunting sounds of Blind Willie Johnson on an interstellar journey into the unknown.

LIGHTNIN' HOPKINS

A key player whose career stretches across modern blues history, from backing Blind Lemon Jefferson in the 1920s to playing festivals worldwide in the 1970s, Lightnin' Hopkins was a living link between the country blues and its modern legacy. Playing publicly from the age of ten, he served a two-decade apprenticeship on the road, playing juke joints and bars, before being spotted in Houston, Texas by the LA record label Aladdin. Hit followed hit in the national R&B charts through the late 1940s and early '50s, and he went on to become a fixture on the folk and blues revival circuit, his live performances a potent example of unadulterated Texas blues.

> **"I hate to think of not having a Lightnin' Hopkins, the blues would never have been like it turned out to be . . . because he was a great player, he didn't put sugar on anything, he just played it. And to me that's the kind of blues we need . . ."**
>
> B.B. KING

Born
Sam John Hopkins, March 15, 1912, Centerville, Texas

Died
January 30, 1982, Houston, Texas

Instruments
Vocals, Guitar, Piano, Organ

Recording Debut
"Katie Mae Blues" [as Thunder & Lightnin']
Recorded November 4, 1946, Los Angeles, California
Aladdin Records

Awards
Inducted into Blues Hall of Fame, 1980

Playlist
"Short Haired Woman" [1947]
"Shotgun Blues" [1948]
"Tim Moore's Farm" [1949]
"T-Model Blues" [1949]
"Give Me Central 209" [1952]
"Coffee Blues" [1952]
"Lightnin's Boogie" [1954]
"Penitentiary Blues" [1959]
"Mojo Hand" [1960]

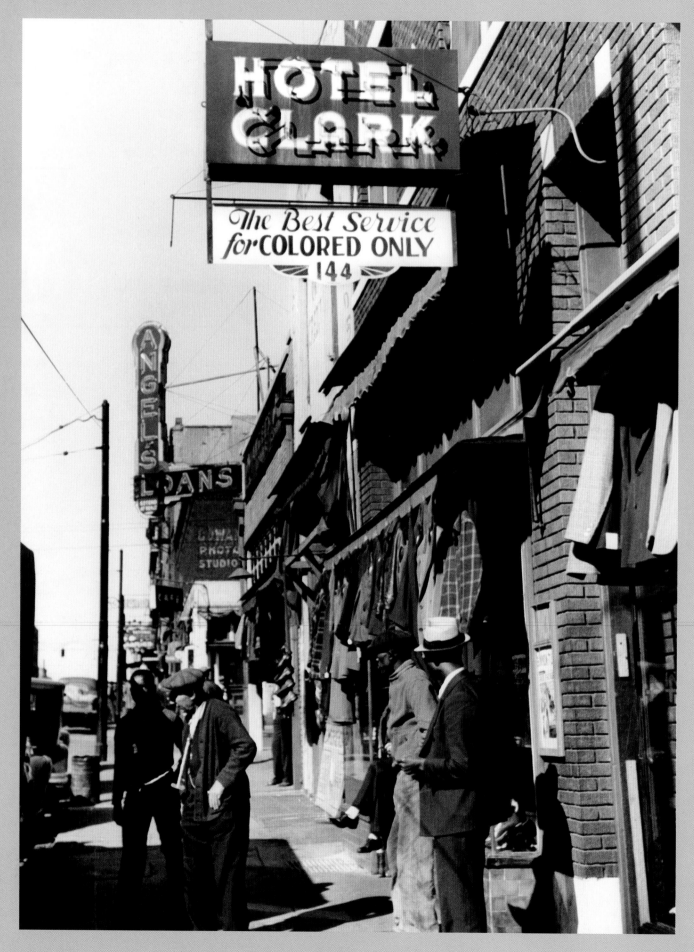

LEFT:
A bustling Beale Street in Memphis, during the 1930s.

W.C. Handy's
BEALE STREET BLUES
"BEALE STREET...WHERE THE BLUES BEGAN"

SCENES REPRODUCED BY COURTESY OF THE COMMERCIAL APPEAL OF MEMPHIS, TENN., FROM THE DEDICATION OF HANDY SQUARE ON BEALE, MARCH 29, 1931.
UPPER LEFT—THE CROWD GATHERED IN SQUARE. UPPER RIGHT IN CAR LEADING PARADE—W. C. HANDY WITH LIEUT. G. W. LEE. LOWER LEFT—PARADE PASSING DOWN BEALE. LOWER RIGHT, SCHOOL CHILDREN IN FLOATS PASSING REVIEWING STAND. CITY, STATE AND FEDERAL OFFICIALS WERE AMONG THE LONG LIST OF SPEAKERS WHO WERE HEARD OVER RADIO AND CAUGHT BY MOVING PICTURE CAMERAS.
HANDY BROTHERS MUSIC CO., Inc.
PUBLISHERS
"Genuine American Music"
1650 BROADWAY, NEW YORK 19, N.Y.

ABOVE LEFT:
A Memphis legend, co-founder of the Beale Street Sheiks, Frank Stokes.

ABOVE RIGHT:
A sheet music edition of W.C. Handy's "Beale Street Blues," depicting scenes from the dedication ceremony of Handy Square on Beale, on March 29, 1931.

Memphis blues

Located on the Mississippi River and crossed by the two great north-south Highways, 51 and 61 (as well as several major east-west paths), Memphis was a natural hub of the blues as African Americans moved from the cotton fields of the Delta and elsewhere. Even before the Great Migration northward, it had a substantial black population and had become a melting pot for the various strains of music surfacing in the closing years of the nineteenth century.

The thriving center of black entertainment in the city soon established itself in and around Beale Street, which by the first decade of the twentieth century was already buzzing with bars and dance halls, featuring the latest in ragtime, jazz, minstrel music, vaudeville, and of course blues—indeed, there was an early name-check for the city in 1912, when the Memphis-based composer W. C. Handy published his "Memphis Blues," followed by the hugely successful "Beale Street Blues" in 1916.

Popular in vaudeville and medicine shows, the Memphis blues style was often characterized by a more exuberant edge than its Delta counterpart. As well as guitar-based blues, the style was also evident in the jug bands that emerged in the city, most famously Gus Cannon's Jug Stompers and the Memphis Jug Band. And it was partly as a jug band musician that the man considered by many to be the father of the Memphis blues guitar style, Frank Stokes, made his mark.

Frank Stokes

Born on New Year's Day, 1888, Stokes began playing guitar and singing on the streets of Memphis while he was still in his early teens, usually partnered with fellow guitarist Dan Sane. Before he was twenty, Stokes had gone into entertainment professionally, as a blackface "minstrel" singer, comedian, and dancer in the Doc Watts Medicine Show, one of the many tent shows that toured the South. While on the road, Stokes developed not only his guitar skills but also a sense of showmanship not found in the performances of most country blues musicians of the period.

Around 1920 he again teamed up with Sane, and together they began to establish themselves on the local Memphis circuit of dances, parties, and picnics, as a jug band-style double act, the Beale Street Sheiks. It was as part of the Sheiks that Stokes first recorded for the Paramount label, in 1927, and in all he made nearly forty recordings, more than half of them with Dan Sane.

With his booming voice and fluid guitar style—both in counterpoint with Sane and as a solo performer—Frank Stokes was a hugely original musician and a pioneering influence on the Memphis blues sound. In September 1929 he made his final recordings, and despite making no phonograph sales during the Depression years, he remained a popular live performer throughout the 1930s and 40s, before his death in Memphis in 1955 after suffering a stroke.

"By the late 1940s it wasn't as though the jukebox was taking the place of live musicians, but the other way around. A performer had to be prepared to deliver anything the audience might want to hear, because a jukebox certainly could. On record, someone like Memphis Minnie was a blues singer. In performance she was a mechanical-age songster. Many blues performers prided themselves on their versatility—and their ability to gauge an audience's desires. They aimed to please."

FRANCIS DAVIS, *The History of the Blues*

Furry Lewis

In addition to being recorded by field trip "expeditions" (as the record companies sometimes grandly billed their talent-spotting excursions), many bluesmen were invited to record in the North, primarily in New York and Chicago. Among those early musicians who made the trek to the big city recording studios was Furry Lewis. Born in Greenwood, Mississippi, in 1893, Walter "Furry" Lewis's family moved to Memphis when he was a child. Skilled on the guitar from his early youth, he became a traveling musician and songwriter before settling back in Memphis in 1922, where his permanent job as a road sweeper subsidized his prolific musical activity.

In 1927 Furry was invited to Chicago by Vocalion Records, where he cut his debut disc "Rock Island Blues" backed with "Everybody's Blues." He went on to also record many sides for Victor, mixing blues version of folk songs like "John Henry" with straight blues such as his celebrated "Judge Harsh Blues." As with so many other blues artists, Furry's career was slowed down by the Depression, but he carried on playing around Memphis before enjoying a new lease of life in 1959, when he was recorded in the city by musicologist Samuel Charters for the Folkways label. He remained a part of the Memphis musical scene, a connection to the past for many of Memphis's 1960s and 1970s hitmakers. As well as making more records Furry toured worldwide as a result of the blues boom, up until his death at age eighty-eight in 1981.

Memphis Minnie

One of the few female artists to come out the country blues tradition, as her name implied, Memphis Minnie crafted her music on the Memphis blues scene. She was born Lizzie Douglas in Louisiana in 1897; in 1904 her family moved to northern Mississippi, where she began to learn guitar and banjo as a child. Something of a prodigy, she played local parties as "Kid" Douglas; then, as a rebellious teenager, she ran away from home at age thirteen to live on Beale Street in nearby Memphis,

busking for tips. After spending four years on the road playing tent shows with the Ringling Brothers Circus, in the 1920s she returned to Memphis, where she began to make a name for herself both as a single performer and with various ad-hoc jug bands.

In 1929 she began playing with guitarist Joe McCoy, who became her common-law husband, and the pair were discovered by a talent scout for Columbia Records. When the duo went to record in New York City, a record producer dubbed them Kansas Joe and Memphis Minnie.

That first session included Minnie's hit song "Bumble Bee," and within a year she had recorded another five or six sessions, including another version of "Bumble Bee" with the Memphis Jug Band. She was a prodigious songwriter, and composed much of her own material. By the time the Great Depression began to bite into the fortunes of everyone in the music business, Minnie was already firmly fixed as a celebrity; she left Kansas Joe and settled in Chicago.

In Chicago, Minnie began venturing into different styles, adopting a bass and drums accompaniment that anticipated the Chicago blues of the 1950s, and by the 1940s she was playing an amplified "semi-acoustic" electric guitar. She was also now married to another guitar man, Ernest Lawlers—known as Little Son Joe—with whom she began to record.

In May 1941 Minnie cut what would be her biggest hit, the racy "Me and My Chauffeur Blues," and she continued working with Little Son into the early 1950s, when she eventually stopped recording due to declining health. The couple retired to live in Memphis, where Little Son died in 1961, and Minnie (after years of convalescence following a stroke) passed away in 1973.

Minnie had a tough, no-nonsense style—she once beat the great Big Bill Broonzy in a musical "cutting contest". This "down-home" attitude, together with her dynamic guitar playing, made Memphis Minnie—like the city from which she took her name—a link between the country blues of the rural South and the brash, neon-lit music of the big city.

OPPOSITE LEFT:
A glamorous-looking Memphis Minnie photographed with her National semi-acoustic guitar c.1938.

OPPOSITE, TOP RIGHT:
Furry Lewis—having been rediscovered, like so many of his veteran blues compatriots, in the late 1950s blues revival—in full flight in a photograph taken around 1970.

OPPOSITE, BOTTOM RIGHT:
The 1961 Furry Lewis album, *Done Changed My Mind*, released on the Prestige Bluesville label, featured a photograph taken by the eminent blues historian Samuel B. Charters.

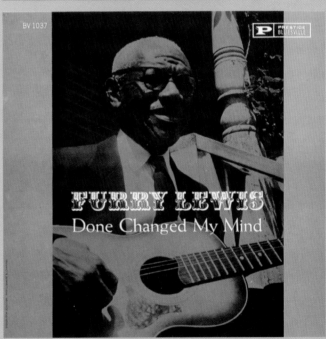

Skilled on the guitar from his early youth, he [Furry Lewis] became a traveling musician and songwriter before settling back in Memphis in 1922, where his permanent job as a road sweeper subsidized his prolific musical activity.

Jimmy YANCEY

VOGUE
EPV 12

ATLANTIC
A-1336
Vocal Quartet
Pub. Progressive, BMI
Time: 2:36
DOIN' THE BEST I CAN
(Jones)
LITTLE JOHNNY JONES
1045

BLACK PATTI
Electrically Recorded
8004-A
Vocal Blues
ROOM RENT BLUES
Mozelle Alderson and Blind James Beck

BIG CITY BLUES

The late 1930s into the war years of the early 1940s was the era of the big swing bands, roaring outfits that crisscrossed the United States coast-to-coast, feeding the jitterbug dance craze that filled the radio airwaves and sold records by the millions. Much of the riffing repertoire of the swing orchestras was solidly based in the blues and provided a platform for the new-style blues shouters who—in parallel with the emergence of flamboyant electric guitar players—anticipated the advent of rhythm and blues after the war.

The blues had been an integral part of jazz from its earliest days, before it first caught on as a pop music craze in the 1920s. Then, with the birth of the big bands in the 1930s, its popularity never really waned. African-American swing pioneers including Fletcher Henderson and Chick Webb ensured that the music retained the potent blues feel of the "hot jazz" that had preceded it, and swing anthems like "One O'Clock Jump," "Stompin' at the Savoy," and "Take the 'A' Train"—huge hits for Count Basie, Benny Goodman, and Duke Ellington, respectively—were all written in blues formats. Even the sweetest-sounding of the big bands, the easy-on-the-ear Glenn Miller Orchestra, had one of its biggest successes with the iconic "In the Mood"—its main theme a simple twelve-bar blues.

The music of the swing bands was, by and large, instrumental, but almost all of them had singers in their permanent lineup, performing small sets as part of live performances, and sometimes appearing (usually billed as "vocal refrain") on recordings. Some of the great song stylists of the mid-twentieth century, including Ella Fitzgerald, Peggy Lee, and Billie Holiday, first made their mark in this way, and although they could all handle blues in one form or another, they were basically jazz singers with a wide repertoire of pop standards, rather than blues performers *per se*.

Goin' to Kansas City

The place where the big swing outfits stuck closer to the blues than most of their contemporaries was Kansas City. Vocalists there developed a style of blues singing that projected the voice—often without the aid of a microphone—over the considerable volume of a full lineup of trumpets, trombones, and saxophones, twenty strong or more. Those who mastered this style became known, fittingly, as the blues shouters. KC, as the city was often called, was a wide-open town from the late 1920s

through the 1930s, largely as a result of the corrupt administration of its political boss, Tom Pendergast. Under Pendergast's regime, a bribed police force allowed gambling and liquor laws to be virtually ignored—even during the nationwide prohibition of alcohol, which lasted until 1933—so clubs and other entertainment spots flourished almost unhindered. With so much work to be found there, KC became a magnet for jazz musicians from all over the country. The town's club scene, with a largely African-American clientele, became famous for all-night sessions where musicians would get together and spontaneously "jam" until dawn.

The first important band to come out of KC was that of Bennie Moten, a native of the city. With his Kansas City Orchestra he pioneered a riffing style of blues-based jazz, based in part on his own boogie-woogie piano technique. But when he recruited Count Basie to play piano in 1929, the band really took off as a blues-based powerhouse, the likes of which had simply never been heard before. And fronting the ensemble on the vocal numbers was Oklahoma-born Jimmy Rushing, the archetypal big-band blues shouter.

OPPOSITE LEFT:
Even by Kansas City's freewheeling standards—not for nothing was it known as the "Paris of the Plains"—the Chesterfield Club was a pretty wild establishment, with the businessman's lunch served by waitresses wearing nothing but shoes and cellophane aprons.

OPPOSITE, TOP RIGHT:
A poster for Kansas City's finest, the Count Basie band, on tour in 1939.

OPPOSITE, BOTTOM RIGHT:
The headquarters of Pendergast Wholesale Liquor in Kansas City, one of various businesses run by mayor Tom Pendergast during his time as the civic supremo of KC.

Mr. Five by Five

Known as "Mr. Five by Five" on account of his rotund build—he was five feet tall, and five feet around his sixty-inch waist—Jimmy Rushing was born in Oklahoma City in 1901. His father played trumpet, and his mother, brother, and sister were all singers. He started, like so many in this volume, as an itinerant blues singer before moving to Los Angeles in 1924, where he sang briefly with the legendary Jelly Roll Morton.

Back in Oklahoma, in 1927 Rushing joined Walter Page's Blue Devils, considered by many to be a prototype for the blues style of the Benny Moten band. Then in 1929, with other members of the Blue Devils, he defected to join Moten. When Moten died in 1935, the band continued under the leadership of pianist Count Basie, with whom Jimmy Rushing would serve as vocalist for the next fifteen years.

With his powerful tenor-baritone voice, Rushing had a distinct blues style, exemplified on his best-known recordings, which included "Sent for You Yesterday and Here You Come Today," "Goin' to Chicago," "I Left My Baby," "Evenin,'" and "Boogie Woogie (I May Be Wrong)."

"The blues are played and sung in a very special way by the majority of Kansas City musicians and singers. They are explosive but fragile; they are intense, but unruffled. They have a kind of beefy sophistication."

WHITNEY BALLIETT, jazz critic and book reviewer for the *New Yorker*

He retired from playing when the Basie band briefly disbanded in 1950, but was soon on the road again having formed a group of his own.

For the next twenty years he performed at jazz festivals, toured with the ex-Basie trumpet star Buck Clayton, guested on albums by Duke Ellington, and even—in an unlikely, but successful teaming—recorded with modern jazz pianist Dave Brubeck. He also took part in several reunions with the Basie orchestra—including the memorable live album *Count Basie at Newport* recorded at the 1957 Newport Jazz Festival.

Jimmy Rushing died in 1971, the year his 1970 album *The You and Me That Used to Be* was named as Jazz Album of the Year by *Downbeat* magazine.

ABOVE LEFT:
A fine study of Jimmy Rushing by the renowned jazz photographer William P. Gottlieb, taken at the Aquarium jazz club in New York City, in October 1946.

BIG JOE TURNER

Nicknamed "the Boss of the Blues," Big Joe Turner was the epitome of the Kansas City blues shouter, equally at home belting out twelve-bar classics over a roaring big band as he was when backed by the potent boogie-woogie of his long-time pianist partner Pete Johnson. Schooled in the hothouse of KC jazz in the 1930s, Joe went on to create the style that would be called rhythm and blues a decade before it was labelled as such. In the first half of the 1950s, he was an early contributor to the birth of rock 'n' roll. Making records and live appearances with some of the finest jazz and blues musicians who ever picked up an instrument, Joe Turner stayed true to his roots for over forty years—as a straight-ahead bluesman of the highest caliber.

> "They didn't have no microphones, they used them pasteboard things. Wha'cha call 'em, megaphones? I didn't have one, didn't need one. You could hear me ten blocks away."
>
> JOE TURNER

Born
Joseph Vernon Turner, May 18, 1911, Kansas City, Missouri

Died
November 24, 1985, Inglewood, California

Instruments
Vocals

Recording Debut
"Going Away Blues" / "Roll 'Em Pete"
December 30, 1938, New York City
Vocalion

Awards
Best Male Vocalist, *Esquire* magazine, 1945
Best New Vocalist, *Melody Maker* (UK), 1956
Inducted into Blues Hall of Fame, 1983
Inducted into Rock and Roll Hall of Fame, 1987

Playlist
"Roll 'Em Pete" [1938]
"Chains of Love" [1951]
"Honey Hush" [1953]
"Crawdad Hole" [1953]
"TV Mama" [1953]
"Shake, Rattle and Roll" [1954]
"Flip Flop and Fly" [1955]
"The Chicken and the Hawk" [1955]
"Boogie Woogie Country Girl" [1956]
"Corrine Corrina" [1956]
The Boss of the Blues: Joe Turner Sings Kansas City Jazz [1956]

The Boss of the Blues

Born in Kansas City in 1911, Joe Turner—or Big Joe Turner, as he was often billed—was a huge figure in every sense of the word. A big man with a big voice, he had an outsized influence on popular music, with a career that linked blues, rhythm and blues, and rock 'n' roll—and, amazingly, without his having to change his style.

Singing on street corners for pocket money while still in his early teens, Joe would try to sneak into the city clubs to hear the music; tall for his age, he would borrow his mother's eyebrow pencil to draw a moustache above his lip to fool the doormen. He quit school at fourteen and started working the clubs regularly, first as a cook, then as a bartender. When he eventually began getting singing gigs at clubs like the Kingfish and the Sunset, it was as "The Singing Barman," still working as a jack-of-all-trades: bartending, carrying crates, serving as a part-time doorman, and other tasks within the clubs.

At the Sunset, he started a permanent musical partnership with boogie-woogie pianist Pete Johnson, stunning the often hard-to-please Kansas City audience with their no-holds-barred renditions of full-bodied blues. Although not usually fronting a big band, Joe Turner's confident style was always that of the pure KC blues shouter, his rich baritone voice soaring elegantly over the seductive pulse of Johnson's classic boogie.

The duo were playing in Kansas City when they were spotted by Columbia Records' John Hammond, who booked them to appear in his "From Spirituals to Swing" concert at New York's Carnegie Hall on December 23, 1938. The show was a landmark in jazz and blues

presentation, with an all-star lineup that included the bands of Count Basie (with Jimmy Rushing) and Benny Goodman, gospel acts the Golden Gate Quartet and Sister Rosetta Tharpe, and bluesmen Sonny Terry, Big Bill Broonzy (who replaced the recently murdered Robert Johnson), and Joe Turner with Pete Johnson. Also on the bill were two of the biggest names in boogie-woogie piano, Albert Ammons and Meade "Lux" Lewis, who performed as a duo before calling Pete Johnson on stage for a three-piano "Cavalcade of Boogie."

The concert was a double triumph for Joe and Pete. They performed and recorded a live version of "Roll 'Em Pete" (listed on the recording as "It's All Right Baby"), which became a hit for the pair. And the hookup with Ammons and Lewis led directly to the Boogie Woogie Trio (with Turner fronting the three pianists on vocal numbers), who enjoyed a year-long residency at the Café Society nightclub in New York, alongside Billie Holiday.

Turner made a number of records for the Vocalion label, including, in 1939, his hit "Cherry Red," which featured a full Kansas City lineup. The following year he signed with Decca Records and recorded with a variety of leading pianists, including Pete Johnson, Art Tatum, Willie "The Lion" Smith, and Oscar Moore. He was now something of a star name, particularly in the African-American community, and Duke Ellington offered him a singing part in his stage show *Jump for Joy*, which opened in Los Angeles in 1941.

Although Turner enjoyed his first national success in 1945 with "S.K. Blues," and famously recorded the ribald "Battle of the Blues" with fellow shouter Wynonie Harris in 1947, things didn't really begin to move for him again

ABOVE LEFT:
Joe Turner's long-term accompanist, the great boogie-woogie maestro Pete Johnson.

ABOVE RIGHT:
A UK release on the London label of Joe Turner's Atlantic classic from 1956, *The Boss of the Blues*. Like much of Atlantic's output during the 1950s, the sleeve design and photography was by Marvin Israel, a much-respected artist and photographer who served as freelance art director for the company.

Poster for a cheaply-produced movie in 1955, with an array of big names including Joe Turner, Count Basie, Amos Milburn, and Ruth Brown, the film—aimed largely at the African-American market—was compiled for theatrical exhibition from made-for-television short films (the promo videos of their day) with newly-filmed host segments to give the impression of a live concert.

until 1951. He was playing the Apollo Theater in Harlem with the Count Basie band, sitting in for a sick Jimmy Rushing, and who should be in the audience but Nesuhi and Ahmet Ertegun, signing up key rhythm and blues acts for their fledgling label Atlantic. Joe's performance that night was, by all accounts, well below par—he'd hardly had chance to rehearse with the Basie band—but the Ertegun brothers liked what they heard, and they signed Joe to their label.

It was the start of a roller coaster ride of hot-selling singles for Big Joe, including such classics as "Chains of Love," "TV Mama," and, in 1953, his first number one in the *Billboard* Rhythm & Blues charts (which had replaced the old Race Records chart in 1949), "Honey Hush." And it was at an Atlantic session in February 1954 that the man dubbed "Boss of the Blues" became, unwittingly, one of the pioneers of rock 'n' roll.

"Shake, Rattle and Roll," written by Charles Calhoun (a pseudonym of Atlantic producer Jesse Stone), was the kind of blues lyric full of sexual innuendo that Joe Turner delivered with great panache. But when it was covered just weeks later by Bill Haley and His Comets—with some cleaned-up lyrics—it was the start of a musical revolution. Both versions became million-sellers, and for a while Joe Turner—then well into his forties—was being promoted to the teenage market as a rock 'n' roll star.

After a number of hits on the national (and indeed international) charts, Joe Turner resumed his place as an established blues shouter, reuniting with Pete Johnson and various alumni of the Count Basie band for the seminal 1956 album *The Boss of the Blues*, a classic in jazz-backed blues singing.

For the next three decades Joe toured the world, continued recording for a variety of labels, and in 1979 took part in the Kansas City jazz reunion movie *The Last of the Blues Devils*, which included "jam session" versions of his classics "Honey Hush," "Chains of Love," and "Shake, Rattle and Roll." He died of heart failure six years later, at the age of seventy-four, on November 24, 1985.

Along with the Benny Moten–Count Basie lineups, the most influential band to come out of Kansas City in the 1930s was that of Jay McShann, an Oklahoma-born pianist who moved to KC in 1936. McShann's lineup in the late thirties included jazz legends-to-be Ben Webster on tenor sax and be-bop pioneer Charlie Parker on alto—both Kansas City born and bred.

Blues was a very big element in the band's repertoire and featured on most of their recordings, with vocals supplied by blues shouter Walter Brown. Hailing from Dallas, Texas, Brown had a somewhat smoother approach than the prime architects of the style, Jimmy Rushing and Joe Turner. But that didn't stop him from delivering Jay McShann's biggest hit, "Confessin' the Blues," in 1941 (the tune, which he co-wrote with the bandleader, would be covered by many artists, including the Rolling Stones in 1964), as well as McShann's subsequent big seller "Hootie Blues."

When McShann was drafted into the Army in 1944, he was forced to disband the group, and Brown continued a solo career, but without particular success. The vocalist recorded for various labels and briefly reunited with his old boss for some sessions in 1949, but an escalating problem with drugs led to his early death at age thirty-eight, in 1956.

HERE COMES BOOGIE-WOOGIE

The sheer potency of the basic twelve-bar blues is never more apparent than it is in boogie-woogie, the deceptively simple piano form that flourished in the rent parties and clubs of Chicago's South Side in the 1920s and '30s and became a huge craze during the big-band era of the 1940s. The pumping left-hand "walking bass" was inspired by the rhythmic clatter of steam locomotives, and the style—originally known as "Fast Western Blues"—had its various roots in Texas and the Mid-West, before coalescing into boogie-woogie in Chicago.

The earliest exponents of boogie to make records were all based in Chicago. Some of them were professional players like Charles "Cow Cow" Davenport—who toured with blues singers Dora Carr, and later Ivy Smith, through the 1920s—and others, like the great Jimmy Yancey, part-time musicians who played casual dates and rent parties to subsidize regular jobs.

"Cow Cow" Davenport was one of the first boogie players to record, cutting his debut sides for Paramount in 1927. He recorded his signature "Cow Cow Blues" the following year for Vocalion, and it became one of the seminal boogie releases, as more boogie players began to enter the recording studios. And it was Davenport who persuaded Clarence "Pinetop" (or "Pine Top") Smith to move from Pittsburgh—where he had worked backing Ma Rainey, among others—to Chicago, recommending him to Vocalion producer Mayo Williams.

On December 29, 1928, Smith recorded "Pine Top's Boogie Woogie." It was the first record to have "boogie-woogie" in its title, and the first boogie record to become a hit. In it, Pinetop talks over the music, breaking in to tell dancers "don't move a peg" and then to "shake that thing."

Pinetop was a big influence on subsequent boogie men like Albert Ammons and Pete Johnson, but his career —and indeed, his life—was cut short in March 1929 when he was hit by a stray bullet in a dance hall brawl, just days before his second session at Vocalion. But his fame lived on; in 1938 Tommy Dorsey's Orchestra recorded a version of the number, kicking off a boogie fashion amongst big bands, and selling five million copies in the process.

In the wake of Pinetop's short-lived success, various boogie players cut their first sides in Chicago, including now-legendary names such as "Cripple" Clarence Lofton, Montana Taylor, Romeo Nelson (his "Head Rag Hop" was another talk-over number), and Rufus Perryman, better known as Speckled Red. Speckled Red's most famous recordings were either side of "The Dirty Dozens, Parts 1 and 2," in which his litany of vulgar remarks and insults was a very early precursor to rap music:

"I want all you women to fall in line
And shake yo shimmy like I'm shakin' mine
You shake yo' shimmy and you shake it fast
If you can't shake the shimmy, shake yo' yes yes yes . . ."

FL 20,002

LONG PLAY 33⅓ COMMODORE RECORDS 33⅓ LONG PLAY

BOOGIE WOOGIE *and the* BLUES

ALBERT AMMONS RHYTHM KINGS

EDMOND HALL SEXTET
with EDDIE HEYWOOD

de PARIS BROTHERS ORCHESTRA
with CLYDE HART

TOP LEFT:
Albert Ammons entertains in a bar in the 1940s.

TOP RIGHT:
Ammon's partner in their celebrated boogie double act, Meade Lux Lewis.

BOTTOM RIGHT:
On the Commodore label, an early 1950s 10-inch album *Boogie Woogie and the Blues*, a compilation of tracks cut as singles during the 1940s, including several by Albert Ammons' Rhythm Kings.

OVERLEAF:
Kansas City boogie man Pete Johnson performing at New York's Café Society in 1946, photographed by William P. Gottlieb.

Although Chicago-born Jimmy Yancey had toured America and Europe, performing in front of King George V at Buckingham Palace, as a teen-aged singer and dancer, he gave up full-time entertaining at the ripe old age of sixteen and began to teach himself the piano. He did not record during the first wave of record company interest in boogie; along with a daytime job as groundskeeper at the Chicago White Sox baseball stadium, he was one of the most sought-after players on the Chicago rent party circuit.

Yancey had a more subtle and light-handed approach than his hard-driving boogie contemporaries, and when he eventually recorded in 1939, it came as a complete revelation to all but those who knew him in Chicago. Despite the repeated left-hand trademark, his music was more blues than boogie, with his small output of elegant recordings—the moving "At the Window" recorded for Session in 1943 is a classic example—enhanced occasionally by his vocals or those of his blues-singer wife, Estelle "Mama" Yancey.

Jimmy Yancey was cited as a prime influence by one of the great popularizers of boogie, Meade Lux Lewis, whose "Honky Tonk Train Blues" was one of the best-selling records in the genre. Lewis played the usual Chicago scene through the 1920s, often as a piano boogie duo with his childhood friend Albert Ammons. And together the pair would become giants of boogie-woogie, after being teamed along with Kansas City boogie maestro Pete Johnson on John Hammond's "From Spirituals to Swing" concert at New York's Carnegie Hall in December, 1938. The "Cavalcade of Boogie," as it was billed, was a sensation, and heralded a boogie-woogie craze that would sweep popular music over the next few years.

Ironically, apart from Lewis and Ammons, it was the big bands that seemed to cash in on the boogie fashion. Tommy Dorsey had already recorded his take on "Pine Top's Boogie Woogie," and over the next few years there were boogie-style hits for, among others, Benny Goodman, Lionel Hampton, Woody Herman, and Artie Shaw, plus boogie hits from vocalists as diverse as the Andrews Sisters ("Boogie Woogie Bugle Boy" was their most famous number), and Ella Fitzgerald, who recorded "Cow Cow Boogie" with the Ink Spots vocal group in 1943. And the boogie style would constitute the backbone of much that transpired in rhythm and blues and, subsequently, rock 'n' roll.

"THE EARLY BOOGIE-WOOGIE PIANISTS ENTERTAINED WORKERS IN THE LUMBER, TURPENTINE AND RAILROAD INDUSTRIES SITUATED IN THE SOUTHERN STATES. THEIR STAGE WAS A BARRELHOUSE, A CRUDE ROOM WITH A PIANO, A DANCE AREA, AND ACCESS TO ROUGH LIQUOR. WHEN THE MUSIC LATER MOVED TO THE CITIES, THE PIANISTS WERE EMPLOYED TO PLAY THE PIANO AT HOUSE-RENT PARTIES, WHERE MONEY TO PAY THE RENT WAS RAISED BY CHARGING AN ADMISSION FEE FOR THE FOOD SUPPLIED AND THE ENTERTAINMENT."

PETER SILVESTER, *A Left Hand Like God*

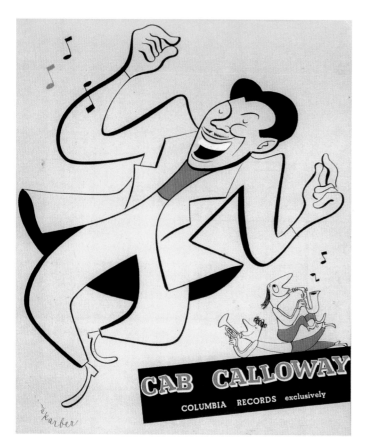

Jimmy Witherspoon

Right after the end of World War II, Jay McShann put together a new band, this time a small-group lineup that suited the post-big-band era, with a new singer in the Kansas City tradition, Jimmy Witherspoon. Born in Arkansas in 1920, Witherspoon was one of the last of the great blues shouters, making his first records with the McShann band for the Philo and Mercury labels in 1945 and 1946 respectively.

His first recording under his own name, but still with the McShann group backing him, resulted in a number one R&B hit in 1949 with "Ain't Nobody's Business, Pts. 1 & 2" on Supreme Records. Two more hits followed in 1950 with live recordings of "No Rollin' Blues" and "Big Fine Girl," although, in an era dominated by small-band rhythm and blues and the first stirrings of rock 'n' roll, his style of jazz-backed blues shouting seemed increasingly out of fashion.

Witherspoon returned to favor with the record-buying public with a 1959 live album, *Jimmy Witherspoon at the Monterey Jazz Festival*, with a 100-percent jazz instrumental lineup—which was what the Kansas City style had always been about. Jimmy Witherspoon nevertheless continued working in a modern blues environment as well, with collaborations ranging from his acclaimed *Evenin' Blues* album with T-Bone Walker in 1963 to 1971's *Guilty* with former Animals vocalist Eric Burdon. Diagnosed with throat cancer in the early 1980s, he passed away on September 18, 1997, at the age of seventy-seven.

Mr. Blues

Another blues shouter who, like Big Joe Turner, crossed over successfully to the world of rhythm and blues was Wynonie Harris. He had already spent some years paying his dues as an entertainer—dancing, singing, and playing drums—when he left Omaha, Nebraska (where he was born in 1915) for the bright lights of Los Angeles in 1940. His travels had taken him to Kansas City, where he had fallen under the spell of Jimmy Rushing and Big Joe, and once he hit LA he was soon singing in nightclubs in and around Central Avenue, in the African-American district of South Central.

Enjoying a growing reputation, in late 1943 Harris was playing at the Rhumboogie Club in Chicago when he was spotted by bandleader Lucky Millinder, who ran a blues-oriented outfit along the lines of the Kansas City groups. He joined Millinder in March 1944, and in May of that year waxed his first single, the exuberant "Who Threw the Whiskey in the Well" for Decca. It would be Millinder's biggest hit, although an embargo on shellac following a two-year Musicians Union strike delayed its pressing until 1945; it topped the R&B charts for eight weeks and also hit the number seven spot in the regular US pop chart.

By the time the record hit the best seller list, Harris and Millinder had parted company after a dispute over money. The singer, flush with the success of the single, soon had a record release under his own name on the short-lived LA label Philo (soon to be changed to the better-known Aladdin Records), "Around the Clock."

ABOVE LEFT:
Columbia publicity material for Cab Calloway. In his trademark zoot suit, the flamboyant "scat" vocalist and bandleader was a big name in the 1930s and 1940s, and a regular attraction at Harlem's Cotton Club. He appeared in several Hollywood films through the 1940s, and in a late-career comeback featured in *The Blues Brothers* movie in 1980, and an episode of *Sesame Street* the same year.

ABOVE RIGHT:
The UK release of a Jimmy Witherspoon album from 1964.

OPPOSITE:
Suave-looking blues shouter Wynonie Harris in a 1948 promotional picture.

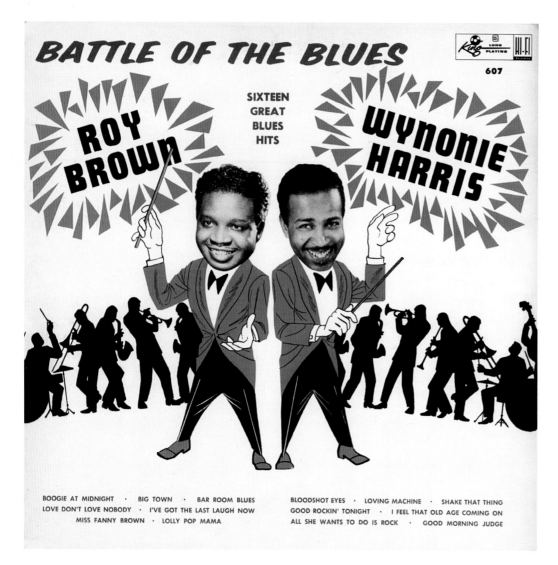

BATTLE OF THE BLUES

ROY BROWN

SIXTEEN GREAT BLUES HITS

WYNONIE HARRIS

607

BOOGIE AT MIDNIGHT · BIG TOWN · BAR ROOM BLUES
LOVE DON'T LOVE NOBODY · I'VE GOT THE LAST LAUGH NOW
MISS FANNY BROWN · LOLLY POP MAMA

BLOODSHOT EYES · LOVING MACHINE · SHAKE THAT THING
GOOD ROCKIN' TONIGHT · I FEEL THAT OLD AGE COMING ON
ALL SHE WANTS TO DO IS ROCK · GOOD MORNING JUDGE

A month later he recorded for Apollo Records, with whom he had two big hits in 1946—"Wynonie's Blues" and "Playful Baby"—the start of a string of releases for various labels including Hamp-Tone, Bullet, and Aladdin. It was on Aladdin that he cut four sides with his hero Big Joe Turner in 1947, including Parts 1 and 2 of their celebrated "Battle of the Blues." But real record stardom came Wynonie's way after he signed with the Cincinnati label King, later that same year.

The first of those hits was a swaggering cover of Roy Brown's "Good Rockin' Tonight" in 1948. Far more boisterous than the original, with its rocking offbeat and honking tenor sax, Wynonie's chart-topping version was a master class in the "jump band" blues that dominated the R&B charts in the late 1940s.

Further hits on King included some of the sexually suggestive numbers that Harris became famous for, songs like "Lollipop Mama," "Sitting on It All the Time," and his other chart-topper, "All She Wants to Do Is Rock." Between 1948 and 1952 he had no fewer than thirteen R&B hits, before the gravy train suddenly came to a halt. The records sounded just as good, but tastes had changed, and they simply failed to sell as they had before.

> **"As for Wynonie Harris, also known as Mr Blues, he summed up the essence of postwar rhythm and blues, his famous raucous voice celebrating good times with sex and alcohol aplenty. He too sang 'Good Rockin' Tonight' in 1948, and performed it swinging his hips and sticking out his chest, as if he sensed the imminence of the coming of rock 'n' roll."**
>
> **FLORENT MAZZOLENI**, music journalist and author

Harris moved labels several times through the 1950s, making some fine records along the way, but none could repeat the old success. His last recordings were with Chess in Chicago in 1964, and his final live appearance was at Harlem's Apollo, in November 1967, appearing with Big Joe Turner, Jimmy Witherspoon, Big Mama Thornton, and T-Bone Walker.

Wynonie Harris, known throughout his career as "Mr. Blues," died of throat cancer just two years later, in 1969, at age fifty-three.

ABOVE:
The first of two *Battle of the Blues* albums released by King Records in 1959, featuring tracks from the 1940s and early 1950s by rivals Roy Brown and Wynonie Harris.

JAMMIN' THE BLUES

Given the importance of improvisation in jazz and blues, the collective "jam session" was an inevitable feature of the music from the earliest days. Wherever musicians gathered, be it in a late-night, after-hours club or someone simply "sitting in" as guest with the band on stage, a "jam" was often the result—and the blues was the perfect musical format. Seasoned jazz players might jam on more sophisticated material of course, but the basic twelve-bar gave anyone a chance to show what they were made of. And that was often the point, from the earliest days of the New Orleans "cutting contests," musicians would compete in this way. In the 1930s Kansas City was famous for its marathon sessions that sometimes went on for hours without a break, but jamming has always been the order of the day when players and singers have wanted to flex their musical muscles without the constraints of a set list or indeed running time.

❝ Now the Sunset [Kansas City] had a bartender named Joe Turner, and while Joe was serving drinks he would suddenly pick up a cue for a blues and sing it right where he stood, with Pete [Johnson] playing piano for him. I don't think I'll ever forget the thrill of listening to Big Joe Turner shouting and sending everybody, night after night, while mixing drinks. ❞
MARY LOU WILLIAMS, pianist

❝ Piney Brown ran the Sunset where I first ran into Joe Turner. I remember we used to play behind Joe there. There was a place close by (across the street in fact) called the Lone Star. Joe Turner would start to sing the blues at the Sunset, and then he'd go across the street and sing the blues at the Lone Star, and we were still playing all this time. Joe would socialize there for a while, and stop in the front and have breakfast, and then he'd come back into the Sunset, go up to the microphone, and sing some more blues, and we'd have been playing all the time. Often we'd play for an hour and a half straight like that. ❞
JO JONES, drummer

❝ Well in the old days, the clubs were places for musicians to meet. There were two clubs that were most predominantly frequented by the musicians, they were the Dew Drop Inn and the Club Tijuana. All the musicians in town would come to these clubs, to hear other musicians play .... and many times they had a chance to participate. And each guy would take a turn to play, and he would play or sing or whatever. It was an atmosphere that today would be a [record] producer's paradise ... because you did not have to be a well-known musician ... you could be an unknown. If you could play an instrument or sing you were allowed up to the mike ... And it was at these clubs that guys really stretched and showed what they could do .... It was like a competition, but with no prizes involved, only the attitudes. It was mostly attitudes. ❞
AL REED, New Orleans singer and songwriter

❝ Saturday night is your big night. Everybody used to fry up fish and have one hell of a time. Find me playing till sunrise for 50 cents and a sandwich. And be glad of it. And they really liked the low-down blues. ❞
MUDDY WATERS

❝ We'd all play for the Saturday night balls, Willie [Brown] and I and Charley [Patton]. Them country balls were rough! They were critical, man! They'd start off good, you know. Everybody happy, dancing, and then they'd start to getting louder and louder. The women would be dipping that snuff and swallowing that snuff spit along with that corn whiskey, and they'd start to mixing fast, and oh, brother! They'd start something then! ❞
SON HOUSE

"Ida Cox—since I was a kid she was one of my favorite blues singers. I went on the road with her on a tour of the South. Twelve girls in the chorus, two principals, two comedians. I used to play thirty-five or forty choruses of 'Tiger Rag' with a table in my teeth and the banjo on the back of my neck. Never had a toothache in my life, and I used to carry tables in my teeth and tap dance at the same time."

T-BONE WALKER

OPPOSITE:
The wide-open cityscape of Los Angeles in the 1930s, its broad streets and relatively low-rise buildings in stark contrast to its East Coast counterpart New York.

West Coast blues

Through the 1920s and 1930s, the main centers of urban blues had been the big cities of the North and Midwest—New York, Kansas City, Chicago, Oklahoma City. The 1940s heralded the appearance of a jazz-influenced jump-blues style, this time associated with the West Coast, more specifically the sprawling aggregation of Los Angeles, California.

Already an important hub of the entertainment industry—with Hollywood firmly established as the movie capital of the world—in 1942 Los Angeles became the site for the first major West Coast record label with the launch of Capitol Records. Up until then all the main companies—RCA-Victor, Columbia, and Decca—had operated from the East Coast, in New York City. But of more importance from a blues perspective was the presence of a number of key independent labels, including Aladdin, Specialty, Imperial, and Modern, who all played a crucial role in the development of the West Coast sound.

The "City of Angels," Los Angeles has always been a city of immigrants, and with a burgeoning recording scene to rival that in other parts of the country, it soon became a magnet for itinerant musicians, especially those from the southern states of Oklahoma and Texas. Hence, despite its name, West Coast blues was actually a style of blues created mainly by artists who originated outside California, but whose music had the chance to develop and flourish there.

T-Bone

Without a doubt, the most influential of the West Coast bluesmen was T-Bone Walker, a key innovator of both the jump-blues style and the whole electric blues guitar sound. Aaron Thibeaux Walker was born in Linden, Texas, in 1910; his family moved to Dallas when he was two years old. Both his parents were musicians, and his stepfather, Marco Washington, played bass fiddle with the Dallas String Band, a seminal group in the local history of Texas blues.

The young Walker soon followed suit, trying out every string instrument he could lay his hands on and learning all he could from the great Blind Lemon Jefferson, a friend of the family. He began playing local parties as a teenager, toured in medicine shows with blues singers Ida Cox and Ma Rainey, and in 1929 made his recording debut on Columbia with "Wichita Falls Blues" and "Trinity Blues." On the 78-rpm single he was billed as Oak Cliff T-Bone—Oak Cliff was the district he lived in, and T-Bone was adapted from his middle name Thibeaux. During those formative years T-Bone kept the best of musical company, including his childhood friend Charlie Christian, who would be as influential in jazz guitar playing as T-Bone became in the blues.

By the mid-1930s, Walker had moved to Los Angeles, where he played the clubs along Central Avenue before signing up as featured vocalist with the Les Hite Orchestra, with whom he made the single "T-Bone Blues" in 1940, though he did not play guitar on the recording.

BLUE DIVAS

Like most of the "classic" blues singers of the 1920s, many of the great female jazz singers of the 1930s, '40s, and '50s were not blues specialists as such, but song stylists steeped in the popular sounds of the era. Nevertheless, coming from a jazz background rather than that of "straight" pop balladeers, singers as diverse as Billie Holiday, Ella Fitzgerald, Peggy Lee, and Dinah Washington showed the influence of the blues in everything they sang.

Despite the title of her celebrated autobiography, *Lady Sings the Blues*, Billie Holiday—often acclaimed as the greatest jazz singer of them all—sang very few actual blues numbers; she was known primarily as an interpreter par excellence of the so-called "great American songbook." But the blues certainly infused every phrase and note she sang in her renditions of standards like "Lover Man" and "Willow Weep for Me," and self-penned songs such as "God Bless the Child" and "Lady Sings the Blues."

Her style was deeply influenced by jazz instrumentalists such as her colleague (and lover) the tenor sax giant Lester Young, and by adopting the phrasing and timing of jazz musicians (for whom the blues was part of their language), she "sang the blues" in any material she was interpreting. And on those occasions when she did sing a blues—her own twelve-bar composition "Fine and Mellow" was a much-recorded regular feature of her repertoire—the result was never anything short of breathtaking.

Rivaling Billie Holiday as the premier jazz vocalist, Ella Fitzgerald was noted for her crystal-clear tone, perfect phrasing and diction, and amazing three-octave range—not to mention her sensational scat singing, improvised wordless vocals inspired by instrumental jazz.

Ella made her singing debut in 1934, winning first prize (a then-impressive $25) at one of the famous Amateur Nights at Harlem's Apollo Theater. She had her first hit with a version of the nursery song "A-Tisket, A-Tasket" in 1938, and for a time her record releases were dominated by fairly lightweight pop songs.

Ella's style moved closer to a jazz orbit—albeit blues-influenced—when she started working in Dizzy Gillespie's big band in the 1940s, where she perfected her scat technique. Her bebop-style recording of "Lady Be Good" caused a sensation when released in 1947. Her biggest mainstream success would come in the 1950s and '60s with her *Songbook* series of albums featuring the classic standards of Cole Porter, Rodgers and Hart, Irving Berlin, and other twentieth-century songwriting giants. But the fact that she never lost touch with her feeling for the blues was reinforced with her 1957 *Ella Fitzgerald Sings the Duke Ellington Song Book*, in which she delivered

ROCK 'N' ROLL REVUE

NAT "KING" COLE · LIONEL HAMPTON AND HIS ORCHESTRA · DINAH WASHINGTON · JOE TURNER · DUKE ELLINGTON AND HIS BAND · LARRY DARNELL · THE CLOVERS · RUTH BROWN

Plus
COLES & ATKINS
MARTHA DAVIS
LITTLE BUCK
DELTA RHYTHM BOYS
MANTAN MORELAND
LEONARD REED
"NIPSEY" RUSSELL

A STUDIO FILMS PRODUCTION

ABOVE LEFT:
Ella Fitzgerald at New York's Downbeat club in 1947, with bebop trumpeter Dizzy Gillespie looking almost love-struck in his admiration.

ABOVE RIGHT:
Poster for *Rock 'n' Roll Revue*, made the same year and by the same company as *Rhythm and Blues Revue* (page 99). The *Revue* jumped on the rock 'n 'roll bandwagon, but with a similar line-up of R&B and jazz artists including the self-styled "Queen of the blues" Dinah Washington.

OVERLEAF:
Publicity shot of the great Peggy Lee in a typically slinky costume.

Ellington classics like "Take the 'A' Train," "Rockin' in Rhythm," and "I Ain't Got Nothin' But the Blues" in a masterwork of jazz vocalizing.

Like Billie and Ella, Peggy Lee learned her trade with the big bands, although with her purring, smoky voice, she offered a more subtle approach to projecting to the ballroom crowds—to put it simply, they had to quiet down and listen to her. Her understated vocals attracted the attention of Benny Goodman, whose band she fronted for two years from 1941, during which time she had her first number one hit, "Somebody Else Is Taking My Place."

Peggy Lee's image was as a smooth purveyor of sophisticated pop, yet her feeling for the blues was apparent in everything she did, and her biggest hit, "Fever," in 1958, was a cover of an R&B hit by Little Willie John. The flip side of "Fever" was a sultry blues "You Don't Know," territory she would explore further in her 1962 album *Blues Cross Country*, which included favorites such as "Basin Street Blues," "Kansas City," and "St. Louis Blues," backed by the Quincy Jones Orchestra. And 1988 saw the release of another riveting blues set, this time in a small quintet setting, simply entitled *Miss Peggy Lee Sings the Blues*.

Dinah Washington, who dubbed herself "Queen of the Blues," had a solid background in blues-based jazz, and she established herself as a mainstream ballad singer only after she hit the big time as an assured R&B artist. Singing with the Lionel Hampton band in the early 1940s, she had her first hits in 1944 with "Evil Gal Blues" and its follow-up "Salty Papa Blues." Leaving Hampton to go solo in 1946, she had no fewer than twenty-seven hits in the R&B Top Ten between 1948 and 1955. It was in 1959 that Washington made her breakthrough into the pop market with "What a Diff'rence a Day Makes," the beginning of a career change that saw her specializing in ballads with lush string arrangements—much to the disdain of many critics, although her basic blues-flavored approach stayed exactly the same. Hers was the voice of someone who, regardless of the setting, couldn't help singing the blues— confirmed (if confirmation was needed) in her 1958 album *Dinah Sings Bessie Smith*, in which the self-styled "Queen" paid passionate homage to "The Empress."

"SINGING THE BLUES IS A SEPARATE ART. THE GREAT BLUES SINGERS HAVE TENDED TO STAY WITHIN THE FORM, ESCHEWING THE CLASSIC AMERICAN POPULAR SONG. AND THE FINEST SINGERS OF THE POPULAR SONG HAVE AS A RULE AVOIDED THE BLUES. PEGGY LEE IS ONE OF THOSE RARE PEOPLE—INDEED, I CAN THINK OF ONLY ONE OR TWO OTHERS—WHO ARE COMFORTABLE AND CONVINCING IN BOTH."

GENE LEES, music critic and lyricist

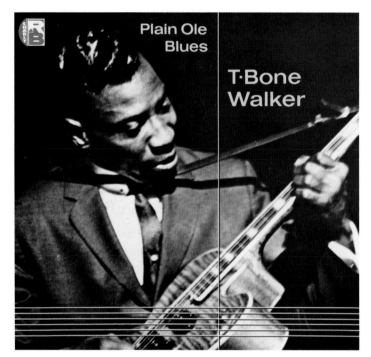

Throughout those first years in LA, T-Bone experimented with amplifying his guitar electrically, and in the early 1940s he began using his gadgets at club gigs, when backed by his own group of musicians. He astounded audiences with the new kind of sound he achieved. And his stage act was almost as revolutionary: doing the splits, playing the guitar behind his head—it was the stuff of rock 'n' roll, but more than a decade ahead of its time.

Record buyers got their first taste of the new sound in 1942, when T-Bone Walker signed with the newly launched Capitol label and released "Mean Old World." Now everyone could hear his fluid riffs, sophisticated jazz chording, and sheer technical prowess, which set a new standard in blues guitar playing.

After spending some time based in Chicago and New York, in 1946 Walker returned to California, signing with Black & White Records, a New York company that had relocated to LA the year before. His first big seller was "Bobby Sox Blues," which made the number three spot in the R&B charts in 1946, followed in 1947 by his most celebrated composition, "Call It Stormy Monday (But Tuesday Is Just as Bad)." The smoky jazz feel of the laid-back, after-hours blues (which is often wrongly referred to as "Stormy Monday Blues") was enhanced by the atmospheric trumpet work of Teddy Buckner, and the song was later cited by B.B. King as the number that inspired him to play electric guitar.

After a run of R&B hits with Black & White, including more classics, like "T-Bone Shuffle" and "West Side Baby," in 1950 T-Bone moved to another LA-based label, Imperial. There he stayed until 1954, where memorable sides among a total of fifty-two songs included "Cold, Cold Feeling," "Glamour Girl," and the ultra-hip instrumental "Strollin' with Bones."

After his Imperial stint, things began to slow down for T-Bone Walker. But in 1955 he signed with Atlantic Records, at that time the cutting-edge label in jazz and blues. This last period of his great recordings included sessions with Chicago bluesmen Junior Wells on harmonica and guitarist Jimmy Rogers, and some sides with the modern jazz guitar star Barney Kessel. In 1959, Atlantic released the best of those sessions as the album *T-Bone Blues*.

In 1962 T-Bone toured Europe as part of the first American Folk Blues Festival, a package he would appear with again later in the decade. He continued to astonish audiences with his live performances, but recordings of note were few and far between. One exception was the 1970 Polydor album *Good Feelin'*, which won him a Grammy award. A stomach complaint (brought on by excessive drinking) got worse during the early 1970s, his gigging tapered off, and he suffered a stroke in 1974. T-Bone Walker died from bronchial pneumonia in the spring of 1975.

In the 1940s, other Texas bluesmen had moved to California, hoping to replicate T-Bone Walker's success. Pee Wee Crayton settled in San Francisco in 1935. Influenced by T-Bone's playing, Pee Wee honed his own aggressive guitar style, earning himself a contract with the Los Angeles label Modern in 1948. Later that year his instrumental "Blues After Hours" topped the R&B chart. Although he never repeated that success, he had at least two more R&B hits with the label.

Clarence "Gatemouth" Brown never actually moved to the coast, but he did have his first release "Gatemouth Boogie" on Aladdin, based in LA. His manager, Houston nightclub owner Don Robey, then set up Peacock Records in the Texas city and released Gatemouth's only national R&B hit, "Mary Is Fine," in 1949. A dynamic guitarist and

ABOVE LEFT:
Released in 1982 on the UK Charly R&B label, seven years after his death, the T-Bone Walker collection *Plain Ole Blues*.

ABOVE RIGHT:
T-Bone Walker in full flight onstage, doing his trademark splits with his guitar behind his head.

RIGHT:
A 1950 concert poster for an appearance by T-Bone in Wichita, Kansas.

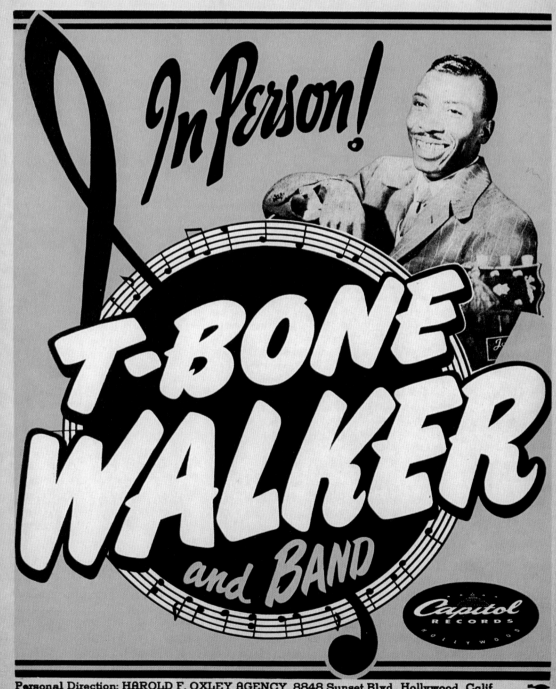

T-BONE WALKER

If one musician could be credited with inventing the electric blues guitar style, then that man would be T-Bone Walker. Raised in the heartland of Texas country blues—as a child he practiced with Blind Lemon Jefferson—he was a pioneer of jazz-edged jump-band blues, and by the mid-1930s was working with primitive prototypes of electric guitar. His flamboyant style of bending and sustaining notes introduced a new language for the instrument—matched only by his onstage acrobatics—which inspired generations of blues axmen. And if only for the all-time classic "Call It Stormy Monday (But Tuesday Is Just as Bad)," his place in the pantheon of blues songwriters is assured.

> "I just naturally started to play music. My whole family played—my daddy played, my mother played. My daddy played bass, my cousin played banjo, guitar and mandolin. We played at root beer stands, like the drive-ins they have now, making $2.50 a night, and we had a cigar box for the kitty that we passed around, sometimes making fifty or sixty dollars a night. Of course we didn't get none of it, we kids."
>
> **T-BONE WALKER**

Born
Aaron Thibeaux Walker, May 28, 1910, Linden, Texas

Died
March 16, 1975, Los Angeles, California

Instruments
Vocals, Guitar, Piano

Recording Debut
"Wichita Falls Blues" / "Trinity Blues" [as Oak Cliff T-Bone]
December 5, 1929, Dallas, Texas
Columbia

Awards
Grammy Award for *Good Feelin'* [Best Traditional Folk Album], 1970
Inducted into Blues Hall of Fame, 1980
Lifetime Achievement Award, *Guitar Player* magazine, 1985
Inducted into Rock and Roll Hall of Fame, 1987

Playlist
"T-Bone Blues" " [1940]
"Mean Old World" [1940]
"Bobby Sox Blues" [1946]
"Call It Stormy Monday (But Tuesday Is Just as Bad)" [1947]
"Strollin' with Bones" [1950]
"The Hustle Is On" [1950]
T-Bone Blues [1959]
Good Feelin' [1970]

ABOVE:
A "disc jockey copy" of Lowell
Fulson's "Reconsider Baby."
It was the essential supply of
advance copies to radio DJs
that led to the payola "pay to
play" scandal, in which many
well-known record companies
were involved.

fiddler, not only was Gatemouth deeply influenced by
T-Bone Walker, but he was first spotted by Robey when
he took over from T-Bone, who was unwell, during a spot
at Robey's nightclub, the Bronze Peacock.

Reconsider Baby

After T-Bone Walker, the single most important name
on the West Coast blues scene of the 1940s and '50s was
that of Lowell Fulson. The son of a Cherokee father and
an African-American mother (a guitar player herself),
Lowell was born in Tulsa, Oklahoma, in 1921. Having
learned guitar as a youngster, in his late teens he hit the
road professionally, touring Texas—for part of 1940, with
the veteran singer-guitarist Texas Alexander—until 1943,
when he was drafted into the US Navy.

After leaving the Navy in 1945, Fulson settled in
Oakland, California, where he met record man Bob
Geddins, who owned local labels Down Town, Downbeat,
and Big Time. It was for Down Town that he went into
the studio and cut his debut "Three O'Clock Blues" in
June 1946, with his brother Martin on acoustic guitar;
the song eventually made the national R&B charts at
number six, in 1948. More classic sides followed,
including a definitive version of Memphis Slim's "Every
Day I Have the Blues"; "Blues Shadows," an R&B chart
topper in 1950; and the two-part Yuletide blues
"Lonesome Christmas."

With his concise, polished guitar work and solid vocals,
Lowell Fulson was a hit everywhere he played. His
sensational ten-piece backing band included a young Ray
Charles on piano and future jazz heavyweight Stanley
Turrentine on tenor saxophone. In 1954 Fulson's music
came to the attention of Chess Records in Chicago, which
signed him to a long-term contract and cut what many
consider his finest single, "Reconsider Baby." Released
on the Chess subsidiary Checker label, it spent fifteen
weeks on the R&B chart, where it peaked at number
three. Fulson would reap far wider benefits from the song
in 1960, when Elvis Presley covered it on his album *Elvis
Is Back!* Countless other artists—from Ike and Tina

Turner to contemporary bluesman Joe Bonamassa—
have covered it since.

After a long period with Checker, which produced some
fine but unsuccessful singles, in 1962 Lowell Fulson
moved to the LA-based Kent Records. There he made
"Black Nights" in 1965, his first R&B chart entry in a
decade. In 1967 "Tramp" (cowritten with pianist Jimmy
McCracklin) did even better, hitting number five and
making the pop *Billboard* Hot 100 as well. A move toward
a mainstream soul sound, the song became a bigger hit
for Otis Redding and Carla Thomas the same year. Lowell
Fulson continued recording and touring through the
following three decades, playing blues festivals and
tribute shows. A long-time resident of Los Angeles
county, he died at his Long Beach home in March 1999
at age seventy-seven.

Mellow Blues

Although T-Bone's influence was crucial, not all the West
Coast jump bands were fronted by guitar men. There was
a new school of mellow-voiced piano players fronting
small blues combos, some of whom—like Amos Milburn,
Charles Brown, and Ivory Joe Hunter—were also
graduates of the Texas blues scene.

A native of Houston, Amos Milburn lied about his age
to enlist in the wartime Navy in 1942 when he was just
fifteen. Leaving the service when the war ended in 1945,
the adept pianist formed a sixteen-piece band and started
playing the Houston club circuit. In 1946 he signed with
Aladdin Records in Los Angeles; one of his first releases
was "Down the Road a Piece," a cover of a 1940 hit by
swing bandleader Will Bradley. Written by pop
songwriter Don Raye, whose other successes included
the Andrew Sisters hits "Boogie Woogie Bugle Boy" and
"Beat Me Daddy, Eight to the Bar," the boogie-based
number was a foretaste of the direction in which small-
band jump music was heading.

Despite steady sales on Aladdin, Amos Milburn didn't
hit the R&B best sellers until 1948 with "Chicken Shack
Boogie," which topped the chart. Then in 1950 "Bad, Bad

"There were parallels between the blues of the East Coast 'classic' singers in the twenties, and the West Coast singers of this school in the late forties: they softened the market and prepared the way for a more vigorous music to follow."

PAUL OLIVER, historian and writer

Whiskey" (another number one) kicked off a whole series of "blues in a bottle" songs over the next few years, including the best-known, "One Scotch, One Bourbon, One Beer" (later retitled "One Bourbon, One Scotch, One Beer") in 1953.

When the booze songs dried up, so did the hits. Amos Milburn parted company with Aladdin in 1957, and subsequent releases couldn't match the fresh vitality of his previous work. He carried on playing into the 1970s, when he suffered a series of strokes, the third of which, in 1980, precipitated his death at age fifty-two.

In his relatively short time at the cutting edge of urban blues music, Milburn was an important figure in the transition from jazz-influenced arrangements to the more basic approach of boogie-based rhythm and blues—and a huge influence on future R&B stars, Fats Domino in particular.

Another Texas émigré to Los Angeles was pianist and singer Charles Brown. He moved to the west coast in 1943 and was soon fronting guitarist Johnny Moore's Three Blazers, who based themselves on the Nat King Cole Trio, but with a bluesier emphasis. Brown's light-handed piano playing and smooth vocals went down well in the more sophisticated black nightclubs of South Central LA.

The trio signed with Philo Records in 1945 and were soon in the R&B chart with "Driftin' Blues," which went to number two and stayed among the best sellers for nearly six months. In April 1946 Philo's name was changed to Aladdin, and with this label Brown had a string of hits, including the definitive version of the much-covered "Merry Christmas Baby," in 1947 (credited as Johnny Moore's Three Blazers), and the chart-topping "Trouble Blues," under his own name, in 1949. The Johnny Moore outfit were also in demand as a studio backing group for singers such as Ivory Joe Hunter.

With some tougher-sounding R&B coming to the fore as the 1950s progressed, Charles Brown's mellow style was sidelined somewhat. Nonetheless, his 1960 release on King Records, "Please Come Home for Christmas," was another seasonal hit, and by 1968 had sold more than a million copies. His influence, however, was far-reaching, with Ivory Joe Hunter, Percy Mayfield,

and Ray Charles all citing him as a key inspiration for their own musical careers.

Born in Kirbyville, Texas, in 1914, Ivory Joe Hunter—his real name—was already playing the blues like a professional when he was recorded by Alan Lomax for the Library of Congress in 1933. He played around the Gulf Coast region of Texas, hosting his own radio show for a time, before moving to Los Angeles in 1942, where he started his own label, Ivory Records. The first release was his own "Blues at Sunrise" (backed by Johnny Moore's Three Blazers), which, when leased to the Exclusive label, became a nationwide R&B hit in 1945.

Ever the entrepreneur, Hunter went on to found Pacific Records, scoring an R&B chart-topper with "Pretty Mama Blues" in 1948. More hits followed on King Records, including "Don't Fall in Love with Me," "Waiting in Vain," and "Guess Who," before he released his all-time classic "I Almost Lost My Mind" on MGM.

With his crooner-like, laid-back delivery, Ivory Joe set a new standard for cool blues, and the single gave him another R&B number one in 1950. The lilting twelve-bar blues later made the top spot in the *Billboard* Hot 100 pop chart, in the 1956 cover version by Pat Boone.

By the mid-1950s Hunter had recorded over one hundred sides, moving to Atlantic Records in 1954, where he followed Boone's "I Almost Lost My Mind" smash with his own similar-sounding "Since I Met You Baby" in 1956. It would be his only pop chart success, climbing to number twelve, but became a pop-blues standard, covered by dozens of artists, including Boone, Sam Cooke, Jerry Lee Lewis, Dean Martin, B.B. King, Johnny "Guitar" Watson, and many more.

The relaxed style of blues played by the likes of Ivory Joe Hunter, Charles Brown, and Amos Milburn, along with the jazz-influenced guitar blues pioneered by T-Bone Walker, and the strident jump music inherited from the big-band blues shouters, were all part of the variety of music coming out of the big cities before and immediately after World War II. Collectively they were the harbingers of even bigger changes to come, as the blues, in its postwar incarnation of rhythm and blues, became the basis for a music revolution that touched every corner of the globe.

OPPOSITE, TOP LEFT:
Smooth-voiced Ivory Joe Hunter, a star of the Atlantic Records R&B roster from the mid-1950s.

OPPOSITE, BOTTOM LEFT:
An Atlantic Records display ad from *Cashbox* magazine in 1956, on the occasion of the annual NAMM (National Association of Music Merchants) trade show, featuring some of the label's biggest rhythm and blues stars including Ivory Joe Hunter, Ruth Brown, Joe Turner, LaVern Baker, and Ray Charles.

OPPOSITE RIGHT:
A vigorous poster for Amos Milburn (the main portion was used for gigs on the road throughout 1952, with the venue information added) for a date at the Mambo Club in Wichita, Kansas.

RHYTHM & BLUES

5

Beginning around 1948, the term "rhythm and blues" (R&B) was a catchall description for the popular music of black America—as "race music" had previously been since the 1920s. And as a label applied to a specific brand of music, it was almost as all-embracing, covering the hippest pop sounds of the postwar years, from the finger-clicking jump 'n' jive bands, and the new electric blues coming out of Chicago, to the gumbo-flavored R&B of New Orleans. In one form or another the blues was all around and, via radio and a booming record industry, there for all to hear—and that included, in ever increasing numbers, the music fans and record buyers of white America.

The years immediately after World War II saw almost all the blues-based big bands give way to smaller outfits, the self-styled "jump bands" fronted by extrovert singers like Wynonie Harris and Big Joe Turner—or, just as often, a new flamboyant breed of saxophone player typified by Arnett Cobb, Big Jay McNeely, and hugely popular sax-playing vocalist Louis Jordan.

Stagecraft was almost as important as musicianship in these new style blues combos: wailing horn men would work the audience to a frenzy, often ending up on their backs screeching up-tempo blues for all they were worth, while the snappily dressed vocalists belted out (and sometimes crooned) the blues, over a riffing backing of saxes, trumpets and—increasingly—amplified guitars.

Blues a Specialty

Among the earliest of these jump bands was Joe Liggins and his Honeydrippers, who topped the Race Music chart in *Billboard* magazine with the first jump single to sell over a million copies, "The Honeydripper," in 1945. Half a decade later Joe Liggins topped the R&B chart for thirteen weeks with "Pink Champagne," on Art Rupe's pioneering Los Angeles-based label Specialty.

Pianist Joe's guitar-playing brother Jimmy Liggins also made the charts several times with his band, the Drops of Joy, first in 1947 with "Cadillac Boogie," also on Specialty. With its insistent boogie piano and riffing saxes, it was archetypal jump music and is sometimes cited as a direct forerunner of rock 'n' roll. Liggins, a sensation on the black club circuit with his frenetic stage act and uninhibited vocals, enjoyed further success with "Tear Drop Blues" in 1948 and, in 1953, "I Ain't Drunk."

Record producer Art Rupe had started Specialty—which was to become one of the key names in the crossover from R&B to rock—in 1946, initially launched as the Juke Box label a year earlier. And it was on Juke Box that singing drummer Roy Milton had his first hit with "R.M. Blues," reaching number two on the R&B chart and number twenty on the pop chart. The swing-style blues went on to sell over a million copies, and it enabled Rupe to properly establish his fledgling company. Roy Milton and his Solid Senders became a major attraction on the road, and had a string of hits with Specialty through the late 1940s and early '50s.

Another Specialty star who helped shape 1950s rhythm and blues was Eddie Jones, better known as Guitar Slim. Inspired by the playing of T-Bone Walker and Gatemouth Brown, Slim soon became known as a wild man of the blues. As well as wearing outlandish zoot suits in garish colors (which he would often match with bizarrely dyed hair), his stage act involved his prowling the audience and sometimes even the street outside, his solid-bodied electric guitar still connected with a 350-foot cable. He played loud, very loud, and his use of feedback and electronic distortion was way ahead of its time.

After a minor R&B hit in 1952 with "Feelin' Sad," Slim had his biggest success in 1954 with "The Things That I Used to Do," recorded in New Orleans and released on Specialty. The record spent six weeks at the top of the R&B chart and sold over a million copies, and as a blues standard has since been covered by innumerable artists including Jimi Hendrix and Stevie Ray Vaughan. Guitar Slim slipped out of the limelight in the latter half of the 1950s, became an alcoholic, and died of pneumonia in 1959, aged just thirty-two.

Less flamboyant by far (but achingly sublime), Louisiana-born Percy Mayfield was influenced by the smooth vocal style of Charles Brown. Although Mayfield's ambitions were as much for songwriting as for singing, in 1950 Art Rupe signed him as a vocalist to Specialty, where he scored immediately with "Please Send Me Someone to Love." His gentle approach lent itself to blues ballads—slow, sentimental love songs written in the blues idiom. He followed its chart-topping success with other R&B hits including "Lost Love," "What a Fool I Was," and "The River's Invitation," all dramatic ballads that verged on the confessional.

Mayfield's career as a live performer was severely limited after an automobile accident in 1952, but that didn't stop the flow of hits into the early 1960s, first on Specialty, then on Chess and Imperial. He also flourished

RIGHT:
One of the favorite "big horn" sax players who were huge stars during the early days of rhythm and blues, Big Jay McNeely hit number one in the R&B chart in early 1949 with "Deacon's Hop." He was pushed off the top of the list just a couple of weeks later by another saxophone blues instrumental, "The Hucklebuck," by Paul Williams.

MID-NITE RAMBLE DANCE
PALACE BALLROOM
FRI., MAY 3rd DERBY EVE
12 TO 4 A.M.
Adv. 99c   Tickets At Usual Places   At Door $1.50

IT'S MR. HONK
Himself. In Person
The GO! GO! BOY
BIG JAY McNEELY
HIS TENOR SAX
and his
All Star Jazz Band
FEATURING
The NEWEST SINGING SENSATION
SONNY WARD ★
"Deacon's Hop"

GLOBE POSTER CORP. BALTIMORE

Tour Direction: SHAW ARTISTS CORP., 565 5th AVE., N.Y.C. & 203 N. WABASH, CHICAGO

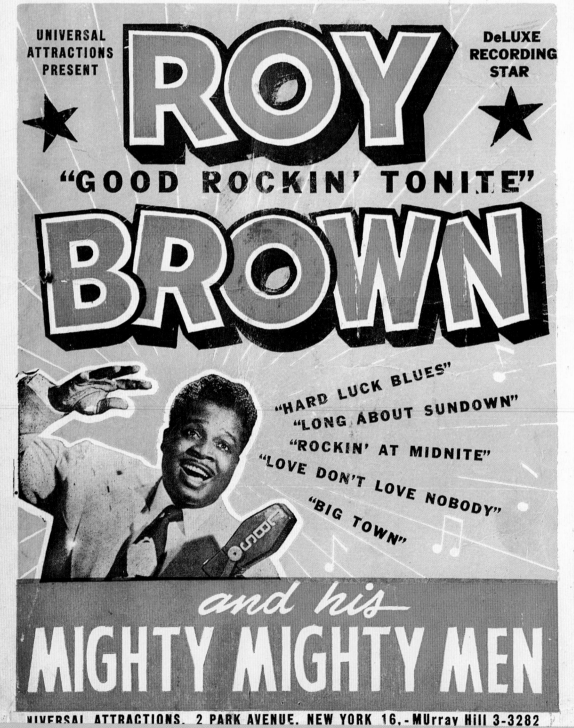

> **"Musical tastes had changed; rock-and-roll had entered the picture and changed the musical equation that had prevailed until the middle '50s. [Roy] Brown—and a host of other performers of his generation—suddenly found their music had been made passé by the very upstart their own innovations had contributed and led to. Talk about sowing the seeds of your own destruction! It was a bitter pill Brown had to swallow."**

PETE WELDING, blues historian and record producer

ABOVE LEFT:
Guitar Slim's 1954 Specialty hit "The Things That I Used To Do" was arranged and produced by Ray Charles, who also played piano on the track, originally released in 1953.

ABOVE RIGHT:
A 1946 line-up of Joe Liggins and his Honeydrippers.

as a songwriter, penning hits for Ray Charles in particular (he signed to Charles's Tangerine label in 1962), including the iconic "Hit the Road Jack" and its apocalyptic flip side "The Danger Zone."

Good Rockin'

With a similarly mellow-sounding voice, but one with a declamatory, gospel edge to it, Roy Brown went from supper-club crooning to establishing an early prototype of rock 'n' roll. Born in New Orleans in 1925, Brown started singing in church before moving to Los Angeles in his teens to sing professionally. Initially a fan of crooner Bing Crosby, Brown was already becoming more comfortable with blues. One song he came up with was his own composition, a jump-blues number called "Good Rockin' Tonight", and when R&B pianist Cecil Gant heard

it, he persuaded Brown to audition—as legend has it, on the phone at 4:00 A.M.—for the boss of De Luxe Records, Jules Braun.

Roy Brown was signed to the label and had his first hit with "Good Rockin'" in 1947, making number thirteen on the *Billboard* R&B chart. Ironically, Wynonie Harris had rejected the song when Brown offered it to him before making his own version, and after Brown's success Harris's cover went on to top the chart later in the year. And the number became even more of a money-earner in 1954, when it became the second single to be released by Elvis Presley, on the Memphis label Sun.

Brown wasn't phased by "Mr. Blues" Harris overtaking him in the chart; between 1948 and 1951 he had no less than fifteen hits, ranging from the emotional "Hard Luck Blues" (his biggest seller in 1950), to up-tempo rockers including "Rockin' at Midnight," "Boogie at Midnight," and "Miss Fanny Brown." For three years the dominant name on the R&B charts, Roy Brown's brand of jump blues has since been recognized as a key contribution in the evolution of rock 'n' roll music.

When rock did break big in the mid-1950s, however, Brown's R&B style failed to connect with the new white teenage market that was rock's core audience. After a period with the Cincinnati label King—with whom he made some impressive sides—his career recovered briefly in 1957 when he moved to Imperial, cutting some dynamic rockers including the original version of "Let the Four Winds Blow," later a hit for Fats Domino. Roy Brown re-emerged in the 1970s with live appearances and an album on ABC-Bluesway, before suffering a fatal heart attack in 1981.

King of the Jukebox

Undoubtedly the biggest star of the postwar "jump blues" era was the singer and alto saxophone star Louis Jordan, whose recording successes actually began in the war years of the early 1940s.

Born in 1908 in Brinkley, Arkansas, in what reads like a classic jazz-blues background Jordan spent time as a youth with the Rabbit Foot Minstrels before working with the famed pianist and composer Clarence Williams, followed by two years playing and singing with the great Chick Webb Orchestra (in which he often duetted with the band's other vocalist, the young Ella Fitzgerald).

He formed his first band in 1938, and almost immediately secured a recording deal with Decca Records, cutting his novelty debut "Honey in the Bee Ball" and "Barnacle Bill the Sailor." The single was credited to the Elks Rendezvous Band, after the Harlem club where they had a residency, but Jordan soon changed it to the Tympany Five—although the band's personnel would often swell to seven or eight in the lineup.

From the start, Jordan's trademark style was humorous up-tempo numbers, typified by his second recording session, from March 1939, which produced five sides including "Keep A-Knockin'" (later covered by Little Richard), "Sam Jones Done Snagged His Britches," and "Doug the Jitterbug." None were hits, but Louis Jordan was establishing himself and the band as a crowd-pulling live act, with topical records to match, such as "Ration Blues" and "Inflation Blues." In November 1941 he recorded one of his classics, "Knock Me a Kiss," a big jukebox hit, followed in 1942 by the blues "I'm Gonna Move to the Outskirts of Town."

Jordan's first chart entry was in *Billboard*'s Harlem Hit Parade, when his amusing "answer record" "I'm Gonna

"I was a real fan of Louis Jordan, that's all I can tell you. He did 'Let the Good Times Roll,' I liked that, and 'Going to Move to the Outskirts of Town' . . . I was a real fan of Louis . . . I was crazy about his music."

RAY CHARLES, 1986

Leave You on the Outskirts of Town" reached number two, followed by "What's The Use of Getting Sober (When You're Gonna Get Drunk Again)," which topped the chart in December 1942. He was on a roll, and one that lasted a decade; between 1942 and 1951 Jordan had no fewer than fifty-seven R&B chart hits—including eighteen number ones—with such well-remembered songs as "Is You Is Or Is You Ain't My Baby" in 1944, "Caldonia" (1945), the multimillion-seller "Choo Choo Ch'boogie" in 1946, and "Saturday Night Fish Fry" in 1949.

Louis Jordan was one of the first black R&B stars to be equally accepted among white audiences, earning the title "King of the Jukebox," and his various appearances in Hollywood films enhanced his popularity with the mainstream public without compromising his music one bit. With the advent of rock 'n' roll—which Jordan once described as simply rhythm and blues played by white performers—his star, like many, faded.

Various comebacks kept him in the public eye before his death from a heart attack in 1975, but ironically his huge-selling comedic hits meant Louis Jordan was taken less seriously as a blues musician and singer than he might have been otherwise. Historically, his importance cannot be overstated; he introduced a form of small-band blues—nearly a decade before the concept of "rhythm and blues"—to mass multiracial audiences across America.

"With my little band, I did everything they did with a big band. I made the blues jump."
LOUIS JORDAN

RIGHT:
An animated Louis Jordan fronting his Tympany Five rhythm section. This is a still from *Swing Parade of 1946*, a musical comedy movie that starred the slapstick trio the Three Stooges, and numbers from Jordan including his 1945 hit "Caldonia."

Atlantic blues

Just as Los Angeles was the West Coast location for several independent record labels key to the history of postwar blues and R&B, so New York—home of Tin Pan Alley and still the center of the music industry—became home to a major "indie" in the late 1940s: Atlantic Records.

The label was formed by Ahmet Ertegun and Herb Abramson in 1947. Ahmet and his elder brother Nesuhi, sons of the Turkish ambassador in Washington, had grown up avid jazz and blues fans. They built up an amazing collection of over fifteen thousand records, and became well connected with the jazz cognoscenti on the East Coast. When Nesuhi moved to California, Ahmet made the decision to go into the record business, starting with an investment of $10,000 from the family dentist. It was at that point he brought in Abramson, a dental student who had worked as a part-time A&R man for a jazz label, National Records.

Although the label's initial releases were primarily instrumental jazz records, from the very start Ertegun and Abramson were keen to explore the burgeoning rhythm and blues market. Following their first big hit, Stick McGhee's "Drinkin' Wine Spo-Dee-O-Dee," Atlantic became the pre-eminent label in R&B.

> **"We were always looking for guitar players who could play the blues, and in New York at that time it wasn't easy. There's a great difference between Duke Ellington or Billy Eckstine and Muddy Waters or Big Bill Broonzy; it's a totally different culture."**
>
> **AHMET ERTEGUN**

Stick was the brother of the Piedmont-style blues guitarist and vocalist Brownie McGhee, who already knew Ertegun. When the Atlantic boss heard that Stick's previous label had closed, he got him to rerecord the yet-to-be-released "Drinkin' Wine . . ." on Atlantic instead. Released in February 1949, it sold nearly half a million copies and made the number three spot in the R&B chart.

Hot on the heels of their success with McGhee's single, in 1949 Atlantic signed a twenty-year-old nightclub singer from Washington, DC, Ruth Brown. Her first release later that year, "So Long" was an R&B hit, although the song was more in the straight pop ballad style of her club repertoire. Things changed, however, in September 1950, when Brown recorded "Teardrops in My

ABOVE:
Years before the foundation of Atlantic Records, the young Ertegun brothers were already acquainted with some of the biggest names in the jazz fraternity. This 1941 get-together at the Maryland home of the distinguished jazz photographer William P. Gottlieb included Ahmet Ertegun, Duke Ellington, Gottlieb, and Nesuhi Ertegun (standing, from far left).

JOHN LEE HOOKER

Although he was from the heartland of the Mississippi Delta, from the start John Lee Hooker nurtured a distinct style that would set him apart from his contemporaries. His insistent, throbbing electric blues came to define a "Detroit sound," if there ever was such a thing, but the magic was really all Hooker's. Numbers like "Dimples," "I Love You Honey," and "Boom Boom," would be part of the soundtrack of the 1960s blues revival, half a decade after he first recorded them. Regarded as a living blues legend in later life, he continued to produce classic albums, often supported by the very musicians who had found their first inspiration via his music.

"The music we play, me, B.B. King, people like that, that music is the roots. Rock music, everything else, is like a branch on the same tree. It all comes from the Blues. They dress it up a little, but it's the same thing."
JOHN LEE HOOKER

Born
John Lee Hooker, August 22, 1917, Coahoma County, Mississippi

Died
June 21, 2001, Los Altos, California

Instruments
Vocals, Guitar

Recording Debut
"Sally Mae" / "Boogie Chillen'"
November 3, 1948, Detroit, Michigan
Modern

Awards
Inducted into Blues Hall of Fame, 1980
Grammy Best Traditional Blues Recording, 1990 for "I'm In the Mood" (with Bonnie Raitt)
Inducted into Rock and Roll Hall of Fame, 1991
Grammy Best Traditional Blues Album 1996, for *Chill Out*
Grammy Best Traditional Blues Album 1998, for *Don't Look Back*
Grammy Best Pop Collaboration with Vocals, 1998 for "Don't Look Back" with Van Morrison
Grammy Lifetime Achievement Award, 2000

Playlist
"Boogie Chillen'" [1948]
"Crawling King Snake" [1949]
"I'm in the Mood" [1951]
"Dimples" [1956]
"I Love You Honey" [1958]
The Country Blues of John Lee Hooker [1960]
"Boom Boom" [1961]
Hooker 'n' Heat [1971]
The Healer [1989]
Mr. Lucky [1991]

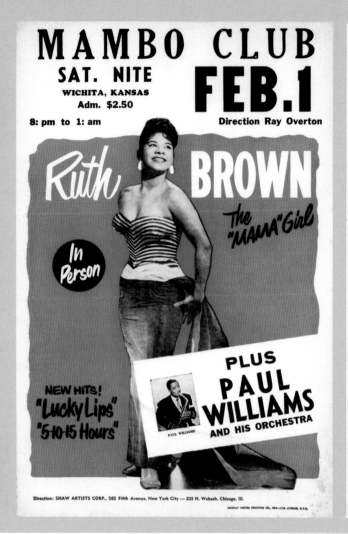

Eyes." Released in October, it would be her first up-tempo hit and an R&B chart-topper for eleven consecutive weeks.

Ruth Brown went on to record more than eighty songs for Atlantic, and with a string of blues-tinted hits, including "I'll Wait for You" in 1951, and two 1953 chart toppers, "5–10–15" and the classic "(Mama) He Treats Your Daughter Mean," she was the acknowledged queen of R&B. Dubbed "Miss Rhythm," she was Atlantic's best-selling artist at the time—indeed, the label became known in the music industry as "the house that Ruth built" (with a nod to the Yankee Stadium nickname, stemming from the feats of baseball legend Babe Ruth).

In 1951 Atlantic successfully rebooted the career of the man they called Boss of the Blues, Big Joe Turner, who was known as a Kansas City-style "blues shouter" in the 1930s and '40s, and enjoyed huge new hits with "Chains of Love," and in 1953 his first R&B number one, "Honey Hush." Then there was the record that guaranteed Big Joe a place in the rock 'n' roll history books, the original version of "Shake, Rattle and Roll," written by Atlantic producer Jesse Stone.

Other key signings to the Atlantic label while Ruth Brown and Big Joe were riding high included R&B vocal group the Clovers, whose "Don't You Know I Love You"

(written by Ertegun) was the label's first R&B number one, hitting the top in September 1951, and Clyde McPhatter, who signed in 1953, with his vocal backing group the Drifters. As Clyde McPhatter and the Drifters, they had an immediate R&B chart-topper with "Money Honey"; with Mickey Baker on guitar and Sam "The Man" Taylor on tenor sax, the single was an instant classic of early '50s rhythm and blues.

The Genius

But the singer who would take over Ruth Brown's crown as the label's top seller was Ray Charles, who signed with Atlantic in 1952. Born in Albany, Georgia in 1930, blind from the age of six and orphaned at fourteen, Ray Charles Robinson began playing professionally in Jacksonville, Florida while still a teenager. By the time he came to the notice of Atlantic, he'd served a solid blues apprenticeship in the Lowell Fulson band, and worked as a solo singer on the Los Angeles label Swing Time, which had also been a launchpad for both Fulson and Percy Mayfield. He delivered blues and ballads in a smooth, relaxed style consciously modeled on the African-American crooner Nat King Cole, and West Coast bluesman Charles Brown.

ABOVE LEFT:
The magnificent Ruth Brown; a poster for a Wichita, Kansas appearance in 1958, along with the "Hucklebuck" hit maker, saxophonist Paul Williams.

ABOVE RIGHT:
Ray Charles in concert, 1957, the poster flagging up some of his Atlantic successes including "It Should've Been Me," "I've Got A Woman," and the sensational gospel-tinged blues "Drown In My Own Tears."

Ray Charles on stage at a concert in Stockholm, Sweden, in 1962.

His first session with Atlantic continued in a similar vein, but both Charles and the studio team knew they were looking for something different. The first sign of things to come came in July 1953 with his third release on the label, the up-tempo jump blues "Mess Around." Written by Ahmet Ertegun and based on a boogie riff from Cow Cow Davenport's "Cow Cow Blues" back in 1928, it put Charles in the R&B chart listings for the first time, with an altogether more strident sound than his previous offerings.

Charles was honing a signature vocal style, poised somewhere between a gospel shout and a blues moan. It was increasingly evident in his next few releases, including his second chart entry, the humorous talking-blues "It Should've Been Me," which was an R&B number five in the spring of 1954. In December that year he recorded his first R&B chart-topper, sending him to national prominence: "I've Got a Woman."

It was the first of a string of seminal recordings made between 1955 and 1959, many with his gospel-style backing vocalists, the Raelettes. They included classics such as "A Fool for You," "Drown in My Own Tears," "Hallelujah I Love Her So," "The Right Time," all featuring a never-before-heard mixture of blues,

gospel, and jazz—in other words, soul music, before it had a name. And Charles capped these with the ultimate call-and-response number, "What'd I Say"—an instant classic, and the gateway into discovering R&B for many a white music-lover.

Ray Charles—dubbed "The Genius" by Atlantic's publicity department—left the company in 1959 for ABC Records, where he continued to deliver blues-based classics including "Hit the Road Jack," "Unchain My Heart," the instrumental "One Mint Julep," and his definitive big-band blues vocal, "I've Got News For You."

Charles was never classed as a blues singer as such. Over the course of a long career, right up to his death in 2004, his repertoire explored many different musical territories, including country music, show tunes, jazz standards, and straight pop songs. But the blues was always at the heart of his vocal style, regardless of the song he was interpreting—like Billie Holiday, he simply sang the blues, whatever the context. And when he did deliver a standard twelve-bar number—his 1963 recording of Leroy Carr's "In the Evening (When the Sun Goes Down)" was a sensational example—it immediately set him apart as an unrivalled blues vocalist of the very highest order.

Chicago R&B

With millions of African-Americans migrating north between the two World Wars, Chicago became a major locus of jazz and blues, and the city was equally pivotal in the history of postwar rhythm and blues. And as was the case in New York and Los Angeles, independent record labels were key to the process.

One of the earliest was Miracle Records, formed in 1946 by businessman Lee Egalnick, which concentrated mainly on jazz, gospel music, and straight pop balladeers. Two names from its small R&B roster made the charts: pianist and bandleader Sonny Thompson, whose instrumentals "Long Gone (Parts 1 and 2)," and "Late Freight" both topped the R&B chart in 1948; and Memphis Slim, one of the giants of postwar blues, who scored for the label with his number one "Messin' Around" that same year.

Every Day I Have the Blues

As the moniker "Memphis Slim" implied, John "Peter" Chatman was born in Memphis, on September 3, 1915. Playing piano in the barrelhouse-boogie style of Roosevelt Sykes in juke joints and dance halls, he moved in 1939 to Chicago where he soon teamed up with guitarist-singer Big Bill Broonzy. He made his first recordings, as Peter Chatman, for OKeh, before switching to Bluebird for a series of recordings that billed him as Memphis Slim, at the suggestion of Bluebird producer Lester Melrose.

The warm-voiced Slim continued to accompany Broonzy, both in live appearances and in the studio, until the end of the war, when he branched out on his own, soon fronting his own seven-piece jump band, the House Rockers. His first postwar records were with the small Chicago label Hy-Tone, before moving to Miracle in the fall of 1946, where his first session included "Rockin' the House," from which his band got its name.

While with Miracle, Slim recorded "Messin' Around" in 1948 and also one of his career staples, "Everyday I Have the Blues", originally titled "Nobody Loves Me." This song has been covered by scores of artists since, including memorable versions by B.B. King, in 1955, and with blues shouter Joe Williams, fronting the Count Basie band, in 1956—both of which received a Grammy Hall of Fame Award.

Through the 1950s Memphis Slim released records on Premium, Chess, and United, all based in Chicago, as well as the Cincinnati label King. It was while he was with United, from 1952 until 1954, that he acquired the services of his first regular guitarist, Matt "Guitar" Murphy, who would put an instantly recognizable stamp on his recordings (and live performances) for years to come. In 1959 Slim signed with Vee-Jay, with whom he would make some of his definitive recordings, releasing classics such as "The Come Back" and "Sassy Mae," with Murphy providing a blistering guitar.

Slim was a featured artist on the first annual American Folk Blues Festival (then billed as the American Negro Blues Festival) to tour Europe in 1962, alongside T-Bone Walker, Sonny Terry, Brownie McGhee, John Lee Hooker, Shakey Jake, and Willie Dixon. The more liberal attitudes in Europe, especially regarding race, led him to take up permanent residency in Paris. Crazy about jazz and blues, the French treated him like royalty—indeed, he would receive an official honor from the Ministry of Culture—and he lived there for the rest of his life, performing regularly across Europe and on return visits to the United States. He died in his adopted home of Paris in February 1988, aged seventy-two, and was buried in his original home town of Memphis, Tennessee.

A much larger enterprise than Miracle Records, Vee-Jay was another Chicago label based on East 47th Street in the City's African-American area, the South Side. Founded by a husband and wife, Vivian Carter and Jimmy Bracken (the "V" and "J") in 1952, it became the most successful black-owned label until the advent of Motown Records in the 1960s. Vee-Jay's golden era spanned the 1950s; its rock and pop catalog included their first non-black act, the Four Seasons, and (albeit briefly) the Beatles. But throughout the 1950s its list of rhythm and blues acts included three seminal doo-wop vocal groups—the Spaniels, the Dells, and the El Dorados—and, in addition to Memphis Slim, two other leading bluesmen who had made the move from the country to the Windy City, Jimmy Reed and (by way of his base in Detroit) John Lee Hooker.

OPPOSITE, TOP LEFT:
Jimmy Reed during a European tour in 1965.

OPPOSITE, BOTTOM LEFT:
The Chicago guitarist Otis Rush. Rush moved to Chicago from Philadelphia, Mississippi, in 1948 and soon made a name for himself after his debut "I Can't Quit You Baby" hit the R&B charts in 1956. He landed a contract with Chess Records in 1960, and extensive touring included the influential American Folk Blues Festival in Europe. Players citing Rush as an influence have included Mike Bloomfield and Eric Clapton.

OPPOSITE, TOP RIGHT:
Memphis Slim in a 1950 publicity photograph.

OPPOSITE, BOTTOM RIGHT:
The third of four albums recorded by Memphis Slim for the Folkways label. Released in 1961, the singer/pianist was accompanied by Arbee Stidham on guitar and Arnold "Jump" Jackson on drums. The cover features a portrait by Raeburn "Ray" Flerlage, who has specialized in Chicago-based blues photography throughout a long career.

HILLBILLY BLUES

Although sometimes referred to as "the white man's blues," country music has more often been incorrectly thought of as music of exclusively European origin. But the mix of European folk music—and Irish and Scottish jigs and reels in particular—that had always been seen as the ancestor of white American rural music also included a strong African-American influence from its earliest days. Indeed, a major instrument in so-called "hillbilly" music, the banjo, had its origins in Africa, and stylistically the blues was a key ingredient of country from the start.

The folk music of the Appalachian Mountains, where the tunes of the European old world persisted in their purest form, was already being influenced by black American, Mexican, and other music by the time the first hillbilly records were made in the 1920s. The communities that initiated what later became known as country music were not isolated hill dwellers, cut off from other cultures but, as far as music was concerned, multi-ethnic melting pots. Despite segregation, working-class whites and blacks shared much of the same deprivation in rural America, especially during the Depression, and this was reflected in many aspects of their culture.

The pioneering hillbilly players, such as "Eck" Robinson and Fiddlin' John Carson, were well aware of the jazz and blues that flooded the record market in the mid-1920s, and experienced it first hand playing around the South in tent shows and vaudeville. It couldn't fail but show in their music—and if blues in its classic eight or twelve-bar form wasn't always predominant in their repertoires, certainly blues intonation, and the use of "blue notes" for emotional effect, was part of the musical currency.

One of the earliest country hits was "Lonesome Road Blues" by guitarist-singer Henry Whitter, released in January 1924. The eight-bar blues was an even bigger hit when subsequently recorded by the Blue Ridge Duo, and it was later released by folk singer Woody Guthrie as "Goin' Down the Road Feelin' Bad," accompanied by blues harp player Sonny Terry.

The blues harp (harmonica) was common to both blues and early country music, as were variations of the slide guitar. The latter was introduced to hillbilly music as the Hawaiian steel guitar, with later developments including the pedal steel guitar, enabling players to achieve much the same sliding effect between notes as the Delta blues bottleneck guitarists. An important early exponent of the Hawaiian steel was Cliff Carlisle, a singer and yodeler who also recorded "Goin' Down the Road Feelin' Bad," with harmonica backing, as well as dozens of blues-inflected singles including "Brakeman's Blues," with the great Jimmie Rodgers, in 1930.

Rodgers fused hillbilly, gospel, pop songs, and blues, selling millions of records and establishing country music among mainstream audiences through the early 1930s. Variously known as "The Singing Brakeman," "The Blue Yodeler," and "The Father of Country Music," he captured a blues feeling in everything he did, and his seminal series of "Blue Yodel" records confirmed the twelve-bar song structure as a universal form in popular music generally, not just in blues, jazz, and swing.

Country music itself came far closer to jazz and blues in the dance hall music known as "western swing," pioneered by Spade Cooley, Milton Brown and His Musical Brownies, and most famously Bob Wills and the Texas Playboys. Brought up playing fiddle and mandolin country style, Wills also picked up blues at an early age from the family neighbors in rural Texas, African-American cotton workers. His "country big band" included horn and saxophone sections, as well as electric and slide guitars. Using jazz-influenced arrangements to deliver such country-oriented classics as "New San Antonio Rose,"

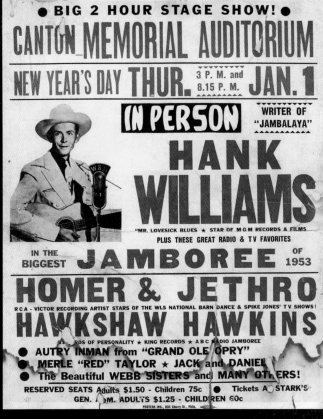

TOP LEFT:
A 1956 poster for an appearance by Bob Wills and his Texas Playboys in Chehalis, Washington.

TOP RIGHT:
This 1953 New Year's Day concert by Hank Williams in Canton, Ohio, never took place. The singer—responsible for such blues-tinged classics as "Your Cheatin' Heart," "I'm So Lonesome I Could Cry," and "Hey, Good Lookin'"—died en route to the show from a heart attack, induced by drugs and alcohol. He was just 29.

BOTTOM RIGHT:
Hillbilly pioneer Fiddlin' John Carson, pictured here with his daughter Rosa Lee, who was known professionally as Moonshine Kate.

OVERLEAF:
Jimmie Rodgers, with his name engraved on the neck of his guitar. When he finished a performance, he would flip the instrument over to reveal the word "Thanks" emblazoned across the back.

"Steel Guitar Rag," and "Take Me Back to Tulsa," the Playboys led the fashion through the 1940s for blues-driven western swing across America, via huge record sales, network radio shows, and sold-out live appearances.

During the postwar years, the new rhythm and blues jump bands also influenced country music, producing another hybrid, "hillbilly boogie." Crossover releases like the Delmore Brothers' 1946 hit "Freight Train Boogie" (yet another contender for "first rock 'n' roll record") and Arthur Smith's pop chart hit "Guitar Boogie" in 1948 heralded the transition of country music into rockabilly in the 1950s.

An even richer seam was mined with "honky-tonk" music, a guitar-based style first popular in Texas and Oklahoma, with its roots in western swing, the Tex-Mex ranchera music of the border states, and Mississippi blues. The earliest mention of the genre in a song was probably "Honky Tonk Blues," recorded in 1936 by Al Dexter, who went on to have a huge hit with "Pistol Packin' Mama" in 1943. Other honky-tonk stars included Ernest Tubb, Kitty Wells, and Lefty Frizell, and its biggest star, Hank Williams, who with over thirty singles in the Top 10 chart (including eleven at number one) was arguably country music's most influential performer.

But at its most basic, honky-tonk was raw, good-time country-rhythm-and-blues, barroom music played primarily for white dancers, in states where segregation was still the order of the day—if it had been on the "colored" side of town, it would have been the music of the juke joint.

"A WHITE TEXAN WHO COULD PLAY THE BLUES AS DEFTLY AS WESTERN NUMBERS AND POPULAR SONGS, HE [JIMMIE RODGERS] MINGLED SONG STYLES TOGETHER WITH A SEEMINGLY EFFORTLESS SHOWMANSHIP."

Big Boss Man

Mathis James Reed (Jimmy Reed), born in 1925, was the son of sharecroppers in Dunleith, Mississippi. He learned the rudiments of his guitar and guitar style from his friend Eddie Taylor, who was already making a name for himself around the clubs and juke joints of the Mississippi "chitlin' circuit." The chitlin' circuit was the collective name given to a string of entertainment venues favorable for black performers during the years of Jim Crow segregation, which in the South lasted until the early 1960s. The name was derived from a soul food staple of stewed pig intestines called chitterlings (or sometimes "chitlins"), served in many establishments.

While still in his teens, in 1943 Reed moved to Chicago; he was drafted into the US Navy soon afterward and served for two years until the end of World War II.

Back in civilian life, he settled for a while in Gary, Indiana, not far from Chicago and its thriving blues scene, working in the Armour Foods meat packing plant while picking up gigs wherever he could. The early 1950s saw him playing with the Gary Kings, a local band led by Chicago guitarist John Brim, and busking on the streets with Willie Joe Duncan (who played a home-made, one-string amplified instrument called a "unitar").

After an unsuccessful audition with Chess Records, which was then fast becoming the premier R&B label in Chicago, in 1953 he signed a contract with the newly formed Vee-Jay. The first sessions with the label reunited him with Eddie Taylor, although it wasn't until his third release, "You Don't Have to Go," in 1955 that he made the R&B chart in *Billboard*, hitting the number five position.

A string of hits in the Hot Hundred pop chart followed, including "Honest I Do" in 1957 and "Big Boss Man" in 1961. Between 1957 and 1963 he appeared in the US singles best sellers twelve times, and in 1964—at the peak of the British blues boom—he even had an entry in the UK Top Fifty with "Shame, Shame, Shame." His relaxed guitar-and-harmonica style was a huge influence on the younger R&B bands emerging in the 1960s—especially in the UK, where his songs were covered by The Animals ("Bright Lights, Big City"), the Rolling Stones (including "Ain't That Lovin' You Baby" and "Bright Lights . . ."), and Van Morrison with Them ("Bright Lights . . ." and "Baby, What You Want Me to Do.")

Jimmy Reed's biggest enemy was himself, and the booze he was addicted to. On some recordings his wife Mama Reed had to sit with him in the studio to whisper the lyrics he couldn't remember. In 1957 he developed epilepsy, although he carried on touring through the 1960s and into the early '70s. He died of respiratory failure in 1976, eight days short of his fifty-first birthday.

Boogie Healer

When John Lee Hooker signed with Vee-Jay Records in 1955, he was already a name in the world of rhythm and blues, especially in his adopted city of Detroit,

"John Lee Hooker . . . was the biggest name in Detroit blues and the one singer who broke out of the confines of its ghetto. He had a guitar technique which made extensive use of 'hammering on' the strings, and his heavily accented foot-beat as he played was integral to his performance. A slight speech impediment in his heavily rich voice gave it an oddly expressive urgency."

PAUL OLIVER

with several R&B chart hits under his belt. By the time he left the Chicago-based label, in 1964, his name was known worldwide.

Born in 1917 near Clarksdale, Mississippi, John Lee was the son of sharecropper parents who separated when he was four years old. His mother soon remarried, and his stepfather, William Moore, was responsible for getting the young boy interested in the guitar. Unlike most of the Delta blues players of the immediate area, Moore—who was originally from Shreveport, Louisiana—played a droning, hypnotic, one-chord style of blues that mesmerized the youngster.

When Hooker was only fifteen, and with just a couple of years of Moore's tuition behind him, he packed his bags and his guitar and set off for the local big city, Memphis, ninety miles to the north. There he found himself a job as an usher in the New Daisy Theater on Beale Street, but that was the nearest he got to being part of the city's flourishing blues scene.

From Memphis he found his way to Cincinnati, working in factory jobs and playing juke joints and bars at night, and then Detroit, where he spent most of the War years working in the giant Ford Motors factory. Picking up regular gigs on the bustling music scene around Hastings Street, Hooker began to get noticed—and, as if anticipating changes in the air, he moved from an acoustic to electric guitar.

In the fall of 1948 Hooker was spotted by a local record producer, Bernard Besman, who offered to represent him. No sooner had the two teamed up than Besman arranged a recording session with the Los Angeles label Modern. The resulting debut single, "Boogie Chillen'" (backed with "Sally Mae," which was released as the A side) was an instant hit, climbing to number one in the R&B chart. With its primitive, repetitive beat, heavily amplified guitar, and Hooker's pounding foot, it set a pattern that "The Boogie Man" (as John Lee had been dubbed) followed into 1949 with three more hits, "Hobo Blues," "Hoogie Boogie," and the hypnotic "Crawling King Snake." Still with Modern, and by now something of a celebrity in the Detroit blues scene, John Lee Hooker topped the R&B chart again in 1951 with "I'm in the Mood," in which his treble-tracked vocals added an extra brooding element to the texture of the song.

RIGHT:
John Lee Hooker in the early days of his career, when he recorded—often under various names—for an array of labels. "I cannot accurately recollect how many times I have cut records" he would admit in 1964, "I think I have made discs for about thirty different labels."

But Hooker never sat still as far as recording was concerned. Although ostensibly contracted to Modern, through the early 1950s he recorded with an array of labels—including King, Savoy, Regal, Swing Time, Chess, and over two dozen more—under an equally bewildering series of pseudonyms that included Delta John, Texas Slim, Birmingham Sam, the easily recognized John Lee Booker, and of course The Boogie Man.

In October 1955, John Lee Hooker traveled to Chicago for his first recording session with Vee-Jay. It was the start of a relationship in which Hooker adopted a more disciplined approach—both by not moonlighting on other labels under assumed names, and by eschewing his previous loose approach to accompaniment in favor of a proper studio backing band. For his first session he had Vee-Jay artist Jimmy Reed on harmonica and Reed's longtime musical partner Eddie Taylor on guitar. His next session for the label, in 1956 still with Taylor on guitar, produced a true Hooker classic, "Dimples," though there were no more chart hits for the time being. That had to wait until 1958, when "I Love You Honey" did the trick.

But during the newly awakened interest in the blues of the early 1960s, among young white audiences in Europe and elsewhere as much as the States, the Vee-Jay relationship really paid off. After "Boom Boom" was a huge hit in 1962, making the pop charts in Britain and the United States, "Dimples," "I Love You Honey," and other Hooker sides were rereleased for the new blues-buying public, with "Dimples" hitting the UK Top Thirty in 1964.

Along with many of his blues compatriots, Hooker toured the new international R&B circuit throughout the 1960s, closing the decade with his acclaimed collaboration with the boogie band Canned Heat, titled *Hooker 'n' Heat*, which in 1971 was his best-selling album for years. This would be his last chart success for nearly two decades, until 1989, when he recorded the award-winning *The Healer*.

Recorded in San Francisco, *The Healer* featured contributions from Carlos Santana, Bonnie Raitt in a riveting version of "I'm in the Mood," and George Thorogood on "Sally Mae," as well as team-ups with harp player Charlie Musselwhite, Tex-Mex group Los Lobos, Canned Heat, and blues guitar virtuoso Robert Cray. The album peaked at number sixty-two on the *Billboard* chart—no small feat for a blues collection—and met with unanimous critical acclaim.

ABOVE LEFT:
John Lee Hooker on the now-legendary UK television rock show *Ready Steady Go!*, in June 1964.

ABOVE RIGHT:
Hooker in his late seventies, enjoying the fruits of renewed success, performing at the Santa Cruz Blues Festival in 1996.

ABOVE RIGHT:
Left to right, Chess Records co-founder Phil Chess with star signing Etta James, and the veteran rhythm and blues record producer Ralph Bass, in 1965.

In 1991 Hooker scored again with another all-star lineup on *Mr. Lucky*, produced by Ry Cooder, which peaked at number 101 in the *Billboard* 200 album chart, and made number three in the UK. And when "Boom Boom" was used for a TV commercial for Levi jeans in 1992, the rereleased record shot to number sixteen in the UK singles chart.

Working to the end, John Lee Hooker died at age eighty-three in June 2001, just before he was due to take off on another tour of Europe. A pure bluesman to the last, who never compromised his basic style, two of his songs—"Boogie Chillen'" and "Boom Boom"—were listed by the Rock and Roll Hall of Fame in their list of "500 Songs That Shaped Rock and Roll."

Chess Players

Vee-Jay, Miracle, Hy-Tone, and various other independent labels all played their part in the history of postwar blues in Chicago, but none as significantly as Chess Records. The company was founded by the Polish immigrant brothers Leonard and Phil Chess, who ran a nightclub on the South Side, the center of the city's African-American population. In 1947 Leonard bought a stake in an existing record label, Aristocrat, which focused on jazz and jump blues, and after bringing brother Phil into the company, he began recording some of the black rhythm and blues he was hearing at his club, the Macomba Lounge.

One of the first Aristocrat sessions under Leonard's watch was with piano player Sunnyland Slim, toward the end of 1947. Slim knew that the Chess brothers were looking to grab a piece of the action being generated by country-style blues players like Lightnin' Hopkins, and he suggested they listen to a guitar player by the name of McKinley Morganfield, who was already billing himself as Muddy Water.

Their first success on Aristocrat was Muddy's debut release, "I Can't Be Satisfied" backed with "I Feel Like Going Home" (a typesetting error added an "s" to his last name on the label, and he decided to keep it), released in April 1948 and soon occupying the number eleven slot on *Billboard*'s Most Played Jukebox Race Records chart. Over the next couple of years Muddy Waters would record over a dozen sides under his own name (and as many again accompanying other artists) for Aristocrat, before the brothers bought out Leonard's original partner and renamed the label Chess in 1950.

The first release on Chess was an instrumental by the jazz tenor sax star Gene Ammons (son of the boogie-woogie legend Albert Ammons), "My Foolish Heart;" released in June 1950, it was the label's biggest success for that year. Straight jazz was soon eclipsed by R&B acts, however, as the fledging label built up its blues catalog with key names including Waters, Jimmy Rogers, Memphis Slim, and Howlin' Wolf (all migrants from the rural South), creating the beginning of a unique "Chicago Sound" in the process.

In 1952 the Chess Brothers started up an alternative label, Checker, partly in order to secure more radio play, as stations were restricted in the amount of music they could broadcast on any one label. That led to a further rash of seminal rhythm and blues signings including Elmore James, Little Walter, and Sonny Boy Williamson. And by the mid-1950s, with Bo Diddley strengthening their R&B arm, and Chuck Berry gaining a foothold in the new rock 'n' roll market, the Chess Records organization was at the very cutting edge of black blues-based music coming out of Chicago.

Hoochie Coochie Man

When he got the call to audition for the Chess Brothers at Aristocrat, it was not Muddy Waters' first experience of recording. That dated back to 1941, when bluesologist Alan Lomax recorded him on one of his field trips for the Library of Congress. Those sessions took place in Waters' own cabin, which was on the vast Stovall Plantation in the Mississippi Delta. Waters was already twenty-eight years old, and since his family's move to Stovall when he was an infant, he'd never really been anywhere else.

McKinley Morganfield was born on April 4, 1913, in a small hamlet called Jug's Corner near Rolling Fork, Mississippi. His mother Berta died soon after he was born—though no record exists, it's possible she was simply swept away in the frequent flooding that was a feature of life near the banks of the Mississippi—and he was adopted by his grandmother, Della.

As a youngster he picked up on the blues music that was all around, listening to the phonograph records of Blind Lemon Jefferson, Blind Blake, and the rest of the

"I wanted to get out of Mississippi in the worst way, man. Go back? What I want to go back for? They had such as my mother and the older people brainwashed that people can't make it too good in the city. But I figured if anyone else was living in the city, I could make it there too."

MUDDY WATERS

early country blues stars. (Not that he could afford a turntable, but he visited the establishments and homes that could.) In his teens he heard both Son House and Charley Patton performing live, experiences that would stay with him as he began playing bottleneck guitar. Gigging where he could in bars and juke joints, he was soon making a name for himself among a widening circle of musicians across the Delta region, including Robert Nighthawk, Big Joe Williams, and Rice Miller (later better known as Sonny Boy Williamson II.)

ABOVE:
A sharecropper's shack, photographed just south of Jackson, Mississippi in June 1937, by the influential photojournalist Dorothea Lange, famous for her Depression-era work for the Farm Security Administration. The almost barren ground and isolation of the homesteads tells its own story.

MUDDY WATERS

More than any other single vocalist or musician, Muddy Waters was the man responsible for transforming the raw music of the Delta into modern electric blues and popularizing it worldwide in the process. His guitar and harmonica-led band would create what became known as Chicago rhythm and blues, a template for the so-called "blues boom" of the 1960s. His influence, the very root of the music of white R&B bands like the Rolling Stones, cannot be overstated. And the sheer sensuality of recordings like "Hoochie Coochie Man," "I Just Want to Make Love to You," and "Mannish Boy," remains as stimulating as it did when they were first released decades ago.

"It's real. Muddy's real. See the way he plays guitar? Mississippi style, not the city way. He don't play chords, he don't follow what's written down in the book. He plays notes, all blue notes. Making what he's thinking."
BIG BILL BROONZY

Born
April 4, 1913, Jug's Corner, Issaquena County, Mississippi

Died
April 30, 1983, Westmont, Illinois

Instruments
Vocals, guitar, harmonica

Recording Debut
"Country Blues" / "I Be's Troubled"
August 1941, Stovall, Mississippi
Library of Congress

Awards
Grammy Best Ethnic or Traditional Folk Recording 1971, for *They Call Me Muddy Waters*
Grammy Best Ethnic or Traditional Folk Recording 1972, for *The London Muddy Waters Session*
Grammy Best Ethnic or Traditional Folk Recording 1975, for *The Muddy Waters Woodstock Album*
Grammy Best Ethnic or Traditional Folk Recording 1977, for *Hard Again*
Grammy Best Ethnic or Traditional Folk Recording 1978, for *I'm Ready*
Grammy Best Ethnic or Traditional Folk Recording 1979, for *Muddy "Mississippi" Waters Live*
Inducted into Blues Hall of Fame, 1980
Inducted into Rock and Roll Hall of Fame, 1987
Grammy Lifetime Achievement Award, 1992

Playlist
"I Can't Be Satisfied" [1948]
"Rollin' and Tumblin'" [1950]
"Rolling Stone" [1950]
"Hoochie Coochie Man" [1954]
"I Just Want to Make Love to You" [1954]
"Mannish Boy" [1955]
"Got My Mojo Working" [1956]
"I Got My Brand on You" [1960]
"Tiger in Your Tank" [1960]
At Newport 1960 [1960]
Muddy Waters: Folk Singer [1964]
Hard Again [1977]

QUEEN CITY RAINBOW
CLARKSVILLE, TENNESSEE
TUESDAY, MAY 1st

9:00 P.M. — — Admission: Advance, $1.75 Door, $2.00

"THAT HOOTCHIE COOTCHIE MAN"

MUDDY
WATERS
★ ★ **AND HIS** ★ ★
ORCHESTRA
Famous for "I'm Ready" and "Mad Love"

ABOVE:
Muddy Waters with James
Cotton on harmonica. Cotton
began working with Muddy in
1955, having already been in
Howlin' Wolf's band and
recorded solo records for Sun.
He alternated with Little Walter
on Muddy's recording sessions,
and toured with the band until
he formed his own outfit in 1965.
A consummate accompanist, he
has backed numerous blues stars
over the years including
contemporary names like Joe
Bonamassa and Keb' Mo'.

By the time Alan Lomax and his African-American colleague Professor John Work arrived at Stovall in late August 1941, Muddy Water (as he had now dubbed himself) had enough of a reputation for the folklorists with their recording machine to actively seek him out. When Waters subsequently received a pressing of two of the songs—"Country Blues" and "I Be's Troubled"—and a check for $20, he renewed his efforts to carve out a career as a full-time musician. He'd already made a move in that direction when he'd briefly relocated to St. Louis in 1940, but the city was not to his liking, and he was back in the Delta within months. But after a second recording visit by Lomax in 1942, Waters decided to take the much bigger step of moving to Chicago.

Driving a truck by day and playing the blues clubs by night, Waters struggled to get a foothold on the highly competitive Chicago blues scene. Veteran star Big Bill Broonzy helped him along the way, letting Waters open dates for him; he struck up a friendship with guitarist

Jimmy Rogers that would last a lifetime; and he got a job backing hot harmonica man Sonny Boy Williamson I. By this time, with his acoustic bottleneck style severely challenged by the rowdy noise in most of the clubs, Waters had switched to electric guitar—and he found the sound that made him famous.

In 1946 he recorded some sides for Mayo Williams at OKeh, of which only one track—"Mean Red Spider"—was released at the time. Then Sunnyland Slim brought him to the attention of the Chess brothers; for them, he initially backed Sunnyland on some songs that were released as "Sunny Land Slim with Muddy Water." His debut on Aristocrat was "Gypsy Woman" and "Little Anna Mae," released in February 1948 to no great success, before the disc that set him on his way via the Billboard R&B chart, "I Can't Be Satisfied," backed with "I Feel Like Going Home."

For Waters' first releases, the studio used tried-and-tested house musicians, even though he now had a regular band playing the Chicago clubs—and what a band, including Little Walter on harmonica, Jimmy Rogers on guitar, and Elgin Evans on drums. Waters was the front man, singing hard driving vocals and playing searing electric guitar, and they became the epitome of the Chicago R&B sound that would sweep the world. By 1951 (with the label name now changed to Chess) they were on Waters' records too, and were soon to add a final piece to the seminal Muddy Waters lineup with Otis Spann on piano, and on many recordings Chess house producer Willie Dixon on bass.

The classic lineup lasted only twelve months or so as a full-time unit, with Little Walter soon branching out with his own band after his instrumental single "Juke" topped the R&B charts in 1952. But Walter's amplified harmonica continued to appear on many of Waters' singles throughout the 1950s, with his regular band replacements Junior Wells, and then James Cotton, also filling the chair. Likewise in the mid-'50s Jimmy Rogers left the band to work with his own group, and Otis Spann also began to forge a career under his own name.

Muddy Waters' output through the 1950s included some of the most powerful recordings in electric blues, serving as a bedrock repertoire for generations of musicians thereafter. Without numbers like "Mannish Boy," "Got My Mojo Working," "I Just Want to Make Love to You," and the iconic "Hoochie Coochie Man," the R&B boom of the early 1960s might never have happened.

With his star in the ascendant worldwide, in 1958 Waters did some concerts in England, where many blues fans—nurtured on the acoustic blues of the likes of Josh White and Big Bill Broonzy—were shocked by his blistering electric guitar. He was simply ahead of his time, but by the dawn of the 1960s things were changing, and his live album *At Newport 1960* helped accelerate that change. Though it never charted, the album was critically acclaimed, and hugely influential on the burgeoning rhythm and blues scene.

Mindful of the simultaneous boom in folk music, in 1963 Waters recorded an acoustic album *Muddy Waters: Folk Singer*, released in April 1964 with Willie Dixon on bass, Clifton James on drums, and Buddy Guy on second guitar. At the same time he continued to tour worldwide with his full electric band, though record-wise it was the young, predominantly white, UK and US blues bands who were reaping most rewards from the R&B explosion that he had helped ignite.

As if to somehow accommodate that state of affairs, in 1968 Chess had Waters in the studio with a psychedelic rock band for the unfortunate *Electric Mud*. This was followed by several more collaborations, including *Fathers and Sons* in 1969 with white American blues players including Paul Butterfield and Mike Bloomfield, and less successfully *The London Muddy Waters Sessions* in 1971—which, with lackluster contributions from Steve Winwood and Georgie Fame, among others, was saved only by the more sympathetic contribution of the great Irish blues guitarist Rory Gallagher.

Through the 1970s Waters was fêted at blues festivals all over the world as a living legend of classic Chicago blues. He also enjoyed a revival of his fortunes on disc, when Chess Records finally folded in 1975, and he signed to Blue Sky Records on the instigation of rock-blues guitarist Johnny Winter. Winter produced (and appeared on) the Grammy-winning *Hard Again* in 1977, plus 1978's *I'm Ready*, and *King Bee* in 1981. Together with 1979's *Muddy "Mississippi" Waters Live*, they would be among Muddy Waters' best-selling albums.

In the early 1980s Waters' health began to decline rapidly; he was diagnosed with cancer, a fact that he kept secret from almost all around him. His last-ever public performance was guesting with Eric Clapton at a Miami concert on June 30, 1982, not long after doctors had told him the cancer was in remission. But that was not to last, and Muddy Waters died at his home in the Chicago suburb of Westmont, Illinois, on April 30, 1983.

Juke

Muddy Waters' various lineups, especially in the 1950s when he made most of his seminal recordings, read like a who's-who of Chicago R&B, including players like Little Walter, who helped to create the sound that Waters made famous. Harmonica man "Little" Walter Jacobs took his inspiration from players like the first Sonny Boy Williamson (John Lee Williamson) and Snooky Prior. Both older players used amplification, playing in front of a microphone to get above the volume of the accompanying guitars and drums, but Walter went one better, cupping a small mic in his hands along with the "blues harp," and achieving various distorted effects that were unique at the time.

Walter had already released some sides on a small Chicago label, but put his own band leading on hold when he got the regular job with Waters' group. In 1952, however, Chess recorded him fronting a session under his own name for their new subsidiary label Checker, and the debut release, the instrumental "Juke," saw him topping the R&B chart for eight weeks in a row. After leaving Muddy's band (replaced by Junior Wells), Jacobs had fourteen top-ten hits (usually with a vocal on one side, an instrumental on the other) on the chart, including another number one, "My Babe,"—a rewrite of Sister Rosetta Tharpe's gospel standard "This Train"—in 1955.

Little Walter continued to appear on many of Waters' recordings through the 1950s, and he backed other R&B stars including Jimmy Rogers, Johnny Shines, Bo Diddley, and Otis Rush. He also starred in a Checker "supergroup" album with Muddy Waters and Bo Diddley in 1967, *Super Blues*. Hugely influential, particularly on the guitar-and-harmonica R&B bands that proliferated in the UK in the early 1960s, Little Walter died after a violent altercation in a Chicago nightclub in 1968.

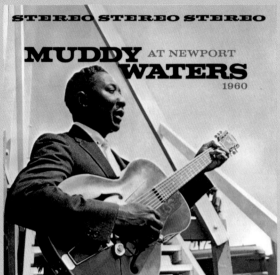

STEREO STEREO STEREO

MUDDY AT NEWPORT
WATERS 1960

PYTHON RECORDS   PLP-KM 20

Little Walter

and his Jukes

JUKE JOINTS

A key social factor in the proliferation of live blues in America—and particularly the rural South—was the juke joint, the often ramshackle venue that had served as dance hall, liquor bar, diner, and gambling den for generations of African Americans since the end of the nineteenth century.

"Juke" (or "jook") is believed to have evolved from the word *joog*, a term of West African descent meaning disorderly, rowdy, or wicked. As in many God-fearing communities across America, the local dance hall or drinking lounge was often described in derogatory terms, the music and good times therein seen as nothing less than the work of the Devil.

In fact, the origin of these modest establishments goes back to the years following the Emancipation, when plantation workers and sharecroppers were grateful for somewhere to relax after their toil, being barred from most white places on account of the "Jim Crow" segregation laws that had been introduced across the South. So by the time ragtime and blues players started entertaining in the jukes of the early twentieth century, there was a thriving network of such venues. Usually located at rural crossroads and on the outskirts of towns, they often occupied decrepit buildings that had been abandoned by previous occupants, many of whom had moved North seeking a better life.

The Prohibition years of the 1920s meant boom time for the jukes, which in most cases were already dealing in bootleg liquor and operating somewhat outside the law— and in many instances the "blind eye" of local police and sheriffs could be bought for a small consideration. It was in such places that the early Delta bluesmen cut their teeth and found their most regular audiences—indeed it was in

typical juke joints around Robinsonville, Mississippi, that a young Robert Johnson listened to the music of Son House, learning his craft from the master. Johnson, Charley Patton, Big Joe Williams—many of the legendary bluesmen of the pre-World War II period relied on the juke joint circuit for a meager income, sometimes living on just tips, with food and drink thrown in for free.

After the War the jukes still flourished, their music provided by the new generation of electric guitar players and rhythm and blues bands—or, on nights when they couldn't afford a band, the ubiquitous jukebox. These nickel-in-a-slot record machines had been around since the early years of the century, but acquired the name "jukebox" only in the late 1930s on account of their popularity in juke joints, roadhouses, and diners across the United States.

The 1990s and 2000s have seen a sharp decline in the number of juke joints operating, especially in the juke heartland of Mississippi. A major reason has been the proliferation of legal gambling casinos, many of which also provide their customers with free live music. At the jukes that still survive—like Po' Monkeys near Merigold, Bolivar County, the Do Drop Inn in Shelby, and the (sadly) recently closed Smitty's Red Top Lounge in Clarksdale—there is now a stronger reliance on the tourist trade, with blues fans from all over the world, wishing for a taste of "where it all began," outnumbering the locals on many nights.

OPPOSITE, TOP LEFT:
Po Monkey's Lounge near Merigold, Mississippi, a surviving juke joint when it was photographed in 2004 by Matthew Craig.

OPPOSITE, TOP RIGHT:
A Florida juke joint in 1944 by the celebrated photographer Marion Post Wolcott, who worked for the Farm Security Administration through the Great Depression and into the war years.

OPPOSITE BOTTOM:
Migratory laborers outside a juke joint during a slack season in Belle Glade, Florida. Another Marion Post Wolcott picture for the FSA, it was also taken in 1944.

OVERLEAF:
A hot night at Mama Rene's Do Drop Inn in Shelby, Mississippi. The joint, still going strong, has been run by Irene Williams for many years, with the band of Wesley Jefferson (pictured here) a regular attraction.

THE MONEY FROM PLAYING IN JUKES, BARROOMS AND PLANTATION HOPS ON WEEKENDS MIGHT NOT LOOK LIKE MUCH, BUT IT PUT THE BLUESMEN AHEAD OF MOST OTHER FOLKS IN THE DELTA PLANTATION WORLD. BLUESMEN COULD AFFORD TO DRESS BETTER, DRINK MORE, GAMBLE MORE, HAVE MORE GOOD-LOOKING WOMEN, MAYBE EVEN GIVE UP FARMING."

ALAN LOMAX

The Wolf

Muddy Waters' biggest rival on the Chicago blues scene was undoubtedly a guitarist, harmonica player, and singer with a powerful, booming voice, born Chester Burnett but known as Howlin' Wolf. Born in 1910 in West Point, Mississippi, as a young man he listened to Charley Patton in local juke joints, picking up tips on guitar technique and learning about showmanship from this early blues master.

Like any aspiring bluesman growing up in the Delta, Howlin' Wolf was also influenced by other popular performers, such as Ma Rainey, Tampa Red, and Blind Lemon Jefferson—whose "Match Box Blues" was one of the first songs he learned to play. And Wolf mastered the harmonica via another blues great, Rice Miller (Sonny Boy Williamson II), who had married his half-sister and taught the youngster the rudiments of the instrument. Howlin' Wolf went on to play with a number of prominent blues musicians during the 1930s including Honeyboy Edwards, Johnny Shines, Son House, and Robert Johnson.

After service in World War II, in 1948 Wolf formed his own band, which included Matt "Guitar" Murphy (prior to his joining Memphis Slim in Chicago), and on harmonica at various times both James Cotton and Little Junior Parker. He began his own daily show on radio KWEM in West Memphis, which came to the attention of Sam Phillips, soon to be the founder of Sun Records.

Phillips had yet to start the label, but had just opened the Memphis Recording Service studio, where in 1951 Howlin' Wolf made his disc debut with two cuts produced by Phillips—"Moanin at Midnight" and "How Many More Years"—which were subsequently released by Chess from their base in Chicago.

The single made the number four position in the R&B chart, and in 1953 Wolf moved to Chicago to live, now under long-term contract to Chess Records.

As soon as he arrived, he began to put a band together, and within a few months he had persuaded the West Memphis (Arkansas) guitarist Hubert Sumlin to follow him. The chemistry between Wolf and Sumlin was remarkable, with the latter weaving notes behind the vocals rather than playing a normal backing of "rhythm" chords. Sumlin's solos were a dazzling continuation of the same style. His guitar complemented Howlin' Wolf's strident delivery perfectly and continued to do so throughout the singer's career.

By 1956 Wolf was in the R&B charts again with "Smokestack Lightnin'," one of his most enduring classics, but his most consistent recording period came at the end of the decade, when he teamed up with Chess staff writer Willie Dixon. For the next five years they produced a string of hits that, like Muddy Waters' best known titles, became the sound track of the transatlantic fashion for Chicago R&B. Songs such as "Spoonful," "Little Red Rooster," "Killing Floor," and "Wang Dang

Doodle" all became standards in the canon of contemporary blues bands everywhere.

For rhythm and blues, as for the rest of the record business, the 1960s saw singles give way to albums as the medium of choice among many record buyers. Although the hit single was still a prized achievement, a best-selling album represented more kudos (though not necessarily more money for many veteran blues stars) in the long term. Beginning with *Moanin' in the Moonlight* in 1959, Howlin' Wolf racked up a string of successful long-players between then and the early 1970s, including *Howlin' Wolf* in 1962, *The Real Folk Blues* in 1966, and in 1971 *The London Howlin' Wolf Sessions*, featuring Eric Clapton, Bill Wyman, Steve Winwood, and Ringo Starr among the guests—a more satisfactory effort than the similar venture with Muddy Waters that same year.

In the early years of the 1970s, Wolf's health declined, although he continued playing and recording. His last album was *The Back Door Wolf* in 1973. But a heart attack, followed by kidney damage after a car accident, took their toll, and he died in 1976, just two months after what turned out to be his final gig, an appearance with B.B. King in Chicago.

ABOVE:
A big man in every way, Howlin' Wolf Burnett towered over his fellow musicians, and with his rich, sonorous voice and commanding guitar style, completely dominated any venue with his presence.

HOWLIN' WOLF

With his six-foot-six, three-hundred-pound-plus frame, Howlin' Wolf was a towering presence, matched by a booming voice that gave every note he sang a commanding authority—when you listen to his records you know this is the blues, unadorned. Despite the fact that Muddy Waters helped him get established on the Chicago blues scene, the rivalry between Howlin' Wolf and Waters was the stuff of legend. Their vocal approaches were quite different, but these blues giants had one thing in common: their legacy of crucial recordings (in Wolf's case including "Smokestack Lightnin'," "Little Red Rooster," and the sublimely confessional "Goin' Down Slow") that came to define the essence of Chicago rhythm and blues.

> **"When you ain't got no money, you've got the blues. When you ain't got no money to pay your house rent, you've still got the blues. A lot of people holler 'I don't like no blues,' but when you ain't got no money, and you can't pay your house rent, and can't buy no food, you damn sure got the blues."**
>
> HOWLIN' WOLF

Born
June 10, 1910, West Point, Mississippi

Died
January 10, 1976, Hines, Illinois

Instruments
Vocals, guitar, harmonica

Recording Debut
"Moanin at Midnight" / "How Many More Years"
August 1941, Memphis, Tennessee
Chess Records

Awards
Inducted into Blues Hall of Fame, 1980
Inducted into Rock and Roll Hall of Fame [Early Influences], 1991
"Smokestack Lightnin'" inducted into Grammy Hall of Fame, 1999
Inducted into Mississippi Musicians Hall of Fame, 2003

Playlist
"Moanin at Midnight" [1951]
"Smokestack Lightnin'" [1956]
"Spoonful" [1960]
"Goin' Down Slow" [1961]
"Wang Dang Doodle" [1961]
"Little Red Rooster" [1961]
"Killing Floor" [1964]
Moanin' in the Moonlight [1959]
Howlin' Wolf [1962]
The Real Folk Blues [1966]
The London Howlin' Wolf Sessions [1971]

Etta James

One of the few female R&B singers to be signed to Chess, Etta James' hit-making career began in the mid-1950s, five years before she signed with the Chicago brothers, Leonard and Phil Chess.

She debuted on the LA label Modern in 1955, as a member of the Peaches vocal group, with a cover of Hank Ballard's racy "Work with Me Annie," "Roll with Me Henry." It made the R&B chart after being retitled "The Wallflower," with "Good Rockin' Daddy" following it into the best sellers.

The Peaches broke up soon afterward, and Etta had little luck until 1960, when she signed with Chess. There she enjoyed a string of successes, including "All I Could Do Is Cry," an R&B number two in 1960, and her sensational 1961 album *At Last!* which included blues-drenched cover versions of jazz standards, doo-wop songs, R&B, and straight blues—featuring a riveting version of Willie Dixon's hit for Muddy Waters, "I Just Want to Make Love to You."

Throughout her subsequent career, which had its share of ups and downs and personal traumas, Etta James demonstrated—as on that debut album—that she could handle most material with a passion that came through in every line. She acknowledged Billie Holiday, Dinah Washington, and Ray Charles as her key influences—and as it was for them, her delivery of any song was, in the words of one writer, "blues personified."

ABOVE:
The most iconic photograph of Etta James, as used here on her third album release *Etta James*, in 1962. The album included her Top 40 hit "Something's Got a Hold on Me," as well as two tracks by the Chess in-house composer, arranger, producer, and bass player Willie Dixon—"Nobody But You" and "Spoonful," best known as the classic by Howlin' Wolf.

Elmore James: first released on Trumpet Records, James' signature "Dust My Broom" later appeared on Enjoy, a Harlem-based label. Enjoy was founded by veteran R&B producer Bobby Robinson in 1962, and specialized in blues, doo-wop, and rock 'n' roll. The label later pioneered early hip-hop music before closing in 1987.

Dust My Broom

Instrumentally, probably the most influential musician to come out of the Chicago blues scene was guitarist Elmore James. Basically a country player steeped in the blues of the Mississippi Delta, his trademark style nevertheless had its biggest impact on electric rhythm and blues.

Raised in the heart of the Delta, he taught himself as a child the rudiments of guitar picking on a one-string homemade diddley bow, which was strung up on a wall of the shack the family called home. By the time he was fifteen he'd bought his first proper instrument, a $20 National guitar, and begun playing local parties and juke joints, before spreading his wings and hooking up with other players across the Delta. They included Howlin' Wolf, the second Sonny Boy Williamson, and, crucially, Robert Johnson.

It was Johnson's song "I Believe I'll Dust My Broom" that served as the basis for James' signature number "Dust My Broom," with its instantly recognizable intro lick. Indeed, there has been some dispute over the years as to which guitarist actually wrote it in the first place.

After serving in World War II, James settled in Canton, Mississippi, where he worked in his adopted brother's radio repair shop. There he devised his particular sound, using parts from the shop to amplify his guitar with not just one, but two pickups. He also started playing with the slide guitarist Homesick James—his cousin—and Sonny Boy Williamson, and was one of the first "guest stars" to appear on the popular *King Biscuit Time* radio show on

KFFA in Helena, Arkansas. And it was through Sonny Boy that Elmore James released his first record under his own name.

James had already been in the studios of Trumpet Records in Jackson, Mississippi, backing Williamson on various sessions. In 1951 he signed with Trumpet as an artist. The result of his first session, under the name of Elmo James, was "Dust My Broom," which became a surprise R&B hit, making the Top Ten and catapulting James to blues celebrity status.

He moved to Chicago, where he formed his band the Broomdusters, and secured another Top Ten hit with "I Believe" in 1953. Through the 1950s he recorded for a variety of labels including Modern, Chess, and in 1959, Fire Records, with whom he made some of his most memorable blues sides, including "Stranger Blues," "The Sky Is Crying" (an R&B number 15), and "Shake Your Moneymaker." His fourth chart hit, "It Hurts Me Too," came in 1965, two years after his death from a heart attack at age forty-five.

But it was as an influence on future guitar players, rather than as a hit maker in his own right, that Elmore James earned his place in the pantheon of blues greats. His raw, soaring slide style was a key element in the sound of 1960s blues, impacting the work of legions of musicians ranging from Chicago bluesmen like Hound Dog Taylor and J. B. Hutto, to blues-rock masters including the Rolling Stones, Canned Heat, and most famously Jimi Hendrix.

Walking to New Orleans

From its days as the "cradle of jazz" in the early twentieth century, New Orleans had always been a unique melting pot of musical influences and, like Chicago, had a long-standing blues tradition that in the 1940s and '50s formed the basis for its own unique brand of rhythm and blues.

With the strength of the jazz tradition in the Louisiana seaport, it's no surprise that New Orleans blues evolved with more emphasis on the piano and saxophone, rather than the guitar, which was dominating music elsewhere in the postwar years.

Of course, there were major guitar names, like Guitar Slim and Earl King, who came out of the Crescent City, but the general thrust of the music there has always been horn-led, good-time party music, flavored with Dixieland jazz and the syncopation of the second line, that was considered simply old-fashioned in other parts of the country. The proximity of the Caribbean and its relaxed musical vibe also exerted its influence, while conversely

New Orleans R&B, with often complex but laid back rhythms falling just behind the beat, was a major influence on West Indian ska, rocksteady, and reggae, that developed out of "blue beat" in the late 1950s.

I Hear You Knocking

With a big voice comparable to Joe Turner's, blues singer and guitarist Smiley Lewis was one of the pioneers of the New Orleans R&B sound. He arrived in the city from his native Lake Charles, Louisiana, in his mid-teens. It was the late 1920s, and he was soon playing the bars and clubs around the French Quarter, often accompanied by the pianist Tuts Washington. World War II came and went, with Smiley Lewis building a reputation over the years that paid off in 1947, when he was offered a session with DeLuxe Records.

Nothing spectacular happened with his debut single, but in 1950 a move to the Imperial label and budding producer Dave Bartholomew (a seminal figure in the

ABOVE:
New Orleans' Bourbon Street in the 1950s, in the heart of the city's historic French Quarter. The district was a musical hub as the birthplace of jazz in the early 20th century, and mid-century was at the center of a flourishing blues and R&B scene.

SHARP DRESSERS

ontrary to the image of the country bluesman strumming his guitar on the front porch of a broken-down shack, dressed in regular working clothes, most of the professional players were cool-looking dudes, eager to make an impression on audiences—and as Ray Charles' "It Should've Been Me" testifies, it was the sharp dressers who got the girls. Rufus Thomas' picture of the zoot-suited cat on the corner of Beale Street in Memphis—probably right by Lansky's clothes shop where a youthful Elvis Presley would gaze in the window before he could afford the threads therein—says it all.

"We herewith submit a preview of men's Easter fashions from the world's least inhibited fashion center, Harlem. Trousers will be deeply pleated, with waistband just under the armpits, 30-inch knees, and 15-inch cuffs. A popular suit jacket is one that measures 36 inches down the back seam and has a fly front, shoulders padded out 3½ inches on each side, two breast pockets, and slashed side pockets. This may be worn with a white doeskin waistcoat. Shoes are pointed, the most popular leathers being light-tan calfskin and colored suede. Hats may be worn in the porkpie shape or with crowns 6 inches high. Colors, as always, are limited only by spectrum."
The *New Yorker*, 1941

"When I got to the corner
I saw a sharp cat
With a three-hundred-dollar suit on
And a hundred-dollar hat
He was standing on the sidewalk
By a DynaFlow
When a voice within said,
"C'mon daddy, let's go."
RAY CHARLES, "It Should've Been Me," 1953

"The first clothes that I got attached to was my uncle, we called him Dude. He'd come down from Chicago and I'd see the threads he'd have on. He was wearing those shirts that buttoned diagonally across your chest and I thought that was so sharp.
Do black shoes go with black socks?
Sure. Only. Everything I wear is going to match. You got blue shoes you got blue socks, you got gray shoes you got gray socks. That's the way I am. Some people can wear black with brown, but I just can't, I wouldn't feel right. I used to match up green and yellow, like a winter green and a canary yellow shirt with the proper tie, but it was just a little too loud. Loudness is not one of my things."
BOBBY "BLUE" BLAND

"The outfit that I remember him [Earl Hooker] best for, he had a black cowboy hat, and he wore a black suit and a lilac ruffled shirt and lilac shoes, any wild kinda shirts. Now he wasn't a real fancy dresser, but you know he dressed up to a certain extent."
DICK SHERMAN, friend of singer Earl Hooker

"No 1950s blues guitarist even came close to equalling the flamboyant Guitar Slim in the showmanship department. Armed with an estimated 350 feet of cord between his axe and his amp, Slim would confidently stride on-stage wearing a garishly hued suit of red, blue, or green, usually with his hair dyed to match!"
BILL DAHL, music journalist

"The clothes I remember [on Beale Street, Memphis], they called 'em drapes. They had all those pleats in front and the pants legs were small at the bottom. They had big hats and they wore a long watch chain, and they used to stand on the corner and twirl that chain. It was the zoot suit, the drape we called it."
RUFUS THOMAS

"Smiley was one of those cats who could sing his own songs, scat sing, do solos, improvise, sing horn parts and stuff like this. He was really talented. He had Dixieland tradition and be-bop tradition. He was not only a blues singer, but he was a pop singer. In fact he was an all-round guy. Just like Percy Mayfield there's only one Smiley Lewis."

DR. JOHN ("MAC" REBENNACK)

New Orleans rhythm and blues scene) proved fortuitous. The harder-hitting local R&B sound was just beginning to develop, with Imperial and Bartholomew very much at the helm, and it seemed like Smiley, with his rocking, bluesy delivery, was in exactly the right place at precisely the right time.

His first Imperial release was "Tee Nah Nah," with "The Bells Are Ringing" in 1952 becoming his first national hit. In 1954 Lewis recorded the original version of "Blue Monday," a Bartholomew composition that would be a hit for Fats Domino a couple of years later, but he saw his biggest success in 1955 with "I Hear You Knocking," with a memorable piano contribution from Huey "Piano" Smith.

That should have been the turning point for Smiley, but unfortunately his fortunes began descending thereafter. Songstress Gale Storm shot to number two in the *Billboard* Hot 100 pop chart with an innocuous version of "I Hear You Knocking," and in 1958 Elvis Presley had similar success with his watered-down cover of Smiley's 1956 R&B hit "One Night." Even having "Shame, Shame, Shame" on the soundtrack of the high-profile 1956 movie *Baby Doll* didn't help his record sales. Smiley Lewis died from cancer in the fall of 1966, all but forgotten outside his beloved New Orleans, where he was remembered as one of the true greats of the city's blues heritage.

Earl King was another highly respected singer-guitarist who played an essential role in the development of New Orleans R&B. A native of the city, King was born in 1934. He became a devotee of Texas bluesmen T-Bone Walker and Gatemouth Brown, but was also a big fan of local stars Smiley Lewis and the great Guitar Slim, who became a close friend.

His first disc releases were with the Savoy label, still under his real name of Earl Johnson, where he had his sensational 1953 debut, "Have You Gone Crazy." The following year a local talent scout, Johnny Vincent, produced his first disc as Earl King, on the pioneer R&B label Specialty. The release caused quite a buzz locally, but it was when he cut "Those Lonely, Lonely Nights" for Vincent's new Ace label in 1955 that things began to happen. The steamy two-chord blues took King to number seven in the R&B charts nationally, making him a bona fide star in the New Orleans firmament, and was just the first of a string of great sides on Ace—usually accompanied by the house band at Cosimo Matassa's celebrated recording studio.

Recording engineer Cosimo Matassa was a key name on the city's rhythm and blues scene. In 1945, when he was just eighteen years old, he opened the J&M Recording Studios on Rampart Street, moving to the larger Cosimo studio in 1955. Across both facilities he was hugely responsible for the development of the "New Orleans Sound," with its emphasis on solid drums, heavy guitar and bass, a prominent piano sound, and light horns behind the ever-up-front vocals.

Often working with producers Dave Bartholomew and Allen Toussaint, Matassa recorded the cream of the city's R&B output, including Fats Domino, Smiley Lewis, Dr John, blues singer Billy Mitchell, Tommy Ridgley, and many more.

In 1960 Earl King moved over to Imperial to work with Dave Bartholomew, recording his classic "Come On," and charting again in 1962 with "Always a First Time." King, who died in 2003, was one of the mainstays of the New Orleans scene; as well as his making his own records and playing guitar on innumerable sessions, he wrote a number of important songs for locally based R&B stars including Fats Domino, Professor Longhair, and soul man Lee Dorsey.

Longhair

But it was the piano men who stood out in the gestation of rhythm and blues in New Orleans and created an essential link to the emergence of rock 'n' roll in the early 1950s—and no piano man commanded more respect in the New Orleans musical community than Henry Roeland "Roy" Byrd, better known as Professor Longhair.

Born in Louisiana in 1918, Roy Byrd didn't start playing the piano seriously until he was in his thirties. He made his professional debut in 1948, at the Caldonia Club, where he was initially noticed after sitting in with trumpet player Dave Bartholomew's band while their pianist was taking a break. It was around this time he was dubbed Professor Longhair on account of his shaggy, unruly hair.

"'Fess" (the shorter version of his nickname devised by fellow musicians) made his first records for the Dallas-based Star Talent label, imaginatively credited to Professor Longhair and his Shuffling Hungarians (who came up with that group name, or why, is anybody's guess.) The four tracks he cut for the label included the original of what would become his signature tune, "Mardi Gras in New Orleans," and his most popular song with club audiences "She Ain't Got No Hair."

The latter number was key in Longhair's only R&B chart success, when he remade it as "Bald Head" for Mercury Records in 1950, for contractual reasons calling himself Roy Byrd once again. The single made number five in the *Billboard* chart in August 1950, but hassles with Mercury cut short his tenure at the label, curtailing any follow-up releases.

A meeting was arranged in New Orleans with Ahmet Ertegun, head of Atlantic Records, although the subsequent sessions didn't produce any great results saleswise. Longhair went on to make some sides for Federal in 1951, with "Gone So Long" being a moderate hit in his home territory, before Atlantic renewed their interest and cut some more sides in November 1953—including "Tipitina," a classic example of early New Orleans R&B which made the local charts in March 1954.

Although he made a comeback in the 1970s with successful appearances at jazz and blues festivals in the US and Europe—and album releases of his back catalog—until his death in 1980, Longhair's importance was really in his influence on other New Orleans piano players. One potent element of his style was the introduction of Afro-Cuban rhythms like the rumba (his particular style was known locally as "rumba-boogie") into rhythm and blues, which can be found in the work of Fats Domino, Huey "Piano" Smith, Dr. John, and scores of other Louisiana R&B piano players, who called Roy Byrd "the Professor" with good reason.

ABOVE:
Professor Longhair during his comeback in the 1970s, when he was lauded by a new audience across America and Europe as one of the truly original spirits of New Orleans rhythm and blues.

OPPOSITE, ABOVE LEFT:
Little Richard's highest-ever US chart position—number six in the *Billboard* list in the summer of 1956—came with the unforgettable "Long Tall Sally."

Rockin' Pneumonia

Following in the footsteps of New Orleans heavyweights Professor Longhair and Fats Domino, Huey "Piano" Smith represented a key stylistic link between New Orleans rhythm and blues and emergent rock 'n' roll, which from 1955 took the country, and the rest of the world, by storm.

Born in New Orleans in 1934, in the early 1950s Smith was backing local guitar heroes Earl King and Guitar Slim, and he became a much-in-demand session pianist, providing backing for some of the biggest names on the scene, including Lloyd Price, Little Richard, and Smiley Lewis (on his classic "I Hear You Knockin'"). He formed his own band, the Clowns, which also featured blues singer (and female impersonator) Bobby Marchan on lead vocals.

After signing with the Ace label, Huey had his most memorable R&B hit in 1957 with "Rockin' Pneumonia and the Boogie Woogie Flu," which went on to become a rock 'n' roll standard. The following year saw him reach

number nine in the *Top 100* pop chart with "Don't You Just Know It." He should have had another big hit with "Sea Cruise" in 1959, but Ace chose to release a version sung by the good-looking (white) teenager Frankie Ford instead, his vocals overdubbed on Smith's original backing track!

Blues to Rock 'n' Roll

Huey Smith's rocking piano style was a perfect example of the lineage of blues—rhythm and blues—rock 'n' roll exemplified in New Orleans. Suffice to say that some of the very first rock 'n' roll records to hit the charts had a strong connection with the city, including Little Richard's "Tutti Frutti," recorded at Cosimo's with Fats Domino's backing band in 1955, as was the follow-up "Long Tall Sally" and many other Richard hits.

Fats Domino himself was the biggest star in New Orleans years before he had his first national hit with "Aint That a Shame" in 1955. He was signed to Imperial Records in 1949 and was a long-time collaborator with

ABOVE MIDDLE:
Poster for a sensational double bill in Seattle, Washington, in August 1957. A graduate of the Chess school of Chicago R&B, Chuck Berry took the music into solid rock 'n' roll territory with self-penned classics that captured the imagination of white teenagers more than African-American record buyers. From New Orleans, Specialty star Lloyd Price likewise crossed over into the mainstream after first shaking up the R&B world with his 1952 hit "Lawdy Miss Clawdy."

ABOVE RIGHT:
A 1959 poster for a Fats Domino date in Topeka, Kansas.

161

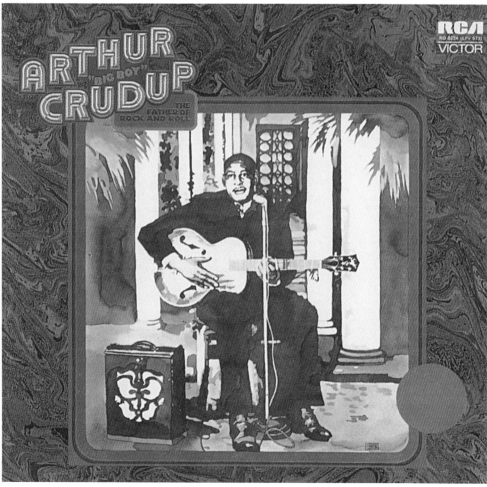

Dave Bartholomew; his first recording that year, "The Fat Man," was a million-seller and has since been a contender for the accolade of "first-ever rock 'n' roll record."

The connection between blues and rock wasn't manifested only in the R&B of the Crescent City. Every strand in rock 'n' roll's genesis could be traced back through postwar rhythm and blues to the various influences of the jump bands, the Delta blues, boogie-woogie, and so on.

Another popular nominee for the title of "first rock record" was an up-tempo twelve-bar R&B song by Jackie Brenston and his Rhythm Cats, "Rocket 88," recorded by Sam Phillips in his Sun studio in Memphis and leased to Chess Records in Chicago in 1951. Phillips' studio was a hotbed of blues material back in the early 1950s, with names like Howlin' Wolf, James Cotton, Little Milton, and B.B. King all gracing its portals several years before a young Elvis Presley walked in and launched his first potent mix of blues and hillbilly music on an unsuspecting world.

As with much early rock 'n' roll, Elvis's repertoire mined the playlists of blues and R&B artists for suitable material. His first release in 1954 was a cover of Arthur "Big Boy" Crudup's song "That's All Right." Presley returned to Crudup's material for his 1956 single "My Baby Left Me." And one of his biggest hits ever, the

multimillion-selling "Hound Dog" in 1956, was originally an R&B number one for the great Texas rhythm and blues singer Willie Mae "Big Mama" Thornton, selling nearly two million copies in 1953.

Before Elvis, Little Richard, or Fats Domino hit the best-seller charts however, the undisputed "King of Rock 'n' Roll" for a year or so was undoubtedly Bill Haley, with his band the Comets. Musically a hybrid of jump band music and country-and-western, Haley chalked up a string of hits through 1954 and 1955, including his biggest, "Rock Around the Clock." Like so much pop music before and since, this was actually a simple twelve-bar blues—as was his 1954 hit "Shake, Rattle and Roll," recorded just weeks after Big Joe Turner's far more powerful original, and Haley's anthemic "See You Later, Alligator," originally written and recorded by the New Orleans R&B maestro Bobby Charles, in 1955.

With rock 'n' roll totally dominating popular music from the mid-1950s onwards, its blues and R&B ancestors could have easily been relegated to obscurity—as indeed some veteran artists were for a time. But just as rock music was in the ascendant, a simultaneous revival of interest in "authentic" blues began to take place, triggering an unprecedented "blues boom" and revival in the early 1960s, which would go on to change the face of rock music itself.

ABOVE LEFT:
Willie Mae "Big Mama" Thornton toured the South with Sammy Green's Hot Harlem Revue before signing with Peacock Records in 1952 and topping the R&B charts with the original "Hound Dog." In the 1960s she recorded for the folk-and-blues Arhoolie label, toured Europe with the American Folk Blues Festival, and made the album *Big Mama Thornton—In Europe* with Buddy Guy, Walter Horton and Fred McDowell. She died aged 57 after a heart attack, in 1984.

ABOVE RIGHT:
A 1972 collection of recordings by Arthur "Big Boy" Crudup.

RIGHT:
Bill Haley topped the bill in "The Biggest Show of 56" package tour. Also featured were R&B vocal groups the Platters, Clovers, and Frankie Lymon and the Teenagers, plus emergent solo stars Clyde McPhatter and Chuck Berry.

BROONZY

...ncert

ALL OUT AND DOWN
Lead Belly
(Huddie Ledbetter)
M 13326-A

RPM
HE DON'T MOVE ME NO MORE
(King)
B. B. KING
And His Orchestra
348

...DON COLISEUM, MARCH 9th, 195...

NEGRO FOLK SONGS

FOR YOUNG PEOPL...

Melotone
LONG 'TALL MAMA
Big Bill
M 13049-B

SUNG BY LEADBELLY

THE BLUES REVIVAL

By the 1950s, the blues in its purest form had all but disappeared from the general cultural landscape, yet the influence of the blues was to be heard everywhere—in jazz, country music, mainstream pop songs, rhythm and blues, and, from the middle of the decade, in the ubiquitous sounds of rock 'n' roll. As this was only half a century from the birth of the blues, many of its original exponents were still active, though now often consigned to the backwater of the local dance hall or crumbling juke joint. The revival of traditional blues came as part of a wider renaissance of American folk music, which by the early 1960s had spread from student campuses and bohemian cellar clubs to concert stages around the world.

The first murmurings of the folk music revival came very early on in the 1940s, in the unlikely context of left-wing radicalism based in New York City. The Almanac Singers were a folk group formed by Woody Guthrie, Pete Seeger, Milard Lampell, and Lee Hays. Part of the Popular Front, an alliance of liberals and leftists, they felt they could promote causes like workers' rights and anti-racism through their music. The group existed from 1940 to 1943, and featured other singers in their ranks, on an ad-hoc basis, including blues artists Josh White, Brownie McGhee, harp player Sonny Terry, and the great Huddie Ledbetter—aka Lead Belly.

Through the 1940s and early '50s a new folk movement began to develop from the seeds sown by the Almanac singers—and later the Weavers, a group that also included Seeger and Hays, whose 1950 cover of Lead Belly's "Goodnight Irene" was a *Billboard* number one for thirteen weeks. Featuring mainly acoustic guitar–backed singing—including blues—this new folk scene was dubbed the "coffee house circuit," as it flourished in bohemian and beatnik-style coffee houses, college campuses, open-air concerts, and folk sing-alongs (self-styled "hootenannies"). Still the territory of earnest enthusiasts, the folk scene nevertheless proved crucial in promoting traditional blues to a new young, white, middle-class, urban audience.

Folkways
A key player in the folk music revival was Folkways Records, founded by Moses Asch and Marian Distler in New York City in 1948. With an ambitious mission to record and document oral histories and music from all over the world, Folkways, in its first few years, was an early promoter of the work of Seeger, Guthrie, Lead Belly, and other prominent names in the folk movement—and that included a rich seam of blues music. Among the many musicians it helped "rediscover"—much in the fashion of the Lomaxes' recordings for the Library of Congress—were Lightnin' Hopkins, Big Bill Broonzy, Josh White, Sonny Terry and Brownie McGhee (often recording and performing as a duo), Blind Gary Davis, and the boogie-woogie pianist Speckled Red.

One of the releases on Folkways that stimulated interest in America's folk and blues heritage was the *Anthology of American Folk Music*, released as a set of six albums in 1952. Made up of eighty-four folk, blues, and country music recordings that were originally released as 78-rpm singles between 1927 an 1932, it was the brainchild of an experimental filmmaker and record collector, Harry Smith.

From the early 1940s Smith had amassed a collection of several thousand old 78s, and soon after Folkways was

OPPOSITE LEFT:
Woody Guthrie in 1943, with his trademark guitar labeled "This Machine Kills Fascists"

OPPOSITE, TOP RIGHT:
Folkways Records founder Moses Asch.

OPPOSITE, BOTTOM RIGHT:
The intricately designed booklet that accompanied Harry Smith's *Anthology of American Folk Music*, a 28-page montage of collage, cut-outs, and hand-typed material put together by Smith himself, forming a song-by-song analysis of the collection.

Featuring mainly acoustic guitar–backed singing— including blues—this new folk scene was dubbed the "coffee house circuit," as it flourished in bohemian and beatnik-style coffee houses, college campuses, open-air concerts, and folk sing-alongs (self-styled "hootenannies").

PROTEST BLUES

It could be said that the blues was born out of a sense of protest, given the abject conditions of most African Americans through the 20th century, and reference to such hardships can be found in thousands of songs. Even natural disasters, referred to in blues like Charley Patton's stark account of the 1927 Louisiana flood, "High Water Everywhere," impacted disproportionately on the black population. And hard-line protest against social ills featured in innumerable songs such as in Josh White's celebrated collections of political blues in the 1940s, and the songs of J.B. Lenoir in the 1950s and 60s.

" Oh the water rising, families sinking down
Now the water was rising, at places all around
It was fifty men and children, come to sink and drown "
CHARLEY PATTON "High Water Everywhere" 1929

As well as the Patton classic, referenced in 2001 by Bob Dylan in his tribute "High Water (For Charley Patton)," other songs about the disastrous flood included Memphis Minnie's "When the Levee Breaks," released by Minnie in 1929 and later recorded by Led Zeppelin.

" Well, I always been in trouble, 'cause I'm a black-skinned man,
Said I hit a white man, [and they] locked me in the can,
They took me to the stockade, wouldn't give me no trial,
The judge said, 'You black boy, forty years on the hard rock pile'. "
JOSH WHITE "Trouble" 1940

Josh White's "Trouble" was from the 1940 album of 78s (before the long-player, "albums" were collections of 78rpm singles bound in a photo-album format) entitled *Chain Gang*. White, a much-loved musical spokesman of the American left, followed in 1941 with an equally hard-hitting collection, *Southern Exposure: An Album of Jim Crow Blues*.

Among other African Americans prominent in the folk song revival, Lead Belly—though not overtly political in most of his material—made a huge impact with "The Bourgeois Blues," an incisive critique of racism to be found right there in the nation's capital.

" I tell all the colored folks to listen to me
Don't try to find you no home in Washington, DC
'Cause it's a bourgeois town
Uhm, the bourgeois town
I got the bourgeois blues
Gonna spread the news all around "
LEAD BELLY, "The Bourgeois Blues" 1938

Born in 1929, so experiencing the rise of the civil rights movement while still in his twenties, J.B. Lenoir was a major exponent of blues as a vehicle of protest, with topical themes addressed in numbers like "Eisenhower Blues" and "Korea Blues" in the 1950s, and "Vietnam Blues" in which he draws a parallel between President Lyndon Johnson's rhetoric regarding the war and the conditions in the Deep South:

" How can you tell the world we need peace,
And you still mistreat and killin' poor me? "
J.B LENOIR, "Vietnam Blues" 1966

Lenoir's most celebrated song is "Down in Mississippi," which he also recorded in 1966, a potent reminder of conditions at the time despite the recent Civil Rights legislation.

" They had a huntin' season on a rabbit
If you shoot him you went to jail.
The season was always open on me:
Nobody needed no bail. "
J.B LENOIR, "Down in Mississippi" 1966

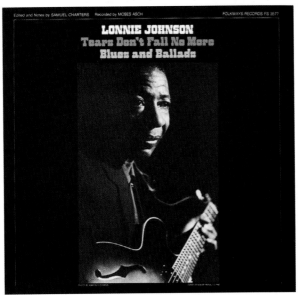

ABOVE LEFT:
The undeniably eccentric Harry Smith, the artist and experimental filmmaker who was also an avid record collector—hence his ambitious *Anthology* project. In many ways, with his interest in alternative religion for instance, he was a forerunner of the Hippie movement.

TOP RIGHT:
The folk-blues musician Lonnie Johnson was one of the artists on Folkways' 1959 release *The Country Blues.* The label was still going strong more than twenty years later—the album here dates from 1982.

BOTTOM RIGHT:
A business card for Folkways Records, the Aztec-inspired logo suggesting the "world music" aspect of the company's mission.

established, he approached Moses Asch with a view to releasing a selection on the new label. The result was an amazing archive of music, much of which would otherwise have been lost in the mists of time. Among the blues recordings committed to a long-playing record for the first time were tracks by Mississippi John Hurt, Blind Willie Johnson, the Memphis Jug Band, Blind Lemon Jefferson, and Sleepy John Estes.

The compilation made a huge impact in the folk community, with many largely forgotten songs given a new lease of life on the burgeoning club scene. It also shone a new light on the work of seminal blues artists and was a major source of inspiration for the new generation of folk and blues players emerging during the 1950s.

Although not as influential on the folk scene generally as the Harry Smith *Anthology*, Folkways' 1959 release *The Country Blues* certainly had a similar impact on blues aficionados. Another collection of records cut as 78s during the late 1920s and early '30s, the fourteen tracks included numbers by Leroy Carr, Lonnie Johnson, Peg Leg Howell, Blind Willie McTell, Big Bill Broonzy,

Bukka White, and Robert Johnson—who was virtually forgotten at the time—as well as several singers featured in the Smith package (the producers taking care not to duplicate any songs from the latter).

The album was put together by the jazz and blues writer Samuel Charters to accompany his landmark book of the same name, which was described by the eminent jazz critic and music historian Ted Gioia as a "signal event in the history of the music, a moment of recognition and legitimization." Several of the songs—including Gus Cannon's "Walk Right In," Big Bill Broonzy's "Key to the Highway," and Bukka White's "Fixin' to Die"—were taken up by contemporary folk and blues singers, subsequently becoming standards, as a direct result of having been heard first on the album.

Appropriately, after Moses Asch's death in 1986, Folkways ended up being acquired by the Smithsonian Institution in Washington, DC, in recognition of its importance as a living archive of American history and culture, with the blues and blues-related music a central part of that culture.

The Legend of Lead Belly

Of all the blues artists who came to prominence (or in some cases, returned to prominence) in the folk music revival, none was more closely associated with the movement than Huddie Ledbetter, better known as Lead Belly (sometimes written Leadbelly). Although his repertoire embraced folk songs, gospel music, and children's songs, as well as blues, his importance in the blues revival as a living symbol of the African-American musical heritage is inestimable.

Ledbetter was born near Mooringsport, Louisiana, in January 1888, and by the time he was a teenager he was already entertaining around the red light district of nearby Shreveport. He moved to Texas in his early twenties—where he acquired a twelve-string guitar that would be his trademark instrument for the rest of his life—and began absorbing folk songs as well as the blues, playing in the Dallas area with Blind Lemon Jefferson.

In 1915 Ledbetter had the first of several brushes with the law; he was convicted of carrying a pistol and served time on the Harrison County chain gang. He escaped—one of many "adventures" that would serve him well when recounting his colorful life in later years—and lived under an assumed name before getting into trouble again in 1917, after killing one of his relatives in a fight over a woman. In January 1918 he began a seven-to-thirty-five-year sentence at the Imperial prison farm in Sugar Land, Texas, but in 1925 was released with a pardon after the

minimum seven years. Another episode in the eventual legend of Lead Belly, the pardon came after the governor was impressed by Ledbetter's good behavior, including entertaining the guards and fellow prisoners, and in response to a song he wrote directly for the governor, pleading for his freedom.

Lead Belly—the nickname possibly earned in prison, as a corruption of his surname—had an explosive temper, and it put him back into custody again in 1930. He was charged with attempted murder after stabbing a white man in a fight, and committed to the notorious Angola Prison Farm in Louisiana. It was at Angola that he was "discovered" by folk collectors John and Alan Lomax in 1933 on their first field trip for the Library of Congress. They recorded him on their portable equipment, impressed by his sonorous vocals, strident guitar playing, and wide-ranging repertoire, and they returned to make more recordings the following year.

Once again Lead Belly was released early on account of his good behavior, although the Lomaxes always held that their petition to the governor on his behalf helped things along. Whatever the case, Lead Belly was a free man again, and started employment as an assistant for John Lomax on his field trips across the South. Then, early in 1935, the two arrived in New York City, where very soon the newspapers were writing about the "singing convict"—he was even the subject of a newsreel short shown in cinemas nationwide.

ABOVE LEFT:
A highly staged portrait photo of Lead Belly, emphasizing the stereotype of the son-of-the-soil country working man that record companies and others were often keen to promote.

ABOVE RIGHT:
Compound No 1 at the Angola Prison Farm, with Lead Belly visible in the foreground, nearest to the fence.

LEAD BELLY

A romantic character at a time when traditional country blues singers were a forgotten factor in popular music, Lead Belly was promoted as an ex-convict troubadour, and the new folk music audience of the 1940s loved it. A formidable figure, with his strong tenor voice and ever-present twelve-string guitar, Lead Belly's vast repertoire fed the folk revival with ballads, blues, work songs, spirituals, and children's songs. From Blind Lemon Jefferson's "Matchbox Blues" and the prison song classic "Midnight Special," to the angry protest of "The Bourgeois Blues" and his much-loved signature tune "Goodnight Irene," Huddie Ledbetter's huge legacy provided the bedrock songbook for a generation of blues enthusiasts, both amateur and professional, around the world.

> "The blues is like this. You lay down one night and you turn from one side of the bed to the other, all night long. It's not too cold in that bed, and it ain't too hot. But what's the matter? The blues has got you. When you get up and sit on the side of your bed, soon in the morning, you may have a mother and a father, a sister and a brother around, but you don't want no talk out of them. They ain't done you nothing, but what's the matter? The blues has got you."

LEAD BELLY, radio introduction to "Good Morning Blues"

Born
Huddie Wiliam Ledbetter, January 15, 1888, Shiloh, Louisiana

Died
December 6, 1949, New York City

Instruments
Vocals, Guitar

Recording Debut
"The Western Cowboy" / "Honey Take a Whiff on Me"
Recorded July 16, 1933, Louisiana State Penitentiary, Angola, Louisiana
Library of Congress

Awards
Inducted into Nashville Songwriters Association Hall of Fame, 1980
Inducted into Blues Hall of Fame, 1986
Inducted into Rock and Roll Hall of Fame, 1988
Inducted into Louisiana Music Hall of Fame, 2008

Playlist
"Matchbox Blues" [1934]
"Midnight Special" [1934]
"CC Rider" [1935]
"Rock Island Line" [1937]
"Goodnight Irene" [1938]
"The Bourgeois Blues" [1938]
"Good Morning Blues" [1940]
Huddie Ledbetter [1951]
The Library of Congress Recordings [1966]
Leadbelly Sings Folk Songs [1990]

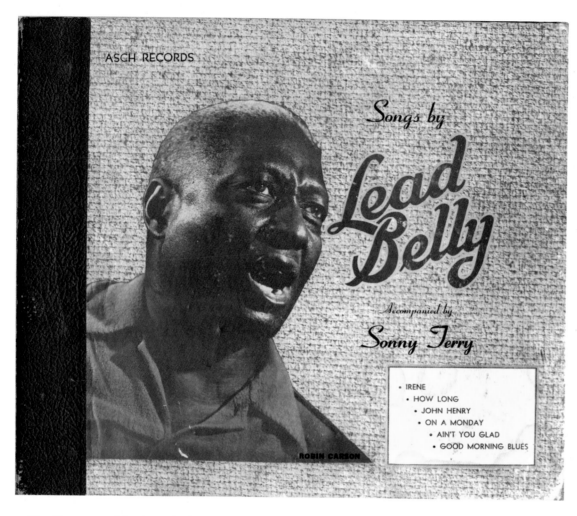

ASCH RECORDS

Songs by Lead Belly

Accompanied by Sonny Terry

- IRENE
- HOW LONG
- JOHN HENRY
- ON A MONDAY
- AIN'T YOU GLAD
- GOOD MORNING BLUES

ROBIN CARSON

The film, part of the *March of Time* series produced by *Time Magazine*, gives an indication of how the Lomaxes—despite their benevolence in taking him under their wing—had a complicated relationship with Ledbetter. The scripted account of the singer's release from prison hints at Lead Belly's feeling of subservience towards John Lomax, not least in dialogue (somewhat uncomfortably delivered by the singer) in which he constantly refers to the folklorist as "boss."

Lead Belly's first commercial recordings, made a week or so after his arrival in New York, were for Columbia Record's "race" division, ARC, although the few sides they released from the sessions didn't sell particularly well. Lomax was also promoting his discovery on lecture tours to colleges across the Northeast, but this exposure in academia didn't make Lead Belly's financial position any better, and in the spring of 1935 he and his wife Martha traveled back, by bus, to Louisiana.

Lead Belly decided to give New York City, and its promise of fame, another try, and in early 1936 he moved back to the Big Apple. From 1936 to 1939 he made more recordings for the Library of Congress with Alan Lomax, during which period he began to be patronized by the left-wing groups who laid the foundations of the 1940s folk revival. Although he had little political commitment himself, his passionate espousal of anti-racist views, in

songs like "The Bourgeois Blues," made him a hero of the people in their eyes.

Through the Popular Front activists and his occasional appearances with the Almanac singers, Lead Belly quickly became a regular on New York's emerging folk scene, alongside Woody Guthrie, Pete Seeger, and fellow folk-bluesmen Sonny Terry, Brownie McGhee, and Josh White, with whom he made many nightclub appearances. A darling of the liberal intelligentsia, Lead Belly was certainly more popular with white audiences than black, as were his records, and he was the first country blues musician to be acclaimed by enthusiasts in Europe.

At the end of the decade he was recording for, among others, the newly launched Folkways label. He had a weekly radio broadcast on station WNYC in New York, and in 1949 undertook his first European tour. The tour was cut short due to illness, later diagnosed as motor neurone disease, from which he died at the end of the year.

Lead Belly was a consummate songster rather than solely a blues singer, but he was the first celebrated name performing country blues (as well as other essential aspects of black American folk music) to connect with a significant segment of white listeners. As a key figure in the folk music revival, he played a pivotal role in the consequent renaissance of traditional blues.

ABOVE LEFT:
Songs by Lead Belly (with harmonica accompaniment by Sonny Terry), an album of 78s issued by Asch Records, Moses Asch's label prior to his setting up Folkways Records.

Lead Belly, looking the serious professional in marked contrast to the 'farm hand' image of the photograph on page 170.

FOLKNIKS AND SKIFFLERS

Although initially the US folk music revival was manifested mainly in singers' clubs, hootenannies, and college campuses—the coffeehouse circuit—by the end of the 1950s its influence had spread to the general pop mainstream, with blues and blues-related folk music reaching a much wider public as a result. And earlier in the decade, a quite separate development was taking place across the Atlantic, where the "skiffle" phenomenon had a similar effect on the youth of Great Britain, making a generation of teenagers aware of the blues for the first time.

As in America, the 1940s folk revival touched only a small section of the UK populace, the dedicated enthusiasts who met in pubs and clubs maybe once a week, earnestly reading the "Folk" section of the *Melody Maker* and discussing the latest few releases that filtered through from the pop-dominated record industry. In terms of traditional blues, there was Big Bill Broonzy and Josh White, and that was about it.

Then, at the end of 1955, something amazing happened. A record of an old Lead Belly song, "Rock Island Line," performed by the Lonnie Donegan Skiffle Group, started climbing the pop charts. Donegan, at the time the banjo player with Chris Barber's jazz band, fronted the trio, which consisted of himself on guitar, Beryl Bryden on washboard, and trombonist Barber on double bass; it was a spin-off outfit that played intervals in the band's main set, and never planned to be anything more than that.

When the single rocketed to the top ten of the US *Billboard* chart as well, Donegan promptly left the Barber band and formed a regular group of his own. There followed a huge string of UK hit singles and best-selling albums over the next couple of years, with Donegan's repertoire very much tied to the American folk and blues of the likes of Ledbetter, Woody Guthrie, and Leroy Carr.

What set the youth of Britain alight, however, was the homemade possibilities of skiffle, not unlike the instrumentation of the 1920s jug bands. With a few rudimentary chords on the guitar and a washboard and tea-chest bass rhythm section, anyone could launch into songs like "Midnight Special," "John Henry," and the pure blues of "(In the Evening) When the Sun Goes Down" and "How Long, How Long."

Historically the importance of the skiffle craze was setting a generation of guitarists on the path to professional music making; the seeds of the 1960s British blues boom were sown by skiffle, with everyone, from the Rolling Stones to Van Morrison and Jimmy Page, starting out in a do-it-yourself group. But of equal importance, through Donegan's records young people in Britain, not just budding musicians, were exposed to a rich vein of previously unheard American folk and blues songs, and they soon wanted to hear the "real thing" in its original form.

In America, the big crossover of folk and blues into the pop arena came at the end of the 1950s, although artists like the Weavers, Odetta, and Harry Belafonte had whetted the public's appetite with best sellers of folk-related material. The Weavers had hit number one with their cover of Lead Belly's "Goodnight Irene" back in 1950,

OPPOSITE LEFT:
Joan Baez and Bob Dylan, figureheads of the early 1960s folk revival, singing together at the 1963 Civil Rights March in Washington, August 28 1963. From his debut album in 1962—and despite his move out of the folk orbit when he "went electric" later in the decade—Dylan's work has always been informed by a total connection with the blues form and blues musicians.

Historically the importance of the skiffle craze was setting a generation of guitarists on the path to professional music making; the seeds of the 1960s British blues boom were sown by skiffle, with everyone, from the Rolling Stones to Van Morrison and Jimmy Page, starting out in a do-it-yourself group.

ABOVE RIGHT:
Backstairs Session, a seminal EP from 1956 by Lonnie Donegan, the four tracks including Leroy Carr's "When the Sun Goes Down," and the traditional song "Midnight Special," previously recorded by Lead Belly among others, in his Angola prison sessions.

OVERLEAF:
A hand-drawn flyer from 1961 for Gerde's Folk City club in Greenwich Village, with upcoming attractions including a second-on-the-bill Bob Dylan.

and through their live concerts and albums help popularize folk revival standards such as "On Top of Old Smokey," "Kisses Sweeter Than Wine," and "Pay Me My Money Down." Odetta was a classically trained singer who made successful albums of spirituals, folk, and blues songs. Belafonte—a leading light in the political wing of the folk revival and the civil rights movement—was a regular in the charts with calypso-influenced songs like "Jamaica Farewell," "Cocoanut Woman," and "Banana Boat Song," the latter also a hit for the Tarriers folk group.

It was the success of a clean-cut group called the Kingston Trio that catapulted folk music into the mainstream proper, with their three-million-selling hit, the old folk ballad "Tom Dooley," in 1958. The three singers helped redefine "folk" in marketing terms, with their preppy-looking image, a far cry from the beard-and-

sandals beatnik look associated with folk singers up until then. For three years the Trio could do no wrong sales-wise, with their first five studio albums all making number one, and altogether selling a total of more than eight million records.

The subsequent boom in folk music—with its new army of young fans often derided as "folkniks" by the old guard—opened the door to other up-and-coming singers like Joan Baez (whose debut album reached the top ten in 1960 and stayed in the chart for the next two years); the trio Peter, Paul, and Mary; and the newfound hero of the folk scene, Bob Dylan. Although the blues wasn't predominant in the folk boom, the embracing of traditional American "non-commercial" music included a strong blues element in many singers' repertoires, and certainly paved the way for blues-inspired rock a little later in the decade.

"LONNIE USED TO DO A LEAD BELLY BLUES CALLED 'LEAVING BLUES' AND HE REALLY HAD THE FEEL OF IT. ONE DAY I PLAYED THAT RECORD TO SONNY TERRY WITHOUT COMMENT, AND THEN I ASKED 'WHO'S THAT?' AND HE SAID 'LEAD!' LONNIE WAS *THAT* CONVINCING."

CHRIS BARBER

gerdes

FOLK CITY

new york's center of folk music

PRESENTS

A HISTORIC REUNION • SEPT. 12-24

LONNIE JOHNSON • VICTORIA SPIVEY

DEAN OF BLUES GUITARISTS

QUEEN OF THE BLUES • MGM STAR

"A GENERATION OF GOLDEN BLUES TRADITION" • PRESTIGE RECORDS

& DAVID GUDE •

• september 26 thru october 8 •

GREENBRIAR BOYS

PICKING & SINGING THRU BLUEGRASS –

• WITH THE SENSATIONAL

BOB DYLAN

SHOW BEGINS 9:30
11 W. 4th STREET • AL 4-8449
1 BLOCK WEST OF BRD'WAY

EVERY MONDAY •
HOOTENANNY &
GUEST NIGHT

OPEN EVERY NIGHT • NEVER A COVER CHARGE

AIR CONDITIONED

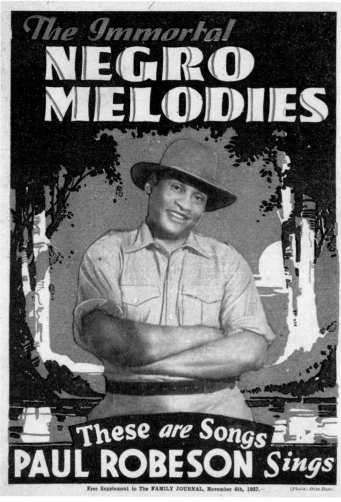

White House Blues

Like Lead Belly, Josh White came to be regarded as a folk revival artist rather than a bona fide blues player of the old school. Yet the New York-based singer established an impressive track record as a singer and guitarist in the Piedmont blues style, after moving from his native South in the early 1930s.

Joshua Daniel White was born in 1914 in Greenville, South Carolina, and his early life was like something out of a novel. After his preacher father was committed to a mental institution, Joshua left home at just seven years of age to accompany a blind singer, Blind Man Arnold, collecting coins for him as he busked. He soon got similar work from more eminent sightless itinerants, including Blind Blake and Blind Joe Taggart, and from them he learned to master blues guitar in the finger-picking Piedmont style, sometimes even singing with their accompaniment.

Arriving in Chicago with Taggart in 1927, he made his recording debut with some sessions at Paramount, before singing lead and playing lead guitar on "Scandalous and a Shame," billed as performed by Blind Joe Taggart and Joshua White. It was a minor hit and led to White's eventually signing with ARC in 1930, after which he moved permanently to New York City.

Record-wise, he began leading a double life, recording both gospel music and blues—the "music of the devil." For his gospel sides he was credited as Joshua White, the Singing Christian; for the blues releases he went by the name of Pinewood Tom. Both incarnations were relatively successful, and along with session work for the likes of Leroy Carr, Lucille Bogan, and the old-timey country group the Carver Boys, he was carving a comfortable niche for himself.

White's big break, however, came from the unlikeliest source—the Broadway stage. He was cast in a play, *John Henry*, based on the legendary railroad man, with the celebrated singer Paul Robeson in the title role and White (as Blind Lemon Jefferson) narrating the story in song. The show opened in January 1940; it didn't run for long, but it brought Josh White into the orbit of the burgeoning New York folk scene, and he was soon working with Woody Guthrie, Burl Ives, and Lead Belly in a radio series *Back Where I Belong*, written by Alan Lomax.

From there on things seemingly couldn't go wrong. White had a six-month residency at the Village Vanguard nightclub alongside Lead Belly, followed by more stage work, and his album of 78s on the Blue Note label *Harlem Blues*, which included a hit single "Careless Love." (The song, of unknown origin, is one of the oldest in the blues

ABOVE LEFT:
A 1962 publicity shot of blues singer and activist Josh White.

ABOVE RIGHT:
A sheet music songbook of "Negro Melodies" by Paul Robeson, included as a supplement to *Family Journal* magazine in 1937. Robeson was not a blues singer by any means, but his outspoken political and anti-racist statements brought him into the orbit of Josh White and others on the folk revivalist left.

BIG BILL BROONZY

Although an established blues player on the Chicago blues scene before World War II, Big Bill Broonzy found his biggest audiences when he was reinvented as a folksy country blues player. Recording for Folkways and other seminal labels, he was a key figure in the folk-blues revival, idolized by young white blues fans. In Europe, he was greeted as a hero by a generation who had literally never seen a black American bluesman perform live. And with iconic songs like "Key to the Highway" and "Black, Brown and White," he helped write the soundtrack for the rediscovery of traditional blues in the 1950s.

> "Blues is a natural fact, is something that a fellow lives. If you don't live it you don't have it. Young people have forgotten to cry the blues. Now they talk and get lawyers and things."
>
> BIG BILL BROONZY

Born
Lee Conley Bradley, June 26, 1893, Scott, Mississippi [possibly 1903, Jefferson County, Arkansas]

Died
August 15, 1958, Chicago, Illinois

Instruments
Vocals, Guitar, Mandolin, Fiddle

Recording Debut
"Big Bill's Blues" / "House Rent Stomp"
Recorded February 1928, Chicago, Illinois
Paramount

Awards
Inducted into Blues Hall of Fame, 1980
Inducted into Rock and Roll Hall of Fame, 1990
Inducted into Gennett Records Walk of Fame, 2007

Playlist
"Big Bill's Blues" [1927]
"Good Boy" [1937]
"Key to the Highway" [1941]
"Black, Brown and White" [1947]
"Guitar Shuffle" [1952]
"Southbound Train" [1957]
His Story—Interviewed by Studs Terkel [1957]
Big Bill Broonzy Sings Folk Songs [1989]

ABOVE:

Josh White with his wife, appearing before the notorious House Un-American Activities Committee in 1950, after being accused of Communist sympathies in 1947, as a result of his civil and human rights activism.

canon, and was adapted as "Loveless Love" by W.C. Handy.) But it was his 1940 Columbia album *Chain Gang*, produced by John Hammond, that caused an outcry as the first race record to be promoted on "white" radio stations and in the South. The controversy caught the attention of President Roosevelt, and the two men became close friends. Josh White became the first black singer to perform at the White House, in January 1941.

Famous for his civil rights songs, and throughout the 1940s a political activist at rallies and demonstrations, Josh White had run afoul of Senator Joseph McCarthy's "red scare" by the early 1950s, which damaged his career considerably. He was blacklisted by US television for many years, a ban lifted only in 1963, when President John F. Kennedy invited him to appear on a civil rights special.

Through the 1960s and up to his death from a heart complaint in 1969, Josh White starred in TV specials and international concerts, celebrated as a "folk-blues" performer rather than a member of the "authentic" blues fraternity who were being hailed worldwide as part of the blues boom of that decade.

Sonny and Brownie

Another master of the Piedmont guitar style, Brownie McGhee also had a background in the prewar world of country blues, before he found fame as part of the 1940s folk revival alongside his long-time performing partner, the harmonica virtuoso Sonny Terry.

Born in 1915 in Knoxville, Tennessee, as a teenager McGhee sang with a local vocal group, the Golden Voices Gospel Quartet, before teaching himself to play guitar. When he was twenty-two he set out as a traveling musician, working in the famed Rabbit Foot Minstrels and meeting guitarist Blind Boy Fuller, whose playing was a big influence on his own. Fuller died in 1941, by which time Brownie was recording for OKeh in Chicago. A record company scout, J. B. Long, persuaded him to adopt the great bluesman's name, billing him as "Blind Boy Fuller No. 2." But it was after moving to New York in 1942, when he teamed up with Fuller's old harmonica player Sonny Terry, that McGhee's career really took off.

From Greensboro, Georgia, Sonny Terry was born Saunders Terrell four years earlier than Brownie

FOLKWAYS RECORDS FA 2006

SONNY TERRY'S WASHBOARD BAND

WINE HEADED WOMAN
MY BABY IS GOIN' TO CHANGE THE LOCK
SONNY'S JUMP
LOUISE BLUES
CUSTARD PIE
DIGGIN' MY PATATOES
WOMAN IS KILLING ME
MAN IS A CRAZY FOOL

TOP LEFT:
Brownie McGhee (right) with his brother Stick McGhee. Stick was the first hit-maker for Atlantic Records with his single "Drinkin' Wine Spo-Dee-O-Dee" in 1949.

BOTTOM LEFT:
Sonny Terry (left) and long-time partner Brownie McGhee.

ABOVE RIGHT:
Sonny Terry's Washboard Band was a 1955 release from Folkways featuring a skiffle-like ensemble consisting of washboard, a washtub bass (a one-string variation on the diddley bow), frying pans, bones, and of course Sonny's instantly recognizable harmonica.

McGhee, in October 1911. After suffering two separate accidents that damaged his eyes, by age sixteen Sonny Terry was blind. His father had taught him the rudiments of the blues harmonica (or blues harp) when he was a youngster, so when he found himself unable to work on his father's farm, he decided to make a living as a musician. He began playing in nearby Raleigh and Durham, North Carolina—starting out, like many a bluesman before him, playing on street corners for tips.

In 1934 he met up with Blind Boy Fuller, who persuaded him to move to Durham, where the two teamed up, and they soon had a strong local following. In 1937 they were recording for the Vocalion label in New York, where Terry would return the following year to take part in John Hammond's *Spirituals to Swing* concert at Carnegie Hall, performing one of his most celebrated numbers, "Mountain Blues." Back in Durham, he met his future partner McGhee in 1938, though the two would not hook up professionally until after Fuller's death in 1941.

With Sonny's energetic style, full of vocal whoops and hollers—and sometimes even imitations of railroad

trains—and Brownie's smooth vocals and stylish guitar picking, the duo was an immediate success. Like Lead Belly and Josh White, they were promoted as "folk" artists in the 1940s, and they went on to collaborate with Lead Belly, Guthrie, and the other members of the New York folk revival axis, making some memorable recordings for Folkways in the process.

And although they were considered "pure" folk musicians by their enthusiastic fans, during the 1940s the duo also fronted a jump blues band with a honking tenor sax and boogie piano, variously billed as Brownie McGhee and his Jook House Rockers, or Sonny Terry and his Buckshot Five.

R&B outings notwithstanding, after the folk revival had given way to the blues boom of the 1950s and '60s, Sonny and Brownie were still going strong, the highlight of blues festivals and package tours—as well as making dozens of albums—until they parted company in 1982. Sonny Terry died in 1986, the year he was inducted into the Blues Hall of Fame, and Brownie McGhee passed away, after fighting stomach cancer, in 1996.

BLUES+GOSPEL =SOUL

In the churchgoing communities of black America, the blues was long considered "the music of the Devil," to be found only in the bars and juke joints of the chitlin' circuit. Indeed, like its equally dubious offspring, jazz, the first instances of the blues outside the rural fields of the South were in the vice-district bordellos of New Orleans, Memphis, and other big cities.

Despite sharing many musical characteristics, the music of the church—sacred music—was treated as a world apart from the blues, and even a hint of mixing the two was greeted with horror by preachers, teachers, and other respectable Christian folk. But the common links that bound African-American culture, forged in the days of slavery, would not be ignored forever. Through the 1950s an unholy musical alliance of the sacred and secular developed, and by the 1960s it had a name—soul music—which by the middle of the decade defined the blues-based popular music of black America.

Most blues musicians—and jazz musicians for that matter—had their earliest musical experience in the church, and the pioneers of soul like Ray Charles and James Brown took that heritage with them into the world of commercial pop music and rhythm and blues. When Charles wrote "I Got a Woman" for his tight seven-piece R&B combo in 1954, it was a radical move, to say the least, bringing a gospel resonance to his bluesy piano style and horn arrangements. The record was a huge success, topping the R&B charts, and Ray knew he had found a winning formula. More hits followed in a similar vein through the 1950s—songs like "Hallelujah I Love Her So," "Yes Indeed," and his classic in gospel-based call-and-response, "What'd I Say."

Charles wasn't alone in paving the way for soul music, of course. Other innovators moving in a similar direction in the 1950s included Chicago R&B queen Etta James; the original lead singer with the Drifters vocal group, Clyde McPhatter; and Sam Cooke, who was famous as part of the Soul Stirrers gospel outfit before controversially moving into secular music with his 1957 hit "You Send Me."

And in the world of jazz there was also a move back to the roots, with cutting-edge players like Cannonball Adderley, Jimmy Smith, and Charles Mingus all acknowledging their blues and gospel heritage in the "soul jazz" movement of the late 1950s. Even their album titles, such as *Them Dirty Blues, The Sermon,* and *Blues & Roots,* harked back to the down-home values they felt had been ignored as jazz became more sophisticated.

But it was in the 1960s that soul music as such came into its own. James Brown, who had his first hit with the emotive "Please, Please, Please" in 1956, had developed a sensational stage act reminiscent of a "hot gospel" preacher at a Southern prayer meeting, which made his *Live at the Apollo* album a huge hit in 1962. He was later dubbed the "Godfather of Soul," and other peers from the early 1960s were singers like Solomon Burke and Ben E. King. But by the middle of the decade, the focus of the soul revolution had moved to Memphis—and the Stax record company.

Formed as Satellite Records in 1957, the label first hit with local R&B stars Rufus Thomas and his daughter Carla, before changing its name and making a distribution deal with New York giant Atlantic in 1960. With a house band led by pianist Booker T. Jones (as Booker T. and the

OPPOSITE, TOP LEFT:
Mahalia Jackson, a major voice in popularizing black gospel music during the 1950s.

OPPOSITE, TOP RIGHT:
The "Queen of Soul" Aretha Franklin, whose musical background was firmly rooted in the church.

OPPOSITE, BOTTOM RIGHT:
James Brown, the man dubbed the "Godfather of Soul," brought a hot gospel dynamic to his onstage R&B shows.

OPPOSITE, BOTTOM MIDDLE:
Charles Mingus' 1960 release *Blues & Roots,* one of the key albums to come out of the "soul jazz" movement.

OPPOSITE, BOTTOM LEFT:
Ray Charles, with a pivotal item in the genesis of soul music, the 1956 single and 1957 album (illustrated) *Hallelujah I Love Her So!*

"SOUL IS WHEN YOU TAKE A SONG AND MAKE IT A PART OF YOU—A PART THAT'S SO TRUE, SO REAL, PEOPLE THINK IT MUST HAVE HAPPENED TO YOU . . . IT'S LIKE ELECTRICITY—WE DON'T REALLY KNOW WHAT IT IS, DO WE? BUT IT'S A FORCE THAT CAN LIGHT A ROOM. SOUL IS LIKE ELECTRICITY, LIKE A SPIRIT, A DRIVE, A POWER."

RAY CHARLES

JESSE FULLER

MARCH · 1960

Transatlantic Blues

The folk and blues revival was not connected solely with American left-wing activism, although it was certainly initially triggered by groups like the Almanac Singers and later the Weavers. In the mid-1950s the coffeehouse circuit expanded, and began to attract a much broader coalition of followers. But these venues were still associated with political dissent, folk, and blues (the two musical styles still very much linked together in the public mind), and artists like Sonny Terry and Brownie McGhee were very much at the center of this newfound popularity, as far as blues was concerned.

As well as having spread across the United States and Canada, the folk-blues fashion was evident across Europe and especially in the UK, where the shared language gave it something of a head start. Although, as in America, the blues were part of a growing folk music scene, in Britain the blues was also promoted as part of a simultaneous revival of "traditional" jazz, Dixieland-style music harking back to the early days of New Orleans jazz.

One of the leading bandleaders on the "trad" scene, as it was dubbed, was trombonist Chris Barber, who was instrumental in bringing over to England a number of blues stars, including, in April 1958, Sonny and Brownie. The duo played as guests of Barber's band at London's Royal Festival Hall, followed by a tour of the UK. A few months later Barber staged a similar tour with Muddy Waters and his pianist, Otis Spann. Muddy's use of an electric guitar shocked many of the "folkie" fans, who

> **"The first time I saw him was when he did the Albert Hall concert with [gospel singer] Mahalia Jackson. Big Bill was most upset. He felt he shouldn't have been put on a concert with Mahalia because his was secular devil's music and it wasn't correct to be on with Mahalia. Mahalia, of course, only cared about the money."**
>
> **CHRIS BARBER**

expected to hear a pure country-blues acoustic set. Those were not Chris Barber's first exercises in importing major names to a blues-hungry Britain; the previous year, he brought over the gospel-folk singer Brother John Sellers (another active participant in the New York folk revival), the gospel singer-guitarist Sister Rosetta Tharpe, and one of the major names in the 1950s blues revival, Big Bill Broonzy.

It wasn't Broonzy's first visit to England, he'd toured in 1954 and '55, and before that in September 1951, a short visit following some dates in Paris. Big Bill's 1951 date was followed in 1952 by a similarly brief stopover by the jazz-blues guitarist Lonnie Johnson, but the first country blues star to appear in the UK was Josh White. All three men represented a more accessible style of blues, exemplified in the context of the folk revival, but of the three, Big Bill Broonzy's approach remained most faithful to his country blues roots.

ABOVE LEFT:
Magazine of London's 100 Club, announcing a 1960 appearance by Jesse Fuller, the blues one-man-band famous for his song "San Francisco Bay Blues."

ABOVE MIDDLE:
A folk and blues concert at the Royal Festival Hall in London in 1961, featuring Josh White, and Memphis Slim.

OPPOSITE, ABOVE RIGHT:
Mose Allison's 1957 debut album
Back Country Suite. A modern
jazz pianist firmly rooted in the
blues of his native Mississippi,
the relatively few but highly
influential vocal tracks from his
albums included "Parchman
Farm," "One Room Country
Shack," and Willie Dixon's
"The Seventh Son."

ABOVE LEFT AND RIGHT:
Despite being promoted as a
straight-from-the-country rural
blues musician during the 1950s
blues revival, Big Bill Broonzy's
career was largely forged in
the big city since his move to
Chicago in the early 1930s—
with sharp-looking clothes to
match. The *Big Bill Blues* album
was released on the UK Vogue
label in 1957.

Big Bill's Blues

Most sources state that Lee Conley Broonzy was born
in the small town of Scott, Mississippi, in June 1893
(though recent research suggests his birthplace might
have been in nearby Jefferson County, across the river in
Arkansas, and the year 1903). His family moved to Pine
Bluff, Arkansas when he was an infant, and at the age of
ten he fashioned himself a fiddle out of a cigar box, which
he played at country picnics and such while still working
as a farmhand.

In 1920, he moved to Chicago, and it was there he
started playing guitar, tutored by the veteran minstrel
show singer Papa Charlie Jackson, whom he occasionally
accompanied. As his technique improved and he began
playing dates at rent parties, it was through Jackson
that Broonzy was introduced to Paramount Records'
legendary producer Mayo Williams. In 1927, he released
his first record "Big Bill's Blues," with the credits on the
recording listing Big Bill and Thomps (his friend and
vocalist John Thomas).

He recorded for several labels as well as Paramount
during the early 1930s, sometimes using his full name,
other times Big Bill Johnson, Big Bill Broomsley, or just
Big Bill. Becoming a regular figure on the flourishing
Chicago blues scene, by 1938 he had earned such a
reputation that when John Hammond needed a
replacement for the recently deceased Robert Johnson
on his *Spirituals to Swing* concert at Carnegie Hall, he
asked Broonzy.

"I guess all songs is folk songs. I never heard no horse sing 'em."

BIG BILL BROONZY

As well as recording in his own right, Big Bill was a
prolific session musician, backing a number of important
blues artists, including Memphis Minnie, Tampa Red,
Jazz Gillum, and Washboard Sam. And with a wide
range of repertoire that embraced ragtime, big city blues,
country blues, and folk songs, he was the personification
of the blues in various forms, in prewar Chicago
representing the link between the country blues and the
more sophisticated urban style prevalent in the city. With
the emergence of Chicago electric blues in the late 1940s
and '50s, Broonzy began to emphasize his acoustic roots,
adopting a leading position in the folk-blues revival that
was happening at the same time.

With his raconteur's talent for storytelling, easy-to-
listen-to style, and "authentic" persona, he was adored
by the new generation of blues fans across America and
Europe. And many of his lyrics were in tune with the
liberal sympathies of his audiences, in songs like his
celebrated "Black, Brown and White":

"They says if you was white, should be all right
If you was brown, stick around
But as you's black, m-mm brother, git back git
back git back."

ABOVE:
B.B. King (standing center)
with fellow musicians—
including Joe Hill Louis on
guitar and Ford Nelson on
piano—at the WDIA radio
station in Memphis in 1954.

Throughout the latter part of his career (which, despite throat cancer, ended only months before his death in 1958), Big Bill Broonzy's image was, to all intents and purposes, that of a country blues player seemingly "discovered" in his rural environment and set center stage as the embodiment of a vanishing tradition. Nothing could have been further from the truth, with Broonzy living and playing in Chicago since the 1920s; nevertheless, his influence on a new breed of blues player, coming of age during the blues revival of the 1940s and 50s, was enormous.

Blues Boy

The new audience for traditional blues soon became aware of the other blues out there—musicians and bands whose music had long since moved from the country to the city. Their electric-oriented music, since the early 1950s under the banner of rhythm and blues, had largely been the preserve of black American audiences, but now there was a new, white public eager to pick up on what it had clearly been missing for years.

One crucial effect of the blues revival was that these contemporary bluesmen, who had been making records since the 1940s, now were reaping the benefits (or at least some of the benefits) of a new international market for their music. One such musician was B.B. King, whose career straddled the history of modern blues, from humble plantation beginnings to becoming perhaps the most influential blues guitarist of the last half century.

Riley B. King was born and brought up in the heart of the Mississippi Delta, working as a sharecropper while absorbing the music of the church, white country songs on the radio, and the blues all around. Once he began playing the guitar, his big influences included jazz players Charlie Christian and Django Reinhardt, and seminal blues guitarists like T-Bone Walker and Lonnie Johnson. In 1946, at age nineteen, he up and went to Memphis to seek out his cousin, country blues guitarist Bukka White.

King learned much from his older relative, and after a brief return to his hometown, Indianola, he finally settled in Memphis in 1948. There, inspired by Sonny Boy Williamson's success on radio in the *King Biscuit Time* show beamed from Helena, Arkansas, he got a job at WDIA, the pioneering all-black-staff station. He would sing and play, spin discs, and plug his local gigs, now going out as the "Beale Street Blues Boy"—later shortened to Blues Boy, and eventually B.B..

King's popularity around the city led to a session with Bullet Records in 1949, in which he cut the first four tracks in a long recording career. None fared particularly

Born
Riley B. King, September 16, 1925, Berclair, Mississippi

Instruments
Vocals, Guitar, Piano

Recording Debut
"Miss Martha King" / "Got the Blues"
Recorded 1949, Memphis Recording Service,
    Memphis, Tennessee
Bullett

Awards
Inducted into Blues Hall of Fame, 1980
Inducted into Rock and Roll Hall of Fame, 1987
Polar Music Prize, 2004
Grammy Best Male R&B Vocal Performance for "The
    Thrill Is Gone," 1970
Grammy Hall of Fame Award for "The Thrill Is Gone," 1998
Grammy Best Traditional Blues Album 2000, for *Riding
    with the King*

Playlist
"Three O'Clock Blues" [1951]
"You Know I Love You [1952]
"Every Day I Have the Blues" [1955]
"Sweet Little Angel" [1956]
"Sweet Sixteen" [1960]
"Rock Me Baby" [1964]
"The Thrill Is Gone" [1969]
Live at the Regal [1964]
Riding with the King [2000]

B.B. KING

A blues guitar great whose style influenced many of the young blues players coming up through the early 1960s, B.B. King was something of an "old school" player himself—not the old school of the country blues, but following the tried and tested technical expertise of jazz players like Charlie Christian, and the no-shortcuts Texas blues of T-Bone Walker. When applied to straightforward R&B-edged blues, his spectacular mastery of his instrument and warm-hearted vocal delivery have never failed to make an impression on audiences over many decades. With numerous chart hits and best-selling albums to his name, B.B. has managed to transcend categories of blues and rock, without compromising his style for a single bar.

well, and in 1950 he laid down some more sides, this time for local producer Sam Phillips. From his Memphis Recording Service (the precursor to his famous Sun label), Phillips was leasing his recordings to various independent labels, including Chess in Chicago and RPM in Los Angeles.

At the time the Bihari Brothers, proprietors of RPM, were in Memphis looking for talent. They made a deal with Phillips, but again B.B. King's releases failed to sell particularly well, and Joe Bihari decided to return to Memphis and record the guitarist himself. He set up a portable studio in the local YMCA in January 1951, and one side from the sessions, "Three O'Clock Blues," became B.B. King's first national R&B chart-topper.

It was the start of a spectacular run of R&B hits for King through the 1950s, including such classics as "You Know I Love You" in 1952, the definitive remake of Lowell Fulson's "Every Day I Have the Blues" in 1955, "Sweet Little Angel" in 1956, and in 1960 his double-sided version of Joe Turner's "Sweet Sixteen." By then, having moved to the Kent label in 1958, B.B. King had notched up no fewer than twenty chart entries, four of them number ones.

In 1962 he moved to the much bigger ABC-Paramount company, and with that label he cut his now-legendary album *Live at the Regal*, recorded in the famous Chicago theater in 1964. A huge smash with its punchy backing

band, raw chemistry with the audience, and superlative performance even by King's standards, it made an instant impression on the new generation of young blues guitarists like Eric Clapton and Johnny Winter, who had had their first taste of the blues from the "revival" players a few years earlier.

With his rounded, gospel-influenced voice and astounding single-string guitar technique, King's music provided a template for the second wave of rock-oriented players coming through during the 1960s. He would carry on being one of the great blues performers, working incessantly and making more hits—including "The Thrill Is Gone" in 1969, which took him to number fifteen in the US pop charts.

B.B. King crossed over successfully into mainstream music, without losing any of his stylistic integrity, in numerous collaborations including U2 on their *Rattle and Hum* album, jazz-funk group the Crusaders, and his longtime friend Clapton on 2000's Grammy Award-winning *Riding with the King*.

But it was in the early 1960s, riding the shockwaves of the blues revival that had introduced the music to hundreds of new musicians around the world, that the likes of B.B. King and his contemporaries in Chicago, New Orleans, and elsewhere sowed the seeds for the transition from R&B to blues-rock later in the decade.

ABOVE LEFT:
Named for one of B.B. King's many "Lucille" guitars, this UK album was released in 1968.

ABOVE RIGHT:
B.B. King playing with the Bill Harvey band at the Hippodrome, Memphis, in 1950. The saxophone player on the left is Evelyn Young, and on the right is Bill Harvey.

RIGHT:
A contemplative promotional portrait of B.B. and Lucille.

RED HOT FROM ALEX

DECCA
REGD.
MADE IN ENGLAND · THE DECCA RECORD CO. LTD.
45 RPM
K/T
s
(XDR.33543)
F.11934
TRUE HIGH FIDELITY
ffrr
ALL RIGHTS OF THE MANUFACTURER AND OF THE OWNER OF THE RECORD PRODUCTION
RECORDING FIRST PUBLISHED 1964
Kags Music Ltd.

IT'S ALL OVER NOW
(B. & S. Womack)
THE ROLLING STONES
Production: Impact Sound

FAIRFIELD HALL, CROYDON
General Manager: T. J. Pyper, M.I.M.E.M.

FRIDAY 18th OCTOBER
at 6.30 p.m. and 8.50 p.m.

THE NATIONAL JAZZ FEDERATION
in association with HORST LIPPMANN presents the

ONLY APPEARANCE IN BRITAIN OF THE 1963

AMERICAN NEGRO BLUES FESTIVAL

MUDDY WATERS · LONNIE JOHNSON · OTIS SPANN
MEMPHIS SLIM · SONNY BOY WILLIAMSON
VICTORIA SPIVEY · BIG JOE WILLIAMS · WILLIE
DIXON · MATT 'GUITAR' MURPHY · BILL STEPNEY
Compere: Chris Barber

A DOCUMENTARY OF THE AUTHENTIC BLUES

TICKETS: 6/- 8/- 10/6 12/6 15/- 17/6 21/-
Available from FAIRFIELD HALL BOX OFFICE (CRO. 9291); NATIONAL JAZZ FEDERATION,
18 Carlisle Street, London, W.1 (GER. 8923) and usual Agents

PYE INTERNATIONAL
R&B series

THE BLUES VOL.2
NPL.28035
SIDE 1
1. Thirty Days (To Come Back Home) (Berry)
CHUCK BERRY
2. Sugar Mama (Hooker)
JOHN LEE HOOKER
3. Evil (Burnett)
HOWLIN' WOLF
4. Got My Mojo Working (Morganfield)
MUDDY WATERS
5. I'm a Man (McDaniel)
BO DIDDLEY
6. Blues With a Feeling (Jacobs)
LITTLE WALTER
JEWEL MUSIC N.C.B.. B.I.E.M.
An Aristocrat, U.S.A.. Recording

RAW BLUES
ace of clubs

JOHN MAYALL
ERIC CLAPTON
OTIS SPANN
CHAMPION JACK DUPREE
CURTIS JONES
PETER GREEN
STEVE ANGLO

BLUES ROCK

7

The folk boom triggered a new awareness of the blues among white audiences. By the early 1960s, record companies in the United States, Britain, and elsewhere were releasing the latest American rhythm and blues, records that previously would have been targeted at just the urban African-American market. Eager young white musicians became the driving force in the latest manifestation of the blues in popular music, and by the end of the decade the R&B boom led by groups like the Rolling Stones had given way to guitar-driven blues rock, dominated by giants of the genre such as Johnny Winter and Jimi Hendrix.

At the end of the 1950s, blues in the UK was still very much part of the folk or jazz scenes. It was in the latter context that British rhythm and blues was born. Bandleader Chris Barber had already brought over Muddy Waters, Big Bill Broonzy, and others to guest with his band, and they were followed by more American bluesmen, including Champion Jack Dupree, Roosevelt Sykes, Memphis Slim, and Jesse Fuller. And Barber was key in the genesis of home-grown R&B when in 1958 he became a partner in a new jazz club in London, the Marquee.

In 1962, the Marquee began featuring weekly rhythm and blues nights led by guitarist Alexis Korner. Korner, often described as the godfather of British R&B, already had a band, Blues Incorporated , featuring Chicago-style harp player Cyril Davis, that played around the London jazz and folk clubs. For a while, his line-up at the Marquee included Charlie Watts on drums (later replaced by Ginger Baker) and Jack Bruce on bass, while a young student called Mick Jagger would occasionally sit in on vocals.

Rollin' Stones

Nineteen-year-old Jagger already had the nucleus of his own group, assembling his guitarist friend Keith Richards and Brian Jones, a guitarist-harmonica player whom Mick and Keith had spotted playing with Korner at their local jazz club in Ealing, West London. All three were passionate fans of American blues, particularly the electric blues of Muddy Waters and company coming out of Chicago. When they formalized their band with drummer Charlie Watts and bass player Bill Wyman, they named it for Waters' 1950 record "Rolling Stone," initially billing themselves as the Rollin' Stones.

The end of 1962 was a seminal time for British popular music. While the embryonic Stones were putting together their repertoire of contemporary hard-hitting blues by the likes of Muddy Waters, Jimmy Reed, and Bo Diddley, the Beatles—still based in their hometown of Liverpool—had just released their debut single, the

bluesy "Love Me Do." Although their name still didn't mean much outside the northwest of England, that was to change radically in the spring of 1963, when they topped the UK charts for the first time.

The Beatles never claimed to be an R&B band, seeing themselves as a straightforward rock 'n' roll group, although their set list at the time included current rhythm and blues numbers coming out of America, like Richie Barrett's "Some Other Guy," and "Twist and Shout" by the Isley Brothers. And as was true for most pop music before and after the Beatles' reign, the blues informed much of what they played and wrote for the rest of their career. Furthermore, the "beat boom" that their overwhelming success prompted in 1963 included scores of guitar-led groups around the country, among them dedicated R&B outfits like the Rolling Stones.

The Stones' debut album, released in April 1964, was typical of their set at the time, including numbers written by Willie Dixon (a cover of Muddy Waters' "I Just Want to Make Love to You"), Jimmy Reed, Slim Harpo, and Chess Records' two biggest R&B stars at the time, Chuck Berry and Bo Diddley. Later that year the Stones toured America, part of the "British invasion" of beat groups that followed in the wake of the Beatles' US success, and they did some recording in the studios they had long regarded as a shrine, Chess Records in Chicago. They even named one self-penned number—"2120 South Michigan Avenue"—for the studio's famous address.

"We first met Brian Jones at Ealing Jazz Club. He was calling himself Elmo Lewis. He wanted to be Elmore James at the time. 'You'll have to get a tan and put on a few inches, boy.' But slide guitar was a real novelty in England, and Brian played it that night. He played 'Dust My Broom,' and it was electrifying."
KEITH RICHARDS

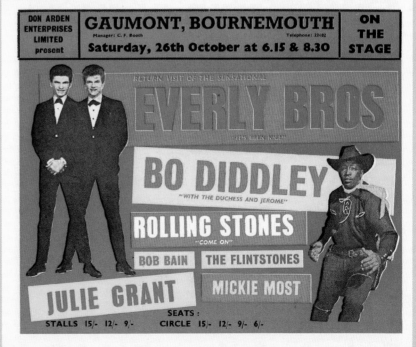

Through the 1960s and ever since, notwithstanding various changes of personnel, the Rolling Stones, despite excursions into seemingly alien territory such as psychedelia and disco, have always had at the heart of their music a close affinity with the blues. And in continually promoting, and often collaborating with, some of the living legends who first inspired them, they have been flag bearers for the music for over fifty years.

Shape of Things

As the Stones raised the profile of British R&B, other groups emerged across the country who had been plowing the same furrow, from the Animals in Newcastle and the Roadrunners in Liverpool, to Van Morrison's group Them in Belfast and Birmingham's Spencer Davis Group—and, from the Stones' former home ground of West London, the Yardbirds.

The Yardbirds were formed by singer Keith Relf and bass player Paul Samwell-Smith, who had previously been in another blues outfit, the Metropolitan Blues Quartet. In May 1963 the Yardbirds performed as a backing band for harp player Cyril Davis, and that September they began to attract attention when they replaced the Rolling Stones as the house band at the

Crawdaddy blues club in Richmond. A month later their lead guitarist left the lineup, to be replaced by a fiery newcomer who would soon be accepted as the finest blues player in the country, Eric Clapton.

The Yardbirds' repertoire was classic blues for a British band of the 1960s, drawn from the work of Howlin' Wolf, Muddy Waters, Elmore James, and the other Chicago greats. They were managed by the Crawdaddy's proprietor, Georgio Gomelsky, and soon had a recording contract with EMI, resulting in their live debut album *Five Live Yardbirds*, recorded at the Marquee and released in December 1964. Prior to that they released two singles, both with solid blues credentials—Billy Boy Arnold's "I Wish You Would," followed by "Good Morning, Little School Girl," a Chicago standard originally recorded in 1937 as "Good Morning School Girl" by the first "Sonny Boy Williamson," John Lee Williamson.

In December 1963 they had recorded a live set at the Crawdaddy Club with the second Sonny Boy Williamson (Rice Miller) on harmonica; shortly afterward they toured with the fifty-one-year-old harmonica legend. It was on that tour that many outside the London area got their first chance to hear the Yardbirds, particularly the sensational technique of their lead guitarist Clapton.

ABOVE:
Mick Jagger gets some harmonica tips from the great Junior Wells. One of the masters of Chicago-style blues harmonica as well as a fine vocalist, Wells made his recording debut in 1952 when he replaced Little Walter in the Muddy Waters band. After an R&B hit in 1960 with "Little by Little," his solo career took off, and in 1965 he teamed up with guitarist Buddy Guy, a partnership that would continue on and off until Wells' death in 1998.

ROLLING STONES

Spearheading the British rhythm and blues boom in the mid-1960s, the Rolling Stones were responsible for shepherding Chicago electric blues into mainstream pop culture. Formed by three young blues fans—vocalist Mick Jagger, and guitarists Keith Richards and Brian Jones—the Stones introduced the music of the likes of Howlin' Wolf and Elmore James to a new generation of white audiences, both in the music's homeland and around the world. Since then the band—in an evolving lineup that today centers on the core group of Jagger, Richards, guitarist Ron Wood, and drummer Charlie Watts—have been among the music's longest-serving exponents and world ambassadors.

> "If you don't know the blues there's no point in picking guitar and playing rock and any other form of popular

KEITH RICHARDS

Formed
July 1962–January 1963, England

Instruments
Guitars, harmonicas, bass guitar, drums

Recording Debut
"Come On" / "I Want to Be Loved"
May 10, 1963, Regent Sound Studios, Lond
Decca (UK)

Awards
Grammy Lifetime Achievement Award, 19
Inducted into Rock and Roll Hall of Fame,
MTV Video Music Lifetime Achievement
Grammy Best Rock Album for *Voodoo Lou*
Inducted into UK Music Hall of Fame (200
World Music Awards, World's Greatest To
    All Time (2005)

Playlist
"It's All Over Now" [1964]
"Little Red Rooster" [1964]
The Rolling Stones (UK) [1964]
Five by Five (EP, UK) [1964]
Got Live If You Want It (EP, UK) [1965]
"Route 66" [1965]
"Honky Tonk Women" [1969]
Let It Bleed [1969]
"Brown Sugar" [1971]
Exile on Main St [1972]

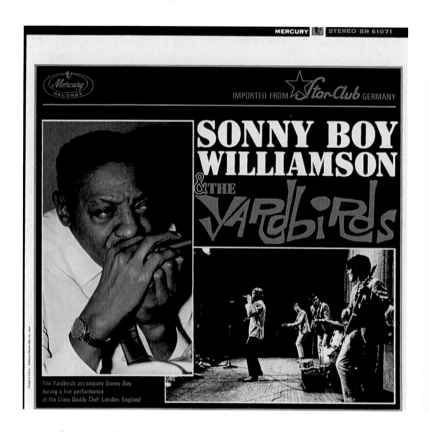

But the man who would soon be called "God" by British blues guitar fans did not last long in the Yardbirds. After their first two singles had done moderately well, in February 1965 the band released "For Your Love," a much more commercial-sounding number, written by songwriter Graham Gouldman. It shot to number three in the UK singles chart (and subsequently number six in the United States), but it also brought to a head Clapton's growing dissatisfaction with the way the band was going. Still very much a blues purist, he despised the compromise that "For Your Love" represented, and the publicity and hype that followed its success, and quit the band in March 1965.

Clapton was replaced only two days later by Jeff Beck, who would prove to be another seminal figure in British blues. Beck's experimental style with feedback and distortion suited the Yardbirds' new direction, though it didn't have the commercial appeal promised by "For Your Love." Singles like the psychedelic-sounding "Shape of Things" indeed heralded the shape of changes to come but, as Clapton had feared, took the band even further from their blues roots.

In June 1966, session-guitarist Jimmy Page was brought into the lineup, and for a brief period he and Beck shared the lead guitar spotlight. Then in October, Beck left the group over various incompatibilities within the band. The Yardbirds soldiered on with Page, but things became increasingly strained, as singer Relf and drummer Jim McCarty wanted to move in a direction influenced by folk and classical music, while Page—intrigued by the new psychedelic blues-rock of Cream and Jimi Hendrix—wanted to explore a "heavy" approach.

Finally, in 1968 the group broke up, and Page formed a new band with singer Robert Plant, bassist John Paul Jones, and drummer John Bonham. They initially called themselves the New Yardbirds, but would shake the very foundations of blues-based rock in the late 1960s when they were relaunched as Led Zeppelin.

Bluesbreaker

When Eric Clapton left the Yardbirds, he had earned a huge reputation as a maestro of blues guitar. Seeking someone who shared his "purist" credentials, he found John Mayall. Born in 1933, Mayall was older than most of the musicians emerging during the 1960s R&B boom, who were mostly wartime babies. He had been playing blues—first on guitar, but later settling on keyboards and harmonica—since his Manchester art school days in the mid-1950s and formed his first band, the Powerhouse Four, in 1956. In 1962 he joined the Blues Syndicate and was still Manchester-based until Alexis Korner persuaded him to try his luck in London.

There he formed the Bluesbreakers in 1963. They began attracting attention, playing the Marquee regularly, and backing John Lee Hooker on his 1964 UK tour. But it was when they recruited Clapton in April 1965 that things really took off for the band. Their debut album, *Blues Breakers*, was released in July 1966 and caused a sensation. Clapton's contribution was acknowledged by featuring his name prominently on the cover. The songs ranged from blues past and present—including Otis Rush, Freddie King, Robert Johnson, Little Walter, and Mose Allison's seminal "Parchman Farm"—and the album remains a true classic of British rhythm and blues.

ABOVE LEFT:
The live set recorded at London's Crawdaddy Club in December 1963, with the Yardbirds backing Sonny Boy Williamson.

ABOVE RIGHT:
An advert for Hohner harmonicas published in a program for a December 1963 UK tour of Sonny Boy Williamson with the Chris Barber band.

OPPOSITE LEFT:
Flyer showing the location of London's Marquee Club.

OPPOSITE, TOP RIGHT:
A membership card for the Crawdaddy Club, in the London suburb of Richmond, another hub of the British blues and R&B boom.

OPPOSITE, BOTTOM RIGHT:
Liverpool's Cavern Club, famous as the "birthplace" of the Beatles, was an essential venue on the mid-1960s R&B and blues circuit.

> "Just when it looked like maybe the blues were gone, the Rolling Stones, the Kinks, the Yardbirds, and John Mayall reminded white America of what its culture was really all about."
>
> TOM PIAZZA

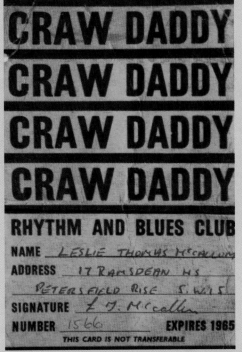

THE AMERICAN FOLK BLUES FESTIVAL CONQUERS EUROPE

The American Folk Blues Festivals were a European phenomenon featuring veteran American blues artists, many touring for the first time outside their native USA. Their concerts were an amazing introduction to live authentic blues for a generation of fans through the 1960s.

The American Folk Blues Festivals were an annual package show between 1962 and 1970. The brainchild of German promoters Horst Lippmann and Fritz Rau, the festival toured various countries across Europe. The first three series of concerts were billed as the American Negro Blues Festival; the name was changed, with the accepted fashion of the times, to the American Folk Blues Festival in 1965.

That very first bill, which played only one UK date in Manchester, featured Memphis Slim, T-Bone Walker, Sonny Terry and Brownie McGhee, John Lee Hooker, harmonica player Shakey Jake, vocalist Helen Humes, bass player Willie Dixon, and drummer Jump Jackson. It was an unprecedented lineup of blues names, some of which were already legendary. The buzz about the Manchester concert was almost entirely word-of-mouth, and in the audience at that first concert were many future stars of the UK blues boom, including singer Paul Jones, guitarist Jimmy Page, and Keith Richards, Mick Jagger, and Brian Jones from a newly formed Rollin' Stones (as the band name was then spelled). Ironically, these players over the following couple of years would "export" the music back to the land where it began.

The tour, which also visited Germany, Austria, Switzerland, France, and Scandinavia, caught the spirit of the blues revival perfectly, and was such a success that Lippmann and Rau were confident enough to stage a second the following year. This time many more British blues fans were able to experience the music of an equally impressive bill, with a week of gigs sold out in advance. The emphasis in 1963 was on Chicago blues, with a bill dominated by Sonny Boy Williamson (who closed the first half) and Muddy Waters, who closed the entire show. Other stars included Memphis Slim again, veteran female singer Victoria Spivey, guitarist Lonnie Johnson, and once more Willie Dixon, who acted as an informal road manager for the tour as well as helping the promoters contact various artists around Chicago.

The list of artists on the Festivals reads like a who's who of the blues, including Mississippi Fred McDowell, Junior Wells, Sippie Wallace, Little Walter, Sister Rosetta Tharpe, Bukka White, Skip James, and many more. As luck would have it, many of the concerts through the 1960s were recorded or filmed (or both), so there is a considerable archival record of what can now be described only as a unique series of events in the history of the blues.

OPPOSITE LEFT:
Guitarist and singer Hound Dog Taylor backstage at a Folk Blues Festival concert in 1967 with promoter Horst Lippman reflected in the mirror.

OPPOSITE, TOP RIGHT:
An album on the UK Fontana label recorded during the 1963 Festival tour.

OPPOSITE, BOTTOM RIGHT:
Howlin' Wolf fronting the Festival ensemble in 1964.

"I think those shows were so important because you didn't get the opportunity to see these guys live. There was something about having seen them live, you just thought, 'Oh man, I'm part of this immense tradition.' . . . I'd heard very little live blues. It was hearing it live and so many of them all on one evening that made me think, 'This is really it. There's nothing else for me.' That was a real kick to see all that on one evening. I was buzzing for weeks. That was very much a catalyst thing."

PAUL JONES, vocalist, Manfred Mann

Just as the album was released, however, Clapton was on the move again, leaving Mayall to form what became known as the "first supergroup," Cream. With Jack Bruce on bass and Ginger Baker on drums (both of whom had played with Korner's Blues Incorporated) Cream was the quintessential blues-rock band, and a harbinger of the powerhouse "heavy" blues to come. Despite exploring the outer limits of what could be strictly defined as blues, their repertoire relied heavily on essential blues and blues-based numbers—such as Skip James's "I'm So Glad," Muddy Waters' "Rollin' and Tumblin'," and the Robert Johnson standard "Crossroads."

Brit Blues II
After Clapton left the Bluesbreakers, the band continued to undergo changes. Peter Green—another blues guitar ace, who stunned everyone with his technique, drawn from B.B. King—came into the fold, soon followed by drummer Mick Fleetwood. But it wasn't long before he, bassist John McVie, and Green left to form their eponymous blues group, Fleetwood Mac, and with the addition of guitarist Jeremy Spencer—a fanatical disciple of Elmore James—this new powerhouse group led what became known as the second British blues boom in the late 1960s.

After two highly regarded albums—one writer has since described their second, *Mr. Wonderful* (1968), as "effectively a homage to Elmore James"—Fleetwood Mac moved away from pure blues to a more mainstream stance, heralded by their single "Albatross." When Green left the band in 1970, they recruited Christine Perfect (already married to John McVie) from the Birmingham blues group Chicken Shack, a change that began the band's eventual metamorphosis into international "soft rock" superstars, radically distanced from the blues that originally inspired them.

Chicken Shack, fronted by guitarist Stan Webb, were typical of the second wave of British blues groups emerging during the latter half of the 1960s. Other blues outfits included the Savoy Brown Blues Band, Ten Years After (led by super-speed guitarist Alvin Lee), the Irish group Taste—whose front man, the late Rory Gallagher, is still regarded as an icon in blues guitar circles—and Free, whose 1970 hit "All Right Now" established them as one of the biggest-selling British blues-rock groups.

ABOVE LEFT:
One of the so-called "Three Kings" of blues guitar (along with B.B. and Freddie), Albert King was a leading figure in the blues boom that informed blues rock of the 1970s, based first in Chicago, then Memphis, where he was a leading name with the Stax label. He was a huge influence on players from Jimi Hendrix to Stevie Ray Vaughan.

ABOVE RIGHT:
Nicknamed the "Texas Cannonball," Freddie King also made his mark on a generation of blues-rock guitarists, such as Eric Clapton and Peter Green.

ABOVE LEFT:
The coffeehouse area of Greenwich Village in 1963, where folk-blues players began to move to an electric sound in the mid-1960s.

ABOVE RIGHT:
A picture taken for his 1984 album *Where Have All the Good Times Gone?*, blues harmonica man Charlie Musselwhite—who is still playing and recording today—was one of the young white American bluesmen to emerge in the mid-1960s alongside the likes of Paul Butterfield and Mike Bloomfield.

RIGHT:
British blues band Chicken Shack c.1968, with (left to right) guitarist Stan Webb, bass player Andy Silvester, drummer Dave Bidwell, and Christine Perfect at the piano.

Folk Rock to Blues Rock

The British Invasion begun by the Beatles and the Rolling Stones was a big influence on young blues musicians in the United States, who had been playing mainly acoustic music, a reflection of the blues revival as part of the flourishing folk scene. By 1965, musicians in Greenwich Village, the hub of folk music in New York, began moving into electric instrumentation.

These players included guitarists Danny Kalb and Steve Katz (and subsequently keyboard player Al Kooper), who got together in 1965 as the Blues Project. The band was named for a 1964 compilation blues album on which Kalb appeared alongside various young folk-blues singers including Dave Van Ronk, "Spider" John Koerner, and Rick von Schmidt. Recorded at one of the leading folk venues in the Village, the Blues Project's 1965 debut album, *Live at the Café Au Go-Go*, was heavily oriented to Chicago rhythm and blues, including numbers by Muddy Waters, Willie Dixon, Chuck Berry, and Bo Diddley. The original band lasted just a couple of years, making their final appearance at the Monterey Pop Festival in 1967, but in that time they made their mark as pioneers of blues rock.

Al Kooper was also a session player on Bob Dylan's key 1965 album *Highway 61 Revisited*, released just a month after Dylan's controversial appearance at that year's Newport Folk Festival, in which the leading voice of the folk revival shocked many of his fans by going electric. This watershed event has since been seen as the signal of Dylan's move from acoustic folk music into folk rock, but his backing band—essentially the Paul Butterfield Blues Band—became a prime mover in American blues rock.

Butterfield and Bloomfield

Vocalist and harmonica player Paul Butterfield was born in Chicago in 1942. An avid blues fan, by the late 1950s he was visiting the city's South Side blues clubs with singer Nick Gravenites, getting to know musicians like Muddy Waters and Little Walter, and even occasionally jamming with them. While in college in the early 1960s, Butterfield met guitarist and National Merit Scholar Elvin Bishop, and soon both had forsaken their studies and formed the racially integrated Paul Butterfield Blues Band in 1963, with Jerome Arnold on bass and Sam Lay on drums—both from Howlin' Wolf's touring band.

Late in 1964 Butterfield added Mike Bloomfield to the lineup—another Chicago guitarist who had served the challenging apprenticeship of sitting in with some of the blues greats in the South Side clubs. It was this version of the Butterfield Blues Band that made a sensational afternoon appearance at the Newport Folk Festival in July 1965—the first time that many of the folk fans had heard high-octane electric blues—and later that day, the group, without Butterfield and Bishop, backed Dylan on his electric set (along with two keyboard players, Al Kooper and Barry Goldberg)

Not long after, the Butterfield group recorded their debut album, *The Paul Butterfield Blues Band*, for the Elektra label. From the opening track, "Born in Chicago" (written by Butterfield's old buddy Nick Gravenites), it represented a milestone in white electric blues. Tracks like Elmore James's "Shake Your Moneymaker," Junior Parker's "Mystery Train," and Muddy Waters' anthemic "Got My Mojo Working" brought a genuine Chicago blues sound to many young white listeners for the first time.

ABOVE:
A vintage Fender Stratocaster belonging to Eric Clapton, and used by the guitarist from the mid-1970s. It was a true collector's item with its classic "sunburst" finish and white pick-guard, dating from the introduction of the iconic instrument in 1954.

ERIC CLAPTON

From his early days as the preeminent guitarist of the 1960s blues boom to his position today as one of the music's elder statesmen, Eric Clapton has been a major voice on the blues stage for over fifty years. Nicknamed "Slowhand" by his adoring fans in 1966, Clapton—already having made his mark as a virtuoso player in seminal bands the Yardbirds and John Mayall's Bluesbreakers—fronted the pioneers of heavy blues rock, Cream. After working in various other cutting-edge lineups and on landmark solo albums, his *Unplugged* collection in 1992 and its 1994 follow-up *From the Cradle* marked a return to the acoustic blues roots of his music. Other albums, like his 2000 outing with B.B. King, *Riding with the King*; his 2004 tribute to Robert Johnson, *Me and Mr. Johnson*; and his collaboration with swamp blues guitarist J.J. Cale on *The Road to Escondido* in 2006, have confirmed Clapton's position as one of the elite standard bearers of guitar blues.

> "For me there is something positively soothing about this music [blues], and it went straight to my nervous system, making me feel ten feet tall."
>
> ERIC CLAPTON

Born
Eric Patrick Clapton, March 30, 1945, Ripley, Surrey, UK

Instruments
Vocals, guitar

Recording Debut
"I Wish You Would" / "A Certain Girl" [with the Yardbirds] February 1964, Olympic Studios, London, Columbia (UK), Epic (US)

Awards
Silver Clef Award for Outstanding Contribution to British Music, 1993
Grammy Album of the Year for *Unplugged*, 1993
Grammy Best Rock Vocal Performance for *Unplugged,* 1993
OBE (Order of the British Empire) for Services to Music, 1994
Inducted into Rock and Roll Hall of Fame, 2000
CBE (Commander of British Empire), 2004
Grammy Lifetime Achievement Award (as member of Cream), 2006

Playlist
Blues Breakers (with John Mayall's Bluesbreakers) [1966]
Fresh Cream (with Cream) [1966]
461 Ocean Boulevard [1974]
Unplugged [1992]
From the Cradle [1994]
Riding with the King (with B.B. King) [2000]
Me and Mr. Johnson [2004]
The Road to Escondido (with J.J. Cale) [2006]

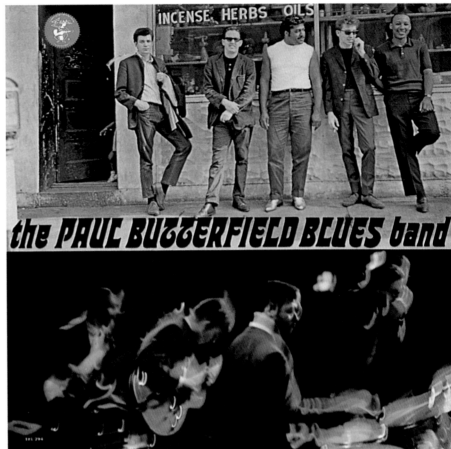

"A lot of people relate me to the blues but I don't think it's a hindrance at this point. I've been doing it long enough that I can do different things and be accepted."

PAUL BUTTERFIELD

In July 1966, billing themselves as the Butterfield Blues Band, the group (with Billy Davenport replacing an ill Sam Lay) recorded their second album, *East-West*. More eclectic than their debut set, and in the spirit of the times, the material ranged from the traditional blues of Robert Johnson and Muddy Waters to the New Orleans R&B of Allen Toussaint to Nat Adderley's soul-jazz standard "Work Song"—plus, as the closing thirteen-minute title track, an instrumental Indian-tinged "fusion" piece with extended solos by Butterfield, Bishop, and Bloomfield.

Hugely influential in his own right, Mike Bloomfield left the Butterfield band in 1967 to form Electric Flag with Nick Gravenites and organist Barry Goldberg (who had appeared with Dylan at Newport), although his tenure with them lasted for only one album, 1968's *A Long Time Comin.'* He went on to team up with Al Kooper for the landmark *Super Session* album in 1968, a "jamming" recording that highlighted his fluid guitar style, garnered rave reviews, and was the best-selling album of his career. Lauded as an instrumentalist, Bloomfield rarely sang on his records, and his reputation was bolstered by his appearance on various all-star albums including the Chess Records 1969 release *Fathers and Sons* with Muddy Waters and Otis Spann. Widely respected as a major figure in blues rock, Bloomfield was hindered by a serious heroin problem through the 1970s, and he died from an overdose, at age thirty-seven, in 1981.

Kozmic Blues

In the late 1960s Mike Bloomfield was involved with the third album by Janis Joplin, who was regarded by many as a modern inheritor of the Bessie Smith blues tradition and was lauded as the finest white blues singer of the blues-rock generation.

Born in Texas in 1943, Janis Joplin from her teenage years onward was a self-described rebel; hanging out with the few like-minded kids in her hometown of Port Arthur, she discovered the records of Bessie Smith and Ma Rainey. She had caught the blues bug, and her life would never be the same.

Shunning small town life, she headed for San Francisco when she was twenty, living in the beatnik enclave on North Beach, and what would become the hippie hub of Haight-Ashbury. Meeting future Jefferson Airplane guitarist Jorma Kaukonen, she informally recorded some blues standards including W. C. Handy's "Hesitation Blues," and "Nobody Knows You When You're Down and Out," made famous by Bessie Smith.

By 1966 she had gained a mixed reputation on the fledgling psychedelic scene as an experimental drug user,

HOW BLUES BEGAT HEAVY METAL

Heavy metal music, long derided by its many detractors as simply a crude wall of noise fronted by posturing guitarists and singers, actually had its roots in the music of 1950s guitar pioneers like Link Wray, the 1960s British blues boom, and the first "heavy blues" bands that followed into the early 1970s.

The move to a heavier, louder approach was anticipated by Pete Townshend of the Who and Jeff Beck of the Yardbirds, as they experimented with feedback and other distortions. But the real breakthrough began with Cream—the guitar, bass, and drums power trio of Eric Clapton, Jack Bruce, and Ginger Baker. Their first two albums, *Fresh Cream* and *Disraeli Gears* in 1966 and '67 respectively, provided a template for much to come, as did Jimi Hendrix's 1967 debut *Are You Experienced.*

One of the few American antecedents to heavy metal at this stage was Vanilla Fudge, a psychedelic rock band that specialized in heavy versions of rock standards such as the Supremes' "You Keep Me Hanging On" and "Ticket To Ride" by the Beatles—both standout tracks on their eponymous debut album released in 1967. And in January 1968, San Francisco band Blue Cheer released a cover of Eddie Cochran's "Summertime Blues" that has since been cited as the first-ever genuine heavy metal record.

But it was later in 1968 when Jimmy Page formed Led Zeppelin, initially as the New Yardbirds, that an increased decibel load was applied to what at that stage was still a basic blues repertoire. It was clearly a sign of the times. Zeppelin's eponymous debut album was released in 1969, and in America the blues-rock trio Grand Funk Railroad made their first major appearance at the Atlanta Pop Festival, followed a month later by the debut of Mountain at Woodstock—both US groups highly influenced by Cream, and very, very heavy.

This was the "second" British blues boom, and from that scene emerged several outfits—such as Ten Years After, fronted by guitar wizard Alvin Lee—that put the emphasis on increased volume and dazzling guitar pyrotechnics. But it was the emergence of more specifically "heavy" bands, though at first still blues based, that instigated heavy metal as a separate genre.

In Britain, the lead came from Black Sabbath (previously a heavy blues group called Earth), whose 1970 albums *Black Sabbath* and *Paranoid* set the agenda, followed by Deep Purple's *In Rock* the same year. Other new names, in what rapidly became both a best-selling genre and UK youth cult, included Uriah Heep, UFO, and Budgie.

Lyrically, especially in the macabre themes explored by the likes of Black Sabbath, the bands were moving into new and darker territory, and although the twelve-bar blues was still the basic format for some songs, the heavy metal groups (as they were universally dubbed after 1970) were effectively becoming distanced musically from their blues roots.

Likewise in the United States, while Led Zeppelin dominated the overall scene with its own brand of blues-infused rock, a specific heavy rock style was being pioneered in the early 1970s by bands like Blue Öyster Cult and Aerosmith. Led by guitar-wielding front men and often over-the-top vocalists, heavy metal established itself as a permanent subgenre of commercial rock, with little musical reference to its blues origins.

OPPOSITE, TOP LEFT: Blue Öyster Cult on stage in the 1970s.

OPPOSITE, TOP RIGHT: Grand Funk Railroad with (left to right) Mel Schacher, Max Carl, and Bruce Kulick performing at the Seminole Casino in Coconut Creek, Florida in March 2012.

OPPOSITE, BOTTOM RIGHT: Led Zeppelin's second album *Led Zeppelin II*, released in 1969 on the Atlantic label.

OPPOSITE, BOTTOM LEFT: Richie Blackmore, lead guitar man with British heavy metal pioneers Deep Purple.

"They credited us with the birth of that sort of heavy metal thing. Well, if that's the case, there should be an immediate abortion."
GINGER BAKER

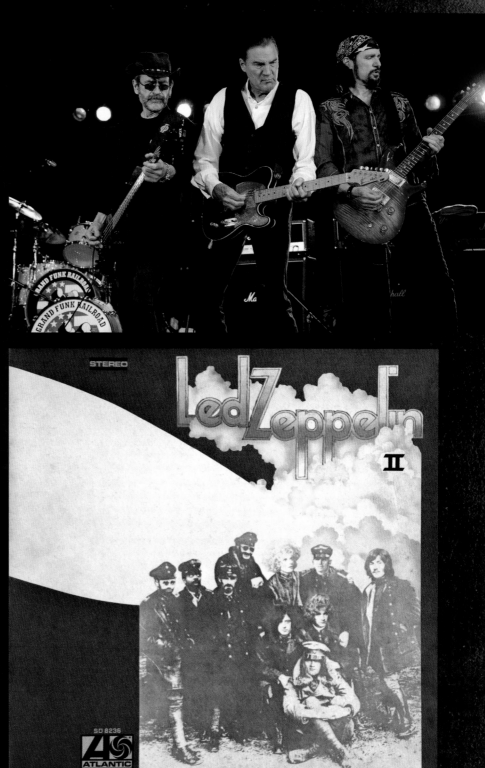

DISCOVERING THE BLUES

When young white people, in both the United States and across the Atlantic in Europe, began to discover the blues during the late 1950s and early 60s, it was a seminal experience that inspired a new wave of singers and musicians. Recalling it in later years, many can still pinpoint precisely the individual singers and songs that first fired their imagination. And for the blues veterans themselves, many brought out of retirement in response to the new audience for the music, it was an opportunity to play to a wider, more international public than they had ever previously enjoyed.

" ... It was at this time that Brian [Jones] heard his first Elmore James recording. Brian was so excited that he bought an electric guitar, a Harmony Stratatone, with one pick-up ... He used a converted tape recorder as an amplifier, until he could afford to buy one. Brian became obsessed with the blues. He constantly practised playing slide guitar listening to any Elmore James, Robert Johnson and Howlin' Wolf records he could get hold of.**"**
BILL WYMAN

" I don't even think I'd heard of Robert Johnson when I found the record [*Robert Johnson: King of the Delta Blues Singers*], it was probably just fresh out. I was around fifteen or sixteen, it was a real shock that there was something that powerful ... It all led me to believe that here was a guy who really didn't want to play for people at all, that his thing was so unbearable for him to have to live with that he was almost ashamed of it. This was an image that I was very, very keen to hang on to.**"**
ERIC CLAPTON

" And there were the seminal sounds—the tablets of stone, heard for the first time. There was Muddy. There was Howlin' Wolf's "Smokestack Lightnin,'" Lightnin' Hopkins. And there was a record called *Rhythm and Blues Vol I.* [ed: actually called *The Blues Vol I*] It had Buddy Guy on it doing "First Time I Met the Blues"; it had a Little Walter track. I didn't know Chuck Berry was black for two years after I first heard his music, and this was obviously long before I saw the film that drove a thousand musicians—*Jazz on a Summer's Day*, in which he played "Sweet Little Sixteen."**"**
KEITH RICHARDS

" They were playing the 50s crap on the radio. It seemed so shallow, all oop-hoop. It had nothing. Then I heard Leadbelly and it was like a flash. It mattered to me. A guy ... introduced me to Bessie Smith's singing. He had some Leadbelly records and I listened to them and I liked them a lot better than what I heard on the radio. They seemed to have some sincerity to them. So then I started listening to blues and folk music. I started reading some books on blues and kept coming across the name Bessie Smith. So I wrote away and got a bunch of her records and just really fell in love with her.**"**
JANIS JOPLIN

" I can imagine how Columbus felt when he came to America. That's what I felt when I went on before the Rolling Stones. You got a great audience out there, but a lot of people don't know you, but they know the Rolling Stones! But I was lucky enough for some reason to get 'em to like me pretty well. So it was a great experience.**"**
B.B. KING

" They call it rhythm and blues, but it's not the same as what I know as rhythm and blues. When I was doing R&B in 1948, and around then, there were only negro singers doing it. Then when Elvis Presley came out and sold well, someone coined the name rock 'n' roll. I mean they couldn't call his music R&B because the negro was singing R&B. Now, among your singers that I've heard, that singer with the Rolling Stones—I don't know his name—gets closest to the blues. He's got a feel ... he's in the right direction.**"**
JIMMY WITHERSPOON

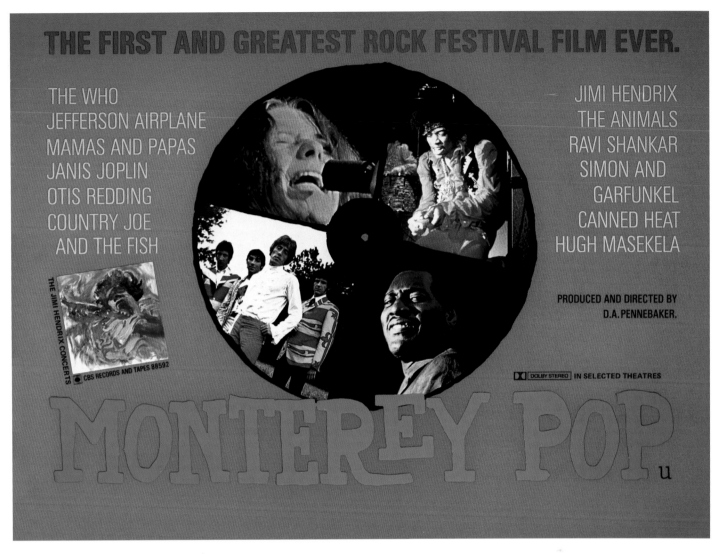

THE FIRST AND GREATEST ROCK FESTIVAL FILM EVER.

THE WHO
JEFFERSON AIRPLANE
MAMAS AND PAPAS
JANIS JOPLIN
OTIS REDDING
COUNTRY JOE
AND THE FISH

JIMI HENDRIX
THE ANIMALS
RAVI SHANKAR
SIMON AND
GARFUNKEL
CANNED HEAT
HUGH MASEKELA

PRODUCED AND DIRECTED BY
D.A. PENNEBAKER.

THE JIMI HENDRIX CONCERTS
CBS RECORDS AND TAPES 88592

DOLBY STEREO IN SELECTED THEATRES

MONTEREY POP u

ABOVE:
Poster advertising the British release of *Monterey Pop*, the acclaimed music documentary that featured some of the greatest names in blues-influenced rock including Janis Joplin, Canned Heat, the British blues band the Animals, and Jimi Hendrix, as well as a show-stopping performance of "I've Been Loving You Too Long" by soul legend Otis Redding just six months before his death in an airplane crash.

heavy drinker, and potentially mind-blowing singer. She came to the attention of a local rock outfit, Big Brother and the Holding Company, gigging with them in June and, in August, joining them in signing a record deal. Their debut studio album—*Big Brother and the Holding Company*—was released a year later, a few week's after their landmark appearance at the 1967 Monterey Pop Festival. One of the highlights of her Monterey set (and of the celebrated D. A. Pennebaker documentary film of the festival), was her riveting performance of Big Mama Thornton's "Ball and Chain."

The band had already nearly made the Top Forty with Janis's version of an old 1920s number, "Down on Me," but it was the Monterey film (released in December 1968) and Big Brother's second album, *Cheap Thrills*, that launched Janis Joplin as the undisputed queen of rock-driven blues. Released in August 1968, the album included the George Gershwin standard "Summertime," and a nine-minute version of "Ball and Chain." The album made it to number one in the *Billboard* chart.

Despite the album's success, by the end of the year Janis had left Big Brother, and soon after formed a new backing group made up of session musicians plus Big

Brother's guitarist Sam Andrews. She dubbed her new outfit the Kozmic Blues Band and shifted her focus to the more contemporary brass-backed R&B of the Stax Records soul sound. In reflecting the current music of black America, she was actually keeping closer to her blues roots than many of her psychedelic-influenced hard rock contemporaries.

I Got Dem Ol' Kozmic Blues Again Mama was recorded in June 1969, released in September, and became another million-seller. But life on the road with Janis could be fractious, and the band broke up at the end of the year. Their final gig at New York's Madison Square Garden was a full-on blues-rock event, with guitar ace Johnny Winter and the Paul Butterfield band also on the bill.

The spring of 1970 saw Janis putting together yet another ensemble, the Full Tilt Boogie Band, whose only album was to be *Pearl*, released in January 1971. The album topped the chart for nine consecutive weeks and sold over four million copies. But for Janis Joplin, it was a posthumous triumph. She had died at age twenty-seven from an overdose in October 1970, ending a brief but brilliant career as potentially the greatest white blues singer of them all.

211

Guitar Virtuoso

A year before Janis's death, she had appeared at the now-legendary Woodstock Festival in upstate New York, held in August 1969. The three-day event (overrunning into four) featured a number of key names in late 1960s rock, with solid blues-based acts including Janis, Joe Cocker, the Paul Butterfield group, Ten Years After, and boogie band favorites Canned Heat. At the other end of the scale there were tastes of where blues-rock was going, with the Cream-inspired heavy rock of the four-piece Mountain, the high-energy blues-rock of guitar man Johnny Winter, and the blues-infused pyrotechnics of Jimi Hendrix.

Hendrix in particular had already redefined the boundaries of blues guitar work in a sensational series of recordings, beginning with his first UK-produced hit in

"I wish they'd had electric guitars in cotton fields back in the good old days. A whole lot of things would've been straightened out."

JIMI HENDRIX

January 1967, "Hey Joe." The Seattle-born Hendrix began playing guitar at the age of fifteen, in 1958. After a brief spell in the Army, he moved to Tennessee and began playing the chitlin' circuit in local R&B outfits. He soon had a regular job with the backing band for the Isley Brothers soul act, moving on to Little Richard's rock revival group into the mid-1960s.

It was after a stint with the R&B group Curtis Knight and the Squires that he was discovered playing in New York by Chas Chandler, ex-bass player with the British

ABOVE:
Boogie rock band Canned Heat playing in Berlin, Germany in 1970, with (left to right) vocalist Bob Hite, guitarist Henry Vestine, and bass player Larry Taylor.

RIGHT:
Rock guitar supremo Jimi
Hendrix c.1968.

JOHNNY WINTER

Johnny Winter was something of a child blues prodigy (as was his brother Edgar), having released his debut single when he was just fifteen. As a teenager he jammed with some of the blues greats, which paved the way for a career as one of the true originals of blues guitar. Always an innovator during a time of explosive changes in rock, in 1969 alone he released two albums and played Woodstock. In the early 1970s he moved to a harder sound, and later in that decade he helped rejuvenate the career of his long-time hero Muddy Waters, producing four award-winning albums. Since then Winter's career has been a consistent reminder that blues is a lifetime commitment, and he has served as an inspiration for a generation of blues rockers that followed in his footsteps.

> "I was about seventeen, and B.B. didn't want to let me on stage at first. He asked me for a union card, and I had one. Also, I kept sending people over to ask him to let me play. Finally, he decided that there were enough people who wanted to hear me that, no matter if I was good or not, it would be worth it to let me on stage. He gave me his guitar and let me play. I got a standing ovation, and he took his guitar back!"

JOHNNY WINTER

Born
John Dawson Winter III, February 23 1944, Beaumont, Texas

Instruments
Guitar, mandolin, harmonica

Recording Debut
"School Day Blues" / "You Know I Love You" [as Johnny and the Jammers]
Beaumont, Texas, 1959
Dart Records

Awards
Inducted into Blues Hall of Fame, 1988

Playlist
The Progressive Blues Experiment [1968]
Johnny Winter [1969]
Second Winter [1969]
Rock and Roll, Hoochie Koo [1970]
Nothin' But the Blues [1977]
I'm a Bluesman [2004]

ABOVE:
The Erlewine Lazer guitar, with its ergonomically shaped body designed to give players increased flexibility. Johnny Winter, who previously played a Gibson Firebird, switched to the Lazer in the 1980s, describing it as "The closest thing I've found to sounding like a Strat and feeling like a Gibson."

blues band the Animals. Chandler wanted to move into record production, and this was his chance. He took Hendrix under his wing, and soon the Jimi Hendrix Experience power trio was born.

Audiences were stunned with his fiery technique, and more hits followed "Hey Joe," which reached number six in the UK top ten. The doom-laden song was perfect for Hendrix's style of reinterpretation, a blues-heavy approach that he brought to bear on his other two UK hits, both self-penned: "Purple Haze" and "The Wind Cries Mary." His first two albums with the Experience were both UK hits in 1967, but his breakthrough in the United States came after a guitar-burning performance at the 1967 Monterey Pop Festival. The documentation of that episode ensured that fame and notoriety would go hand in hand for the rest of his career.

Jimi's third and final studio album was *Electric Ladyland*, which topped the US chart in November 1968. Most of the numbers were written by Hendrix, including an extended blues jam on "Voodoo Child" that occupied fifteen minutes of the first side of the double-disc release. The three covers included "Come On," by New Orleans R&B guitarist Earl King, and a remarkable reworking of Bob Dylan's "All Along the Watchtower."

Jimi Hendrix's injection of blues improvisation into all manner of material—though often outside the strict confines of the accepted chord sequences—came to a glorious head at Woodstock when, closing the event half a day after the scheduled finish, he played a heart-stopping rendition of the US national anthem, "The Star-Spangled Banner." A year later, by then one of the highest-paid performers in the world, he played the mammoth Isle of Wight Festival in England, a thrilling performance captured on film and audiotape. Eighteen days later, Hendrix died from barbiturate-related asphyxia—like Janis Joplin, at the age of twenty-seven.

Winter Blues

Similarly gifted as a virtuoso guitarist, Johnny Winter had a style far more locked into traditional blues playing than that of Hendrix, but he represented as important a contribution to the blues rock period of the late 1960s and early '70s. Both Texas-born Johnny and his brother Edgar were albinos, their ultra-blond look a trademark as they became instantly recognizable musical celebrities.

Johnny was born in 1944, and with his brother was encouraged by his parents to learn music from an early age. He made his first record at fifteen when his teenage band, Johnny and the Jammers, released "School Day Blues" on a local Houston label. He managed to see many of the R&B greats performing live, including Muddy Waters and B.B. King, experiences that set him on a path dedicated to the blues. In 1967 he recorded a single with the rockabilly band the Traits, known for backing Roy Head. The following year he released his debut album, *The Progressive Blues Experiment*, on the Texas indie label Sonobeat.

Winter nurtured his prodigious ability, which paid off when he jammed with Al Kooper and Mike Blomfield at a New York concert and was spotted by Columbia Records. Within days he had secured what was then reckoned to be the largest advance ever, $600,000, for his album *Johnny Winter*. Released in 1969, it featured songs that would become standards of his repertoire, including Sonny Boy Williamson I's "Good Morning Little School Girl," with a lineup that featured Chicago stalwarts Willie Dixon on bass, and Big Walter Horton on harmonica. Suddenly Winter was at the forefront of fashionable rock, playing Woodstock and recording his second album, *Second Winter*, in 1969.

In 1970 he formed a new band with guitarist Rick Derringer, releasing *Rock and Roll, Hoochie Koo*, which marked a move to a new harder rock sound, although he

was still faithful to his background of the blues. However, a problem with heroin marred his career in the early 1970s, effectively taking him off the road for several years, until, having kicked the habit, he recorded *Still Alive and Well* in 1973.

In 1977 Johnny Winter achieved a long-held ambition: playing with Muddy Waters. But it wasn't just a case of sitting in with the blues legend; Winter rebooted the great man's career after Chess Records went out of business, producing three studio albums—*Hard Again* in '77, *I'm Ready* in 1978, and *King Bee* in 1981. Plus there was the 1979 live album *Muddy "Mississippi" Waters—Live*. All four releases included Winter in lineups that featured some of the great names of Chicago blues: harp masters James Cotton and Walter Horton, guitarist Jimmy

Rogers, and pianist Pinetop Perkins. The albums earned three Grammy awards for Muddy Waters, and confirmed Johnny Winter's commitment to the blues, a dedication he has demonstrated since in a long career of performing and recording—including a Grammy nomination for his album *I'm a Bluesman* in 2004.

Johnny Winter remains one of the founding fathers and long-term practitioners of blues-rock, a genre that, following its heyday in the early 1970s, has continued to inform musicians through the 1990s and later, including the White Stripes, ZZ Top, the Black Crows, the Fabulous Thunderbirds, the Jon Spencer Blues Explosion, and most recently Joe Bonamassa—with his debut solo album released in 2000, very much a star of blues-rock for the twenty-first century.

ABOVE:
Multi-instrumentalist Edgar Winter on stage with his keyboard assemblage in 1970.

Johnny Winter at a concert
appearance in June 1973, a rock
superstar who went on to be one
of the modern-day champions of
blues music in its various
manifestations.

THE BLUES TODAY

From the 1980s onward there has been a resurgence in blues music of a wide range of persuasions, from the Texas blues inspired by Johnny Winter's brand of blues rock, through its representation as a part of a bigger "world music," to traditional country blues, which has been revived as part of a general interest in American roots or so-called "Americana" music. And new superstars of the music have emerged, modern-day inheritors of the spirit of Robert Johnson, T-Bone Walker, Muddy Waters, and a thousand other blues legends whose impact on the course of music worldwide is irrefutable.

Two of the founding fathers of contemporary blues started as bandmates in the beat-driven boom of the 1960s. Taj Mahal and Ry Cooder, each of whom put their own stamp on the music they played and helped open it up to a broader audience, were both singer-guitarists who would make unique contributions to modern blues. Their short-lived California group, once described as the American Rolling Stones, was called the Rising Sons.

The Rising Sons first got together in 1964, during the frenetic first days of the British beat "invasion." Taj Mahal was barely out of his teens; Cooder was only nineteen. No wonder the five-piece group (which also included guitarist Jesse Lee Kincaid, bass player Gary Marker and drummer Kevin Kelley) wasn't sure which direction to go in! They were all blues and folk fans, but like a thousand other teenage American "garage bands" at the time, they were dazzled by the impact of the tousled-headed UK beat groups. Signed to Columbia, they recorded enough material for an album, but it was never released, and the band split in 1966. But the experience set Cooder and Taj Mahal on the road to musical careers, which would come to fruition in the 1970s and beyond.

Natch'l Blues

Taj Mahal (as he would later dub himself) was born Henry Saint Claire Fredericks in Harlem in 1942. His mother was from South Carolina, his father from the Caribbean island of St. Kitts. His mixed heritage may well have encouraged his subsequent eclecticism, but from early on he was solidly into the blues, citing Jimmy Reed, Sleepy John Estes, and Mississippi John Hurt among his primary influences.

After the Rising Sons disbanded, he stayed with Columbia Records and released *Taj Mahal* in 1968 and both *The Natch'l Blues* and *Giant Step* in 1969. All were highly acclaimed by critics and well received by the public, making him a celebrity in the rock world elite—regarded highly enough to work with the Rolling Stones (as would Cooder) and perform with them at various times over the years. During the early 1970s he began to incorporate elements of West Indian reggae and

calypso, jazz, Cajun zydeco, and old-time gospel into his music. His 1972 album, *Recycling the Blues & Other Related Stuff*, added African instrumentation to the mix, anticipating the interest in world music that would explode in subsequent decades. .

Despite the respect he enjoyed among a new generation of blues fans, by the end of the 1970s Taj Mahal's career began to lose direction, and in 1981 he moved to Hawaii, where he formed the Hula Blues Band. For the rest of the decade he was largely off the public radar, until the 1988 album *Taj* signaled a return to high-profile music making.

Through the 1990s he released a profusion of albums covering blues, R&B, hip-hop, and rock, collaborating with the likes of Eric Clapton, Etta James, and many others—even the names of his backing groups, such as the Intergalactic Soul Messengers and the Phantom Blues Band, reflected the wide-ranging reach of his music.

In 1997 his album *Señor Blues*—with songs as diverse as Hank Williams' "Mind Your Own Business," Otis Redding's "Mr. Pitiful," "Sophisticated Mama" by Washboard Sam, and the title track, by jazz pianist Horace Silver—won the Grammy Award for Best Contemporary Blues Album, an accolade repeated in 2000 for *Shoutin' in Key*.

But it was his 1999 project *Kulanjan*, a collaboration with the Malian *kora* player Toumani Diabeté, that most positively asserted Taj Mahal's credentials as a visionary in blues-related music. With six other musicians from the Republic of Mali, Diabeté and Mahal created a milestone in world music, a fusion of the blues and its ancient rhythmic past in West Africa that one British reviewer called "a rousing set of eclectic grooves, calling on ragtime, barrelhouse blues and even rock 'n' roll."

OPPOSITE, TOP LEFT:
Taj Mahal facing the crowds at the Gold Rush Festival, held at Lake Amador, California on October 4, 1969.

OPPOSITE, TOP RIGHT:
Taj Mahal's album *Music Fuh Ya'*, released in 1977 on the Warner label.

OPPOSITE BOTTOM:
The Rising Sons, (left to right) bass player Gary Marker, guitarists Ry Cooder, Jesse Lee Kincaid, and Taj Mahal, and drummer Kevin Kelley, in 1966.

> "If you do music long enough, many generations ahead of anybody coming along, your music pops up every now and then. You are ancestor. It is clear that the musicality of my ancient people is still on me and on us as a society."
>
> TAJ MAHAL

Cooder's Story

Like his ex–Rising Sons colleague Taj Mahal, Ryland "Ry" Cooder has made his mark on contemporary music both as a champion of traditional blues and by exploiting his blues-endowed virtuosity in the wider context of world music.

After the two-year apprenticeship of the Rising Sons, Cooder was soon noticed for his remarkable technique, steeped as he was in the acoustic music of the old country players as well as the more recent electric styles of the rhythm and blues era. Following a stint with the anarchic music of Captain Beefheart's Magic Band, he quickly gained a reputation as a session musician, notably with the Rolling Stones on their late 1969 album *Let It Bleed* and *Sticky Fingers* in 1971.

But Ry Cooder really came to prominence in the 1970s, with a series of albums for Warner Bros. The first, *Ry Cooder* in 1970, included numbers by an impressive lineup of blues greats including Lead Belly, Sleepy John Estes, Blind Blake, and—with a hugely atmospheric version of the classic "Dark Was the Night, Cold Was the Ground"—Blind Willie Johnson.

Cooder's big breakthrough came with his next album, *Into the Purple Valley*, in 1972. It was another potent mix of folk and blues, a formula he would follow with *Boomer's Story* the same year, and *Paradise and Lunch*, released in 1974. *Chicken Skin Music*, in 1976, added Tex-Mex music to the recipe, a precursor of Ry's extensive trips into Latin American music more than twenty years later—but as always with his explorations of Americana, deeply indebted to the blues roots of his music.

During the 1980s he began working on film soundtrack music, the most celebrated of all being his work for Wim Wenders' *Paris, Texas* in 1984, featuring a reprise of "Dark Was the Night, Cold Was the Ground."

The stirring depth of feeling that was wrought from the tune's basic, simple structure was a reminder of the potency of the blues.

The similar sensory attraction of other musical forms was demonstrated by Cooder in two "world music" crossover projects in the early 1990s. In 1993 *A Meeting by the River* saw him collaborating with the Indian classical musician V. M. Bhatt, while *Talking Timbuktu* in 1995 featured the African multi-instrumentalist Ali Farka Touré—and, confirming the blues connection in no uncertain terms, the veteran blues man Clarence "Gatemouth" Brown. But Ry Cooder's most famous world music project came in 1997, when *Buena Vista Social Club* highlighted the old-time Cuban pop music from the 1950s still being played in Havana.

Continuing Cooder's love affair with Latin American music, the 2005 album *Chavez Ravine* was the first of a "Californian" trilogy, melding Latino pop, R&B, and jazz in a heady mix. The second album, 2007's *My Name Is Buddy* went back to old Cooder territory of country blues, bluegrass, and honky-tonk music; the third, *I, Flathead*, concentrated on Tex-Mex, country rock, and western swing in its evocation of 1950s West Coast subcultures.

Always socially aware, in 2011 and 2012 Ry Cooder made his most politically motivated musical statements yet, first on *Pull Up Some Dust and Sit Down* and then on *Election Special*—the latter confirming his personal support for the Democratic Party, and Barack Obama, in the 2012 presidential election.

Ry Cooder's story in the evolution of modern blues is unique. His passion for the music often takes him to lands and cultures far from its American origins, but everything he does has been imbued with the commitment of an evangelist—a true missionary, in the broadest sense, for the music of the blues.

ABOVE LEFT:
Music by Ry Cooder from the soundtrack of the 1984 movie *Paris, Texas.*

ABOVE RIGHT:
Ry Cooder in the early 1970s.

STEVIE RAY VAUGHAN

From the rocking country blues of his debut recording with the Dallas band Cast of Thousands at the age of sixteen, it was clear Stevie Ray Vaughan was going places as a remarkable guitar player. After a decade with various local bands in Austin, his sensational debut album with his band Double Trouble, *Texas Flood*, brought instant recognition and a 1984 Grammy Award. A true blues evangelist, he preached the word musically through barnstorming tours and a series of landmark albums. After his death at the tragically young age of thirty-five, posthumous albums of unreleased material confirmed his place in the front line of modern blues performers.

> "Between sets I'd sneak over to the black places to hear blues musicians. It got to the point where I was making my living at white clubs and having fun at the other places."
> STEVIE RAY VAUGHAN

Born
Stephen Ray Vaughan, October 3, 1954, Dallas, Texas

Died
August 27, 1990, Alpine Valley, Wisconsin

Instruments
Vocals, guitar, bass, drums

Recording Debut
"Red, White and Blue" [with Cast of Thousands for compilation album *A New Hi*]
1971, Dallas, Texas
Tempo 2

Awards
Grammy Best Contemporary Blues Album for *In Step*, 1989
Grammy Best Contemporary Blues Album for *Family Style*, 1990
Grammy Best Rock Instrumental Performance for "D/FW," 1990
Grammy Best Contemporary Blues Album for *The Sky Is Crying*, 1992
Grammy Best Rock Instrumental Performance for "Little Wing," 1992
Austin Music Awards Hall of Fame, 1982–1983

Playlist
Texas Flood [1983]
The Sky Is Crying [1991]
In the Beginning [1992]
Soul to Soul [1999]
Blues at Sunrise [2000]
Live at Montreaux 1982&1985 [2001]

Bonnie Raitt

A major name in contemporary roots-influenced blues since the 1970s, Bonnie Raitt—born in 1949 in Burbank, California—was playing guitar from an early age and began playing bottleneck style while still at school. She came to the attention of the veteran blues promoter Dick Waterman, through whom she got to meet—and play alongside—such legends as Howlin' Wolf and Mississippi Fred McDowell. It was while supporting McDowell at New York's Gaslight Café in 1970 that she was spotted by a *Newsweek* reporter, whose coverage sparked a flood of interest in the new singer. She eventually signed with Warner Bros., and her 1971 debut album, *Bonnie Raitt*, was acclaimed but achieved only modest sales. *Give It Up*, in 1972, fared better, but although many critics and fans still regard it as her finest work, it too failed to click commercially, a fate shared by her third album, *Takin' My Time* (1973).

Nevertheless, her reputation was growing, and her passionate slide guitar style was a contributing factor to the growing public awareness of American roots music. This genre became popular through the 1980s, when it was categorized as "Americana" in an increasing number of record stores.

It was with *Sweet Forgiveness* in 1977 that Raitt's blues-saturated style finally connected with a mainstream audience. Her cover of Del Shannon's "Runaway" made the *Billboard* Hot 100 at number fifty-seven—although some of her more purist followers derided the track as too "rhythm and blues." A decade of worthy music followed, but record company hassles didn't help the promotion of her efforts, and she seemed

> ## "The consolidation of the music business has made it difficult to encourage styles like the blues, all of which deserve to be celebrated as part of our most treasured national resources."
>
> **BONNIE RAITT**

to get equal personal satisfaction from her increasing political commitments to causes such as Amnesty International, Farm Aid, and, in 1987, the first joint Soviet/American Peace Concert, held in Moscow.

Her biggest success came in 1989, nearly twenty years after her debut record, with her chart-topping tenth album *Nick of Time*. More million-selling releases followed—*Luck of the Draw* (1991) and *Longing in Their Hearts* (1994)—and since then her records have continued to receive universal acclaim.

One of Bonnie Raitt's most memorable successes came in 1989, when veteran bluesman John Lee Hooker recorded and released *The Healer*, his sensational collaboration with a star-studded roster of contemporary artists. In 1990 it received a Grammy Award for Best Traditional Blues Recording, plus a similar accolade for the stunning version of "I'm in the Mood" featuring Hooker in a duet with Raitt.

More recently, Raitt scored with *Slipstream*, the best-selling blues album of 2012, and she was also declared the best-selling blues artist of 2012. With her career now in its fifth decade, Bonnie Raitt is recognized as a key figure in the continuing influence of blues in the broader field of contemporary music.

ABOVE LEFT:
A teenage Bonnie Raitt photographed in 1969—two years before her sensational debut album.

ABOVE RIGHT:
Bonnie Raitt has long commanded the respect of the entire blues fraternity. She is shown here playing with veteran bluesman B.B. King, photographed by Dick Waterman in 1993.

ABOVE LEFT:
The tour-worn flight case for one of Stevie Ray Vaughan's Stratocaster guitars, c.1970.

ABOVE RIGHT:
Stevie Ray Vaughan in action, c.1988.

Stevie Ray

The success of Bonnie Raitt's *Sweet Forgiveness* in 1977 was a signal to many, among both musicians and the broader music industry, that a traditional blues style could still connect with a far wider audience than just the committed aficionados.

Further confirmation of this came in 1983 with the release of the first album by Texas blues guitarist Stevie Ray Vaughan, *Texas Flood*. Despite reservations expressed by *Rolling Stone*, the album was generally well received by critics and public alike, hitting double platinum sales in the United States and Canada, gaining a 1984 Grammy for Best Traditional Blues Album, and catapulting Vaughan to international fame as a genuinely new and original talent on the modern blues scene.

Born in Dallas in 1954, musically, Vaughan took after his elder brother, Jimmie Vaughan, who played with a blues rock outfit, the Fabulous Thunderbirds. Stevie Ray started playing blues guitar at the age of seven. He was influenced by artists as diverse as B.B. King and Jimi Hendrix and by the modern Texas blues pioneered by Johnny Winter. By the time he was seventeen he had dropped out of high school to pursue a musical career, and in 1977 he formed what would be the nucleus of his band Double Trouble. He was signed by Columbia Records' veteran producer John Hammond for their Epic label in March 1983, and in June of that year Vaughan and the band released *Texas Flood*.

Vaughan was typical of a new breed of players who moved from a strictly blues environment to mainstream rock without compromising their style; among his efforts was session work on David Bowie's *Let's Dance*. He and

Double Trouble took the blues across the world with five hugely successful studio albums.

Their last album, *The Sky Is Crying*, was released posthumously in 1991 after Vaughan's tragic death the previous year. On August 27, 1990, he had just played a gig at Alpine Valley in Wisconsin along with Eric Clapton; the two had jammed together at the concert. After the performance, Stevie and three of Clapton's entourage left in one of four helicopters. In dense fog, the helicopter Stevie was riding in crashed into a nearby hill, killing all on board instantly.

Strong Persuader

Around the same time that Stevie Ray Vaughan was breaking through in Texas, another new name—guitarist-vocalist Robert Cray—was emerging in Eugene, Oregon. Hailing from Columbus, Georgia, Cray was born in 1953 and began playing guitar in his early teens, emulating musicians like Albert Collins (whom he had heard play at his high school graduation) and Freddie King. In the mid-1970s Cray moved to Eugene, where he formed the Robert Cray Band and got a steady gig backing his hero Collins for a time.

After several years of regional success as a live act in his own right, Cray released his debut album *Who's Been Talkin'* on the Tomato label in 1980. But it was his 1983 set for Hightone, *Bad Influence*, and its 1985 follow-up, *False Accusations*, that brought Cray's phenomenal technique into the spotlight in both America and Europe. His major breakthrough came in 1986 on Mercury Records with *Strong Persuader*, which peaked in the main *Billboard* chart at number thirteen.

225

NORTH MISSISSIPPI HILL COUNTRY BLUES

There's a popular misconception that all acoustic Mississippi blues is "Delta blues," but in the rolling hill country east of the flatlands of the Mississippi Delta, there persists another unique blues style, radically different from—though with the same musical roots as—its more familiar neighbor.

A major influence on this divergence of styles has been the geography itself and the consequent social environment. Whereas the flat farmlands of the Delta were owned by a few white plantation owners, the hills in north Mississippi have been home to small farms owned by generations of African-American families. This nurtured a music that was played at family gatherings like picnics and fish fries, as well as at the regular juke joints. And like the white "hillbilly" music of the Appalachian Mountains, the music of the hill country remained relatively isolated from mainstream culture and its musical influences.

Unlike the Delta bluesmen, who had long been the focus of attention of blues collectors and record companies from the big city, the hill country players were settled in their rural lifestyle. They wore truckers' caps and blue-collar work clothes, worked the land and drove tractors, and at night they played for local dancers in the jukes and roadhouses, but they produced a musical style distinct from conventional blues.

As with the Delta blues, guitar players were key to the hill country sound. But whereas the former kept to the orthodox twelve-bar structure (though not always strictly), moving through the basic three chord changes, the latter style involved striking the same chord continuously—

with emphasis on the driving rhythm of the "groove"— to achieve a droning, almost hypnotic effect. In terms of well-known blues players, the style is more akin to that of John Lee Hooker or Howlin' Wolf (think "Smokestack Lightning") than of "straight" bluesmen such as B.B. King.

One of the first bluesmen to be known for the heavily percussive hill country technique—in that respect a mode of playing more akin to its West African roots than Delta blues—was Mississippi Fred McDowell. Discovered and recorded by musicologist Alan Lomax in 1959 when he was already in his mid-fifties, McDowell found unexpected fame as part of the Delta blues revival, though he was not actually a Delta-style guitarist himself.

Among more recent exponents of the genre, R. L. Burnside and Junior Kimbrough are the most celebrated. Born in 1926, Burnside spent much of his life around Holly Springs, Mississippi (a hub of hill country music), running juke joints and playing locally, though he was little known outside the area until the 1990s. In 1992 he began recording for the Fat Possum label based in Oxford, Mississippi, and subsequently toured with the blues rock band the Jon Spencer Blues Explosion; he died in 2005.

Junior Kimbrough also spent most of his life around Holly Springs and recorded for Fat Possum (among others). His 1992 album *All Night Long* received four out

OPPOSITE, TOP LEFT:
Mississippi Fred McDowe[ll] his wife Annie Mae McDo[w] 1959, photographed on his by Alan Lomax after being "discovered" by the latter.

OPPOSITE, BOTTOM LEFT:
Playing "fife and drum" mu another strand of North Mississippi Hill Country n two of its most famous pla[yers] Second left, drummer and musician Othar "Otha" Tu[rner] and playing fife—a six-note instrument home-made fr[om] cane—on the far right, Na[polean] Strickland. Photographed William Ferris in Gravel S[prings] Mississippi, 1970.

OPPOSITE, TOP MIDDLE:
T-Model Ford, who died i[n] 2013, here performing at t[he] New Orleans Jazz and He[ritage] Crescent City Blues & BB[Q] Festival, in October 2009.

of five stars in *Rolling Stone*, doing much to draw attention to the North Mississippi blues scene. That same year he opened a juke joint (the latest of several similar ventures), Junior's Place in Chulahoma, Mississippi, which attracted visitors from around the world. He died in 1998, following a stroke, at the age of sixty-seven.

Fife and Drum Blues

There is another strand of hill country music that, much like the area's distinctive guitar style, sounds little like what is generally accepted as blues. Known as "fife and drum music," it's played at outdoor gatherings like family picnics rather than smoky juke joints. Its essential features are a simple six-note fife made from cane, backed by bass drum and snare drum—much like a European marching band but with strong African undertones in the rhythm and melody.

The fife and drum music unique to North Mississippi persists today; its last representative from the older generation of players was fife player Othar "Otha" Turner, who died at age ninety-five in 2003. Turner's Rising Star Fife and Drum Band, which consisted of friends and relatives, played primarily at farm parties but branched

out into concerts, including appearances in Washington, DC, and New York. They began to receive wider recognition in the 1990s, and in 1998 made the much-acclaimed album *Everybody Hollerin' Goat*. As if to emphasize the music's ancient roots in Africa, their second album was entitled *From Senegal to Senatobia*, with accompanying musicians billed as "The Afrossippi Allstars."

Another famous veteran fife player was Napoleon Strickland, who also played guitar, drums, harmonica, and the diddley bow. Born in 1919, Strickland worked as a sharecropper for most of his life, while teaching other musicians and playing constantly at local functions and, later, at music festivals. He is another Hill Country player who was only "discovered" late in life. He died in a nursing home in 2001.

Every year the North Mississippi area bordering Tennessee plays host to the North Mississippi Hill Country Picnic. Various luminaries take part, including Junior Kimbrough's son David, T-Model Ford (who died in 2013), and North Mississippi All Stars past and present including Duwayne Burnside Jr. (R. L.'s son), brothers Luther and Cody Dickinson, and Kenny Brown, in celebration of the region's unique musical legacy.

"MY SONGS, THEY HAVE JUST THE ONE CHORD, THERE'S NONE OF THAT FANCY STUFF YOU HEAR NOW, WITH LOTS OF CHORDS IN ONE SONG. IF I FIND ANOTHER CHORD I LEAVE IT FOR ANOTHER SONG. MY SONGS DON'T COME FROM THE MUSIC I HEAR OUTSIDE. IT COMES FROM INSIDE MYSELF."

JUNIOR KIMBROUGH

Like those of other newly established players, Cray's career flourished alongside a revival in the popularity of familiar names from the past. As well as headlining his own tours, Cray often opened for artists like Eric Clapton, who was making his own blues comeback. Clapton's 1990 release, the all-acoustic *Unplugged* album, featured traditional numbers by Big Bill Broonzy, Robert Johnson, Jesse Fuller, and the like, but also included a Clapton-Cray composition, "Old Love."

Startling some purists (whom he calls "bluenatics"), Cray's music has been full of experimentation, while keeping faithful to the blues, proven on albums like *Take Your Shoes Off* in 1999 and *Shoulda Been Home* in 2001. Touring regularly with headliners like Clapton and Dylan, his concerts have been as important as his studio recordings—with a catalog of live albums to prove it. A true innovator, Robert Cray has never seen the blues as a static form; to him it is a living music to be interpreted with new concepts and a continually fresh approach.

While Cray was concerned with an evolving music based on the basic tenets of the blues, the 1990s also saw the adaptation of blues in the raw environs of the world of

"In 1976 we had just done this run at this one club in Eugene—four days—and the club owner said, 'Albert Collins is coming through, and he doesn't have a band. Would you mind backing him up?' And we were like, 'Hell no, we don't mind backing him up.' We were doing some of Albert Collins' songs in our set. And so when Albert came through, we got to meet Albert and became his backup band for about a year and a half."

ROBERT CRAY

punk. Artists like the Jon Spencer Blues Explosion, the Oblivians, and more recently the White Stripes, injected a blues sensibility into their challenging music. Spencer in particular, collaborating with North Mississippi blues veteran R.L. Burnside, demonstrated how the raw blues approach of the older guitar man (who died aged 78 in 2005) had much in common with the stripped-down dynamics of the rock new wave.

ABOVE:
Robert Cray performing at the Maryport Blues Festival in Cumbria, England, in 2010.

PLAYING THE BLUES

Blues players of recent generations have more often than not gained their initial inspiration from the originators of the music, be it Robert Johnson, Elmore James, Bessie Smith, or one of the many other early blues men and women. But what inspired those pioneers themselves? Clearly the African-American experience was not unique to musicians; singers, guitar players, and the rest had no special insight into what it meant to be part of the second-class citizenry of 20th century black America. But for each and every bluesman (and woman) there was a trigger, a personal stimulus that transformed those commonly-held feelings into music that was truly of the people.

"All I knew was I wanted to play the piano. And when this fellow Wiley Pittman who was my neighbor would start to play this boogie woogie, I would go sit on the stool and bang on the piano, and he would stop me and try to show me how to play little melodies with one finger. That that was the first music that I recall that attracted me that would stop me from my playing outdoors with other children."
RAY CHARLES

"I grew up singing gospel songs and church was really my thing. I never dreamed that I would be a blues singer. I was singing some blues, but I wasn't sure if that's really what I wanted to do. Until the people started to praise me, and that's when I really decided. Due to the tips I would get from the blues, I decided that that's what I wanted to do."
B.B. KING

"Lightnin' Slim was the first electric guitar I ever seen. I give him my weekly allowance, which was 30 cents, in a hat."
BUDDY GUY

"I caught a ride to Memphis on the 61 highway. I hitchhiked and came into Memphis around Beale Street. I got into the park, I saw so many people, it was like at a concert. People were in the street playing the jugs and guitars. I said to myself, 'Well you're amongst 'em now.'"
HONEYBOY EDWARDS

"We didn't have electricity outside Memphis where I was raised. My oldest brother, he put up the hay baling wire behind our little shotgun house on some nails, he put up six strings and made himself a guitar out of that. And my younger brother, Levi, he made hisself a harmonica out of a corncob. And I was the vocalist. We didn't need no electric or no mikes no none of this we didn't have. But we just had a jam every day behind our little house. I would sing and they would play and we had a good time."
KOKO TAYLOR

"I stone got crazy when I saw somebody run down them strings with a bottleneck. My eyes lit up like a Christmas tree and I said I had to learn."
JOE TURNER

"The blues is true. It's something that everybody goes through, what people go through each and every day. Disappointments, mishaps—if you have a problem and sing something happy, it doesn't help the problem any. You've got to have something that you can relate to. The plantation that you were on, the bosses would wonder why, after all the stuff they put you through, how could you have all that energy to sing? Because it made us happy! Because we couldn't do anything about it, and we had to make the day pass. That's why I sing about life. Love and life. I learn from mistakes and then I learn about life."
BOBBY BLAND

KEB' MO'

Drawing heavily on the traditional country blues of players like Robert Johnson—whom he played in a 1990 docudrama *Can't You Hear the Wind Howl?*—Keb' Mo' has emerged as a modern-day keeper of the flame, while constantly interpreting blues guitar music as a vibrant, living art. Equally adept with acoustic, electric, and slide techniques, he has made excursions into more contemporary musical territories on his most recent albums, which have served only to confirm that the heart of his music is a basic commitment to simply playing the blues.

"Once you're in that club then you're in that club and you don't get to visit any other clubs. You can do whatever you want, but you're still in your lane. It's OK to do something else, but I'm still gonna be the blues. And I'm comfortable with that."
KEB' MO'

Born
Kevin Roosevelt Moore, October 3, 1951, Los Angeles, California

Instruments
Vocals, guitar, harmonica, banjo, keyboards

Recording Debut
Rainmaker [as Kevin Moore]
1980, Los Angeles
Chocolate City

Awards
Grammy Best Contemporary Blues Album for *Just Like You*, 1997
Grammy Best Contemporary Blues Album for *Slow Down*, 1999
Grammy Best Contemporary Blues Album for *Keep It Simple*, 2005
Orville Gibson Award, Best Blues Guitarist, 2002
W. C. Handy Blues Awards:
    1994 Country/ Acoustic Blues Album *Keb' Mo'*
    1997 Acoustic Blues Artist
    1999 Song of the Year for "Soon as I Get Paid"
    1999 Contemporary Blues Male Artist
    2000 Contemporary Blues Male Artist
    2002 Acoustic Blues Artist

Playlist
Keb' Mo' [1994]
Just Like You [1996]
Slow Down [1998]
Martin Scorsese Presents The Blues [2003]
Live and Mo' [2009]
The Reflection [2011]

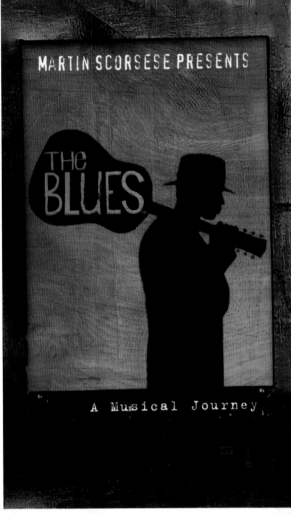

ABOVE LEFT:
Above right: Keb' Mo' on stage at the Nokia Theater, New York City, in October 2009.

ABOVE RIGHT:
CD box set of music from the 2003 Martin Scorsese TV series *The Blues* which featured the work of Keb' Mo'.

Mo' Blues

As the music of Robert Cray and Stevie Ray Vaughan confirms, modern blues can take many forms. They range from the genuinely revivalist, keeping alive early traditions that were once thought almost lost, to the out-and-out eclectic, taking on board myriad influences—be they from the wider world, as explored by Taj Mahal and Cooder, or the rich fabric of American music delved into by artists like Keb' Mo', who has been described as a post-modern blues stylist.

A contemporary of Stevie Ray Vaughan and Robert Cray, blues singer and guitarist Keb' Mo' was born Kevin Moore in 1951, so he was well past forty when he released his debut album as Keb' Mo' in 1994. By that time he had garnered wide-ranging experience, from joining an early 1970s R&B group with ex–Jefferson Airplane violinist Papa John Creach, to jamming with blues legends Albert Collins and Big Joe Turner. In 1980 he released his only album as Kevin Moore, a straightforward blues collection entitled *Rainmaker*.

By 1994 he had adopted the epithet Keb' Mo', a simple street-talk abbreviation of his full name, and that was chosen as the title of his breakthrough album. It was a collection of intense Delta-style blues, and all the tracks on it were (perhaps surprisingly) originals, apart from two Robert Johnson songs, "Come On In My Kitchen" and "Kindhearted Woman Blues."

Two more landmark collections followed. *Just Like You*, in 1996, was again steeped in the rhythms of the Delta; with contributions from Jackson Brown and Bonnie Raitt, it earned Mo' his first Grammy Award as Best Contemporary Blues Album. Then in 1998 came *Slow Down*, another Grammy winner; its opening track was Keb'Mo's dedication to Muddy Waters, called simply "Muddy Water."

When Martin Scorsese made his series of films called *The Blues* in 2003, Keb' Mo' was among twelve artists who had individual compilations of their work released along with the series. He was in prestigious company, on a list that included Jimi Hendrix, Son House, Bessie Smith, Robert Johnson, and Muddy Waters.

In 2011 he released *The Reflection*, in many ways a move away from pure blues to the "folk soul" approach of a Bill Withers or a Bobby Womack. But in bringing together a heady mix of R&B, folk, gospel, and blues, it achieved for Keb' Mo' his stated ambition for the recording: "the culmination of all my influences throughout my career."

BLUES RAP

Contrary to popular belief, rap was not invented in the 1970s. The word itself can be found in dictionary definitions; to rap means "to speak sharply," and in the African-American context, talking rhythmically over a percussive backing can be traced back the work chants of slavery and before that, to the griot storytellers of West Africa. A long way from the streets of Watts or the Bronx, examples of rap-style delivery can be cited throughout the history of the blues.

In terms of content, Speckled Red's celebrated "Dirty Dozen" from 1929, with its risqué sexual insults, is often quoted as an early form of rap, although the words were sung rather than spoken. Likewise, the Memphis Jug Band —with their half-spoken delivery of songs like "On the Road Again" (1928)—have been considered pre-rap musical pioneers.

But it was with John Lee Hooker's "Boogie Chillen" in 1948 that the essence of rap could be said to first appear in modern electric blues. Hooker used the same formula of half-talking, half-singing over an insistent, hypnotic beat to such great effect in dozens of recordings that it became part of his trademark style.

Asked about rap music in an interview in the 1990s, Ray Charles commented that he'd recorded "talk" songs as early as 1953, when he cut Memphis Curtis's comedic jive number "It Should've Been Me." Its laconic spoken narrative ended with the chorus of "it should have been me with those real fine chicks." Charles performed a similar exercise in 1962 with the Percy Mayfield song "At the Club," a classic of talk-over blues, again delivered with a downbeat humor in the lyrics.

There is one rhythm and blues artist above all others, however, who could really be said to be a genuine "Godfather of Rap," and that was Bo Diddley. As part of the Chess Records R&B stable in Chicago, he hit the United States R&B charts with songs like "Who Do You Love" in 1956 and the eponymous "Bo Diddley" the year before—and then (with the same recordings), featured in the UK and US pop charts during the 1960s blues boom. His 1959 single "Say Man" and the sequel, "Say Man, Back Again" were both prime examples of R&B as proto-rap in its most basic form.

In the context of contemporary blues, Chris Thomas King is the acknowledged pioneer of rap/blues fusion, putting together the first sample-based blues concept album, *21st Century Blues . . . From Da Hood* in 1995. He also founded 21st Century Blues Records, signing, among others, the London-based blues/hip-hop band NuBlues, whose *Dreams of a Bluesman* was released in 2004.

Singer-songwriter ZZ Ward (who says the first song she ever sang was Albert King's "As the Years Go Passing By") accompanies herself on guitar, piano, and harmonica and delivers her hard-hitting blues with an edgy, rapping approach. She grew up listening to the blues—she cites Robert Johnson, Big Mama Thornton, Tina Turner, Muddy Waters, and Howlin' Wolf as prime influences—but also rap and hip-hop. When she started singing with a blues band in Oregon, she was singing choruses with a local rap artist too, and from there decided that a crossover of both disciplines was the way forward—"I feel like if I can keep the blues alive and bring the blues back into the lives of new fans then that's awesome."

It's a message that would not be lost on New York blues musician Guy Davis, whose song "Uncle Tom's Dead" from his 2004 album *Legacy* involves a young rapper, disdainful of blues as an old man's music, talking to the elder bluesman. Reminding the youngster that rap didn't start yesterday, Davis points out how both styles of music are part of a common African-American culture—"The blues is in your blood boy, you can't get away, the blues will be with you, till your dying day."

OPPOSITE LEFT:
Gil Scott-Heron (left) was a "spoken word" performer and poet, and, with his emphasis on social and political issues delivered in rapping style, he was an important precursor to hip hop. Singer-songwriter Richie Havens (right) delivered monologue-type songs over an intense rhythmic guitar, and his music can likewise be regarded as an early forerunner of modern rap. The two are pictured together backstage at the B.B. King Blues Club in New York, where Scott-Heron was performing in November 2009.

OPPOSITE RIGHT:
Bo Diddley with "The Duchess" (Norma-Jean Wofford) on guitar, and Jerome Green on maracas.

OVERLEAF:
Michael "Wonder Mike" Wright fronting rap pioneers the Sugarhill Gang at a gig in Birmingham, England, in 2008. In 1979 the Gang were responsible for the first ever rap single to hit the mainstream pop charts with "Rapper's Delight."

...about rap music in an interview in the
...Ray Charles commented that he'd
...ed "talk" songs as early as 1953, when
...Memphis Curtis's comedic jive number
...uld've Been Me." Its laconic spoken
...ive ended with the chorus of "it should
...een me with those real fine chicks."

"IT'S NOT TOO FAR A STRETCH OF THE IMAGINATION TO SAY THAT THE BLUES AND RAP HAVE A LOT IN COMMON. BOTH USE THE LANGUAGE OF THE STREET AS AN EXPRESSIVE TOOL AND BOTH ARE PART OF THE SAME AFRICAN-AMERICAN ORAL TRADITION —FROM FIELD HOLLERS AND PRISON WORK SONGS TO STREET PARTIES AND GANGSTA RAP, IT'S ALL JUST THE BLUES, Y'ALL."

REV. KEITH A. GORDON, *music journalist and critic*

Young Bloods

Whether it be the new postwar electric blues players, the young Englishmen weaned on skiffle and folk blues in the mid-1950s, or the guitar-wielding Texans who took blues rock into the stratosphere, blues has always been perpetuated by an influx of younger generations of musicians and singers. Through the first decade-and-a-half of the twenty-first century, there have been plenty of new names in the pantheon of blues stars.

Corey Harris immediately springs to mind, a blues and reggae musician from Denver, Colorado (no, not Kingston, Jamaica) who focused attention back to acoustic blues in the mid-1990s. His 1995 debut album, *Between Midnight and Day*, revisited the repertoire of Charley Patton, Sleepy John Estes, Muddy Waters, et al. Subsequent excursions—both musical and physical—have included *Mississippi to Mali*, following in the footsteps of Ry Cooder with a collaboration with Ali Farka Touré.

Continuing a tradition that goes back further than many imagine, Louisiana-based Chris Thomas King pioneered blues rap in the early 1990s with *21st Century Blues... From Da Hood*. A seasoned actor, he played the part of R&B bandleader Lowell Fulson in the 2004 Ray Charles biopic *Ray*, and blues singer Tommy Johnson (who, like Robert Johnson, claimed to have sold his soul to the devil) in *O Brother, Where Art Thou?* in 2000.

Susan Tedeschi, the blues and soul singer who fronts the Tedeschi Trucks Band with her husband, Derek Trucks, received no fewer than five Grammy nominations between 2000 and 2010, including Best New Artist and Best Female Rock Vocalist, and three nominations for Best Contemporary Blues Album. Her voice has been called a cross between Bonnie Raitt's and Janis Joplin's, while her guitar playing reflects the influence of her various heroes, including Buddy Guy, Stevie Ray Vaughan, and Freddie King.

ABOVE LEFT:
Chris Thomas King performing in New Orleans in 2011.

ABOVE RIGHT:
Reggae and blues fusion artist Corey Harris.

GARY CLARK, JR

Favorably compared to blues guitar masters Jimi Hendrix and Stevie Ray Vaughan, Gary Clark, Jr. has risen to the heights of musical celebrity in the few short years since the release of his Warner Bros EP *Bright Lights* in 2011. With a unique mix of roots blues and contemporary soul and hip-hop, his music can be heard as both cutting-edge and traditional at the same time. A consummate live performer, in his short time in the limelight Clark has appeared on stage with Eric Clapton, B.B. King, and Buddy Guy, and his major-label debut album *Blak and Blu* made the mainstream pop charts around the world after its release in October 2012.

> "Music is movement. It all moves together, like lifetimes— a continuum. It's all part of the same fabric in the end."
>
> GARY CLARK, JR.

Born
Gary Clark, Jr., February 15, 1984, Austin, Texas

Instruments
Vocals, guitar

Recording Debut
Tribute
2005, Austin, Texas
[Own label]

Awards
Gary Clark Jr. Day, Austin, Texas May 3, 2001
SPIN magazine breakout artist of the month, November 2011
Rolling Stone "Best Young Gun" in Best of Rock issue, April 2011
31st Austin Music Awards (2012–2013):
    Band of the Year
    Musician of the Year
    Song of the Year for "Ain't Messin' Round"
    Album of the Year for *Blak and Blu*
    Electric Guitarist of the Year
    Songwriter of the Year
    Blues/Soul/Funk Artist of the Year
    Male Vocalist of the Year.

Playlist
Tribute [2005]
110 [2008]
Worry No More [2008]
Gary Clark Jr. (EP) [2010]
Bright Lights (EP) [2011]
Blak and Blu [2012]

TOP:
Inspired by British blues players as much as their American forbears, Joe Bonamassa now wows audiences worldwide—seen here at a date in Tel Aviv, Israel.

BOTTOM LEFT:
Sue Foley on stage in August 2001 at the Bishopstock Music Festival in Devon, England.

BOTTOM RIGHT:
Deborah Coleman playing at the San Francisco Blues Festival, September 1999.

The dynamic Susan Tedeschi fronting the Tedeschi Trucks Band at the Lobero Theater, Santa Barbara, in 2009.

Also swelling the ranks of new female blues talent is Deborah Coleman. Born in 1956 and playing guitar by the age of eight, her 1997 debut album *I Can't Lose* included a stunning version of Billie Holiday's "Fine and Mellow" which got considerable radio airplay and helped launch her career. Three albums later, plus an Orville Gibson Award for "Best Blues Guitarist, Female" in 2001, she is a much-in-demand attraction at blues venues and events across America.

Canadian Sue Foley began playing around her native Ottawa when she was just sixteen, before moving to Austin, Texas where she recorded for the blues label Antone's Records. A hugely imaginative guitarist, after her debut *Young Girl Blues* in 1992 she was barnstorming the blues circuit, appearing alongside such names as B.B. King and Buddy Guy, and in 2000 was awarded Canada's biggest music accolade, the Juno Award for Best Blues Album, for her sixth album *Love Comin' Down*.

Born in 1977 in New Hartford, New York, Joe Bonamassa grew up in the perfect environment for a budding musician—his parents' guitar shop. There he remembers getting his first guitar at the age of four, and by the time he was seven he was listening with his folks to Guitar Slim, Bonnie Raitt, Eric Clapton, and so on—and apparently playing Jimi Hendrix tunes note-perfect. A true prodigy, he opened a concert by B.B. King when he was just twelve, and at fourteen he formed the group Bloodline. His first solo album, *A New Day Yesterday*, came out when he was twenty-three, in 2000, followed by nine more solo releases up to 2012, when *Driving Towards the Daylight* reached number two on the UK album chart. Intriguingly, Bonamassa has cited as his prime influences British blues boom guitar players like Jeff Beck, Clapton, and Jimmy Page—and the Irish blues maestro Rory Gallagher—rather then the traditional US blues players who inspired them.

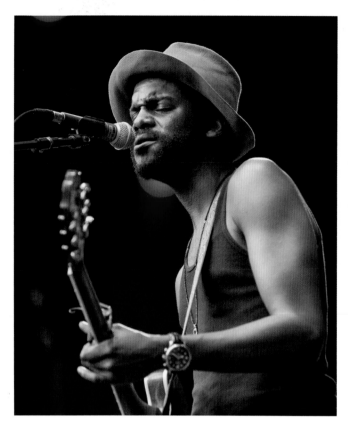

Cutting Edge

One of the youngest of the "new blood" players who has been startling blues enthusiasts and musicians alike in recent years is Gary Clark, Jr. He's another in the long lineage of Texas bluesmen carving out their own unique style while keeping connected to the roots of the blues. In Clark's case, that means a tough, edgy guitar sound reminiscent of Hendrix's fuzz-heavy excursions, applied to a remarkable variety of material.

Born in Austin, Texas, in 1984, Clark began playing at the age of twelve and was soon doing gigs around the city. He got noticed pretty quickly and was taken under the wing of a local club owner, Clifford Antone, whose venue, Antone's, was at the hub of the region's action. That's where the careers of Stevie Ray and Jimmie Vaughan were launched. Antone facilitated Clark's swift development by putting the youngster on stage with some heavy-duty blues veterans, including Chicago legends Hubert Sumlin and James Cotton, and Clark soon earned a name in his own right. While still in his teens he was honored with a Gary Clark, Jr. Day in Austin. By 2007, at the age of just twenty-three, he was named the city's best rock artist and blues guitarist at the Austin Music Awards, and he has gone on to win these titles every year since.

The buzz about Clark was such that in 2010 Eric Clapton invited him to take part in the Crossroads Guitar Festival, the charity event Clapton stages to benefit the Crossroads drug treatment center he founded in Antigua. The event spotlights his pick of distinctive guitar talents, old and new. The event featured Buddy Guy, B.B. King, Jeff Beck, and other luminaries, and when Clark played with Sheryl Crow and Clapton and performed his own originals, it was a breakthrough for the young musician.

Clark had already released a couple of albums on the Hotwire label when he clinched a deal with Warner Bros, resulting in the EP *Bright Lights* in 2010, which he named for the sensual first track, inspired by Jimmy Reed's "Bright Lights, Big City." The highly successful release was just a teaser, however, for his first major studio album, *Blak and Blu*, released in October 2012, which hit number six on the *Billboard* album 200 and number one on the Blues album chart.

In a short time Gary Clark, Jr. has emerged as the most potent name on the modern blues horizon, guesting with musicians and singers as varied as Alicia Keys and the Rolling Stones. As if to confirm his status in the forefront of contemporary blues, he was chosen to appear alongside B.B. King, Mick Jagger, Buddy Guy, and Jeff Beck at the *Red, White and Blues* event held at the White House in February 2012—a long way from Antone's club in Austin. His set included "Catfish Blues," written by the little-known Robert Petway in 1941, and a spine-tingling version of Leroy Carr's "In the Evening (When the Sun Goes Down)." Other songs he took part in that night included Louis Jordan's "Let the Good Times Roll," Eddie Boyd's "Five Long Years" from 1952, and Robert Johnson's blues anthem "Sweet Home Chicago."

With all the musical swagger that comes with being at the cutting edge but knowing that you are doing it right, Gary Clark has shown time and again that his precocious talent—as of this writing, he is just turning thirty—is firmly based on a lifetime's grounding in the blues.

ABOVE LEFT:
Gary Clark Jr opening for Neil Young at the Moon and Stars Festival in Locarno, Switzerland, July 2013.

ABOVE RIGHT:
At the 2010 Crossroads Guitar Festival, a key gig in Gary Clark's rapid rise to the top of the contemporary blues world.

Nearly a century and a half after the abolition of slavery, the first African-American President sings the blues at the White House. Barack Obama joins the all-star line-up on "Sweet Home Chicago" in the East Room of the White House during the "Red, White and Blues" event on February 21, 2012. Also in the picture, left to right, are Troy "Trombone Shorty" Andrews, Jeff Beck, Derek Trucks, Gary Clark Jr., and, seated, B.B. King.

A World Without Blues

Gary Clark Jr.'s music, with its broad base of influences and an eclectic choice of original and classic material, is just one demonstration of how the blues has helped to shape virtually every different form of popular music over the past century.

John Lennon, in an outstanding dismissal of his musical heritage, once solemnly declared "Before Elvis, there was nothing." Had he referenced the blues instead of his rock 'n' roll hero, it would have been a lot closer to the truth. Without the blues there would certainly have been no rock 'n' roll, no soul music, no heavy metal, punk, or hip-hop.

And without the blues, there would have been no jazz as we know it, nor the slide guitars and blue yodels of early country music. George Gershwin wouldn't have written his iconic *Rhapsody in Blue*—nor his opera, *Porgy and Bess*, for that matter either—and similarly, thousands of well-loved standards from the great American songbook of the interwar years would never have seen the light of day.

As the one common element that has characterized nonclassical music since the start of the twentieth century, the simple twelve-bar blues—and its seemingly limitless variations—has truly been the music that changed the world.

A SELECTED BLUES PLAYLIST

Mose Allison
"One Room Country Shack" [1957]
"Parchman Farm" [1957]

Big Bill Broonzy
"Key to the Highway" [1941]
"Black, Brown and White" [1947]
Big Bill Broonzy Sings Folk Songs [1989]

Roy Brown
"Good Rockin' Tonight" [1948]
"Hard Luck Blues" [1950]

R.L. Burnside
A Ass Pocket of Whiskey (with The Jon
    Spencer Blues Explosion) [1996]

Gus Cannon's Jug Stompers
"Walk Right In." [1929]

Leroy Carr
"How Long, How Long Blues" [1928]
"Midnight Hour Blues" [1932]
"When The Sun Goes Down" [1935]

Ray Charles
"Mess Around." [1953]
"What'd I Say" [1959]
"I've Got News for You" [1961]
"In the Evening" [1963]
Ray Charles At Newport [1958]

Eric Clapton
Blues Breakers (with John Mayall's
    Bluesbreakers) [1966]
From the Cradle [1994]
Me and Mr. Johnson [2004]

Gary Clark Jr.
Tribute [2005]
Bright Lights (EP) [2011]
Blak and Blu [2012]

Ry Cooder
Ry Cooder [1970]
Into the Purple Valley [1972]
Paris, Texas [1984]

Robert Cray
Who's Been Talkin [1980]
Bad Influence [1983]
Strong Persuader [1986]

Arthur "Big Boy" Crudup
"That's All Right" [1946]
"My Baby Left Me" [1950]

Sleepy John Estes
"Someday Baby Blues" [1935]
"Airplane Blues" [1937]
"Working Man Blues" [1941]

Lowell Fulson
"Everyday I Have the Blues" [1949]
"Reconsider Baby" [1954]

Guitar Slim
"Things That I Used to Do" [1954]

Buddy Guy
"First Time I Met The Blues" [1961]
Damn Right I've Got The Blues [1991]

Wynonie Harris
"Wynonie's Blues" [1946]
"Good Rockin' Tonight" [1948]

Billie Holiday
"Strange Fruit" [1939]
"Fine and Mellow" [1939]
"Lady Sings the Blues" [1956]

John Lee Hooker
"Boogie Chillen'" [1948]
"Crawling King Snake" [1949]
"I'm In the Mood" [1951]
"I Love You Honey" [1958]
The Healer [1989]

Lightnin' Hopkins
"Shotgun Blues" [1948]
"T-Model Blues" [1949]
"Lightnin's Boogie" [1954]
"Penitentiary Blues" [1959]

Eddie "Son" House
"Preachin' the Blues" [1930]
Father Of The Folk Blues [1965]

Peg Leg Howell
"Broke and Hungry Blues" [1929]

Ivory Joe Hunter
"I Almost Lost My Mind" [1950]
"Since I Met You Baby" [1956]

Mississippi John Hurt
"Stack O'Lee Blues" [1928]

Howlin' Wolf
"Smokestack Lightnin'" [1956]
"Spoonful" [1960]
"Goin' Down Slow" [1961]
"Little Red Rooster" [1961]
Moanin' In the Moonlight [1959]

Elmore James
"Dust My Broom" [1952]
"The Sky Is Crying" [1960]
"Shake Your Money Maker" [1961]

Etta James
"All I Could Do Is Cry" [1960]
At Last! [1961]

Skip James
"Devil Got My Woman" [1931]
"32-20 Blues" [1931]
"Hard Time Killing Floor Blues" [1931]

Blind Lemon Jefferson
"Long Lonesome Blues [1926]
"Matchbox Blues" [1927]
"Black Snake Moan" [1927]
"See That My Grave Is Kept Clean" [1927]

Blind Willie Johnson
"Nobody's Fault But Mine" [1927]
"Dark Was the Night—Cold Was the Ground"
    [1927]
"God Moves On the Water" [1929]

Robert Johnson
"Terraplane Blues" [1937]
"Crossroad Blues" [1937]
"I Believe I'll Dust My Broom" [1937]
"Sweet Home Chicago" [1937]
"Hell Hound On My Trail" [1937]
King of the Delta Blues Singers [1961]

Janis Joplin
Big Brother and the Holding Company [1967]
Cheap Thrills [1968]

Louis Jordan
"Is You Is Or Is You Ain't My Baby" [1944]
"Caldonia" [1945]
"Choo Choo Ch'boogie" [1946]

Keb' Mo'
Rainmaker (as Kevin Moore) [1980]
Keb' Mo' [1994]
Just Like You [1996]

Junior Kimbrough
All Night Long [1992]

Albert King
"Don't Throw Your Love On Me So Strong"
   [1961]
Born Under a Bad Sign [1967]

B.B. King
"Three O'Clock Blues" [1951]
"Every Day I Have the Blues" [1955]
"Rock Me Baby" [1964]
Live at the Regal [1964]

Freddie King
"Hide Away" [1961]
Getting Ready [1971]

Huddie Ledbetter (Lead Belly)
"Midnight Special" [1934]
"Rock Island Line" [1937]
"Goodnight Irene" [1938]
"The Bourgeois Blues" [1938]
Huddie Ledbetter [1951]

Furry Lewis
"Rock Island Blues" [1927]

Smiley Lewis
"I Hear You Knocking" [1955]
"One Night" [1956]

Little Walter
"Juke" [1952]
"My Babe" [1955]

Mississippi Fred McDowell
"You Gotta Move" [1965]

Blind Willie McTell
"Statesboro Blues" [1928]
Southern Can Is Mine [1931]
*Blind Willie McTell: 1940— The Legendary
   Library of Congress Session* [1966]

Memphis Jug Band
"Gator Wobble" [1934]

Memphis Minnie
"Bumble Bee" [1929]
"Me and My Chauffeur Blues" [1941]

Memphis Slim
"Messin' Around [1948]
"Nobody Loves Me" (aka "Everyday I Have
   the Blues") [1948]
"Sassy Mae" [1954]
"The Come Back" [1960]

Charley Patton
"Pony Blues" [1929]
"Screamin' And Hollerin' The Blues" [1929]
"High Water Everywhere." [1929]
"All Night Long Blues" [1930]

Ma Rainey
"Bo-Weavil Blues" [1923]
"See See Rider Blues" [1924]
"Ma Rainey's Black Bottom" [1927]

Bonnie Raitt
Bonnie Raitt [1971]
Sweet Forgiveness [1977]
Slipstream [2012]

Jimmy Reed
"You Don't Have to Go" [1955]
"Baby, What You Want Me to Do." [1960]
"Big Boss Man" [1961]

Jimmy Rushing
"Sent For You Yesterday And Here You Come
   Today," [1938]
"Goin' To Chicago" [1941]
"Harvard Blues" [1944]

Slim Harpo
"I'm A King Bee" [1957]

Bessie Smith
"St Louis Blues" [1925]
"Empty Bed Blues" [1928]
"Nobody Knows You When You're Down And
   Out" [1929]
"Black Mountain Blues" [1930]

Taj Mahal
Taj Mahal [1968]
The Natch'l Blues [1969]

Tampa Red
"It's Tight Like That" [1928]
"You Can't Get That Stuff No More" [1932]
"It Hurts Me Too" [1940]

Sonny Terry and Brownie McGhee
"Fox Chase" [1944]
"Sportin' Life Blues" [1946]
"Whoopin' the Blues" [1947]

Brownie McGhee and Sonny Terry Sing
   [1958]

Big Mama Thornton
"Hound Dog" [1952]
"Ball and Chain" [1968]

Big Joe Turner
"Roll 'Em Pete" [1938]
"Chains Of Love" [1951]
"Shake, Rattle And Roll" [1954]
"Corrine Corrina" [1956]
*The Boss of the Blues: Joe Turner Sings
   Kansas City Jazz* [1956]

Othar Turner
Everybody Hollerin' Goat [1998]

Stevie Ray Vaughan
Texas Flood [1983]
The Sky Is Crying [1991]
Live at Montreaux 1982&1985 [2001]

T-Bone Walker
"Bobby Sox Blues" [1946]
"Call It Stormy Monday (But Tuesday Is Just
   As Bad)" [1947]
"T-Bone Shuffle" [1950]
"Strollin' With Bones" [1950]
T-Bone Blues [1959]

Muddy Waters
"I Can't Be Satisfied" [1948]
"Hoochie Coochie Man" [1954]
"I Just Want to Make Love to You" [1954]
"Mannish Boy" [1955]
Muddy Waters At Newport 1960 [1960]

Junior Wells
"Little By Little" [1960]
"It Hurts Me Too" [1962]

Josh White
"Careless Love" [1940]
"One Meat Ball" [1944]
"House of the Rising Sun" [1947]

Sonny Boy Williamson II
"Don't Start Me Talkin'" [1955]
"Nine Below Zero" [1961]
One Way Out [1968]

Johnny Winter
The Progressive Blues Experiment [1968]
Johnny Winter [1969]
I'm a Bluesman [2004]

BLUES TURNING GOLD

The blues has permeated popular music across all genres, from the obvious areas of jazz, rock 'n' roll, and soul music to country songs, dance band swing, film soundtracks, and straight pop. Here are just twenty examples from the hundreds of big hits that had their roots in the blues, though none of them blues records as such.

Rhapsody in Blue / Paul Whiteman and His Concert Orchestra [1924] *(prior to introduction of Billboard record sales charts in 1936)*

Composer George Gershwin played piano on this abridged version (released on two sides of a Victor 78) of the first major classical work directly influenced by jazz and blues.

Boogie Woogie Bugle Boy / Andrews Sisters [1941] *US Chart #26*

One of many pop hits of the boogie woogie craze in the early 1940s, the song also made the charts in a 1973 version by Bette Midler.

The Birth of the Blues / Frank Sinatra [1952] *US Chart #19*

A kitsch torch-song homage that bears little musical relationship to the blues itself, the number was first published in 1926, became a regular feature with mainstream singers, and a hit for Frank Sinatra in 1952.

Ode to Billy Joe / Bobby Gentry [1967] *US Chart #1*

Written by 23-year-old Gentry, the tragic tale of Billie Joe McAllister who "jumped off the Tallahatchie Bridge" is rich in potent imagery of a humid Mississippi, where all is not always as it seems.

In The Mood / Glenn Miller [1940] *US Chart #1*

A perennial favorite by one of the most popular swing era bands, just one of Miller's many hits based on a blues format, with others including "Tuxedo Junction" and "Pennsylvania 6-5000."

Main Title from "The Man With The Golden Arm" / Elmer Bernstein [1956] *US Chart #16*

An atmospheric movie theme, a big band brassy blues that evoked the neon-lit cityscapes of night-time Chicago, and typical of crime-thriller soundtracks—on TV as well as the big screen—of the period.

Fever / Peggy Lee [1958] *US Chart #8*

A cover of a recording by R&B artist Little Willie John, Peggy Lee's steamy version became her signature tune.

Comin' Home Baby / Mel Torme [1962] *US Chart #36*

Smooth crooner Torme (nicknamed "The Velvet Fog") branched into more bluesy territory than usual on this finger-clicker.

Never Ever / All Saints [1997] *US Chart #4*

The UK-based girl group (comprising two Canadians and two Brits) had a worldwide hit with this self-penned classic of modern soul.

Rock Around the Clock / Bill Haley [1954] *US Chart #1*

One of the biggest selling singles of all time, the straight twelve-bar song that heralded rock'n'roll. Other blues-based hits followed for Haley, including the million-selling cover of Joe Turner's "Shake, Rattle and Roll."

The "In" Crowd / Ramsey Lewis Trio [1965] *US Chart #5*

Pianist Ramsey Lewis had a string of funky blues-based hits, with other soulful chart entries from the Trio including instrumental versions of the old spiritual "Wade In The Water," and the Beatles' "A Hard Day's Night."

Sultans of Swing / Dire Straits [1978] *US Chart #4*

The British blues-rock band's hugely successful debut single was included in the Rock and Roll Hall of Fame's list of "500 Songs that Shaped Rock and Roll."

African Waltz / Johnny Dankworth [1961] *US Chart #101*

British bandleader Dankworth had a chart entry on both sides of the Atlantic with this piece of waltz-time soul-jazz. It was an even bigger US hit for saxophone star Cannonball Adderley that same year, climbing to #41 in the pop chart.

Boogie Woogie / Tommy Dorsey [1938] *US Chart #1*

A swing era smash, the big band arrangement of Pinetop Smith's 1928 classic "Pinetop's Boogie Woogie" was Tommy Dorsey's most popular release, selling over five million copies.

The Swingin' Shepherd Blues / Moe Koffman Quartette [1957] *US Chart #23*

A catchy twelve-bar instrumental from Canadian jazz flautist Moe Koffman, a vocal version of which was a UK hit for Ella Fitzgerald in 1958.

Walk On the Wild Side / Jimmy Smith [1962] *US Chart #21*

From the movie of the same name, an instrumental *tour de force* by organ supremo Smith, preceded by a hefty statement of the anthemic theme tune, arranged by Oliver Nelson.

Mercy, Mercy, Mercy / Cannonball Adderley [1966] *US Chart #11*

A surprise chart entry for jazz saxophonist Adderley, whose soul-infused repertoire included such titles as "Work Song," "A Sack O' Woe," and "Them Dirty Blues."

Rainy Day Women # 12 & 35 / Bob Dylan [1966] *US Chart #2*

With its memorable chorus of "everybody must get stoned," one of Dylan's many songs with a twelve-bar blues structure that have featured on his albums over a fifty-year-plus career.

Green Onions / Booker T and the MGs [1962] *US Chart #3*

Straight from the soul music hit factory of Stax Records in Memphis, Hammond organist Booker T. Jones and the MGs (Memphis Group) were the house band for the label.

Mercy / Duffy [2008] *US Chart #27*

A chart-topper in nine countries worldwide, the UK soul diva's hit stands as a blues-drenched masterpiece of contemporary pop.

BIBLIOGRAPHY

Chris Albertson, Bessie: *Empress of the Blues* [Sphere Books (UK) 1975]

John Broven, *Walking To New Orleans* [Blues Unlimited (UK) 1974]

Roy Carr, *A Century of Jazz* [Hamlyn (UK) 1997]

James Lincoln Collier, *The Making of Jazz* [Macmillan (UK) 1981]

Sebastian Danchin, *Earl Hooker, Blues Master* [University Press of Mississippi (US) 2001]

Francis Davis, *The History of the Blues* [Hyperion (US) 1995]

Ahmet Ertegun, *What'd I Say: The Atlantic Story* [Orion Publishing (UK) 2001]

Mike Evans, *Ray Charles: The Birth of Soul* [Omnibus Press (UK) 2005]

Charles Farley, *Soul of the Man: Bobby "Blue" Bland* [University Press of Mississippi (US) 2011]

Ted Gioia, *The Delta Blues* [W.W. Norton (US) 2008]

Robert Gordon, *Can't Be Satisfied: the Life and Times of Muddy Waters* [Little, Brown (US) 2002]

Peter Guralnick, *Feel Like Going Home* [Penguin (UK) 1992]

W.C. Handy, *Father of the Blues: An Autobiography* [Macmillan 1941]

Patrick Humphries *Lonnie Donegan: The Birth of British Rock & Roll* [Robson Press (UK) 2012]

Deborah Landau, *Janis Joplin: Her Life And Times* [Paperback Library (US) 1971]

Andria Lisle and Mike Evans, *Waking Up in Memphis* [Sanctuary Publishing (UK) 2003]

Alan Lomax, *The Land Where the Blues Began* [Methuen (UK) 1993]

Alan Lomax, *Mister Jelly Roll* [Pantheon Books (US) 1993]

Taj Mahal / Stephen Foehr, *Taj Mahal: Autobiography of a Bluesman* [Sanctuary Publishing (UK) 2001]

Florent Mazzoleni, *Rock 'n' Roll 39-59* [Fondation Cartier (France) 2007]

James Miller, *Almost Grown* [Arrow Books (UK) 2000]

Thomas L. Morgan, William Barlow, *From Cakewalks to Concert Halls* [Elliott & Clark (US) 1992]

Charles Shaar Murray, *Boogie Man* [Canongate (UK) 2011]

Paul Oliver, *The Story of the Blues* [Penguin (UK) 1972]

Robert Palmer, *Deep Blues* [Prentice Hall (US) 2001]

Keith Richards, *Life* [Weidenfeld & Nicolson (UK) 2010]

Paul Roland [ed], *The Jazz Singers* [Hamlyn, 1999]

Nat Shapiro and Nat Hentoff, *Hear Me Talkin' To Ya* [Dover Publications (US) 1966]

Peter Silvester, *A Left Hand Like God* [Quartet Books (UK) 1988]

John Szwed, *Alan Lomax: The Man Who Recorded the World,* [Viking Adult (US) 2010]

Paul Trynka, *Portrait of the Blues* [Hamlyn (UK) 1996]

Elijah Wald, *Escaping the Delta: Robert Johnson and the Invention of the Blues* [Harper Collins (US) 2005]

Geoffrey C. Ward and Ken Burns, *Jazz: A History of America's Music* [Pimlico (UK) 2001]

Steven Watson, *The Harlem Renaissance* [Pantheon Books (US) 1995]

Isabel Wilkerson, *The Warmth of Other Suns: The Epic Story of America's Great Migration* [Random House (US) 2010]

David Williams, *First Time We Met the Blues* [Music Mentor Books (UK) 2009]

Valerie Wilmer, *Mama Said There'd Be Days Like This* [The Women's Press (UK) 1999]

Charles Wolfe and Kip Lornell *The Life and Legend of Leadbelly* [Secker & Warburg (UK) 1993]

Kurt Wolff, *Country Music: The Rough Guide* [Rough Guides (UK) 2000]

Bill Wyman, *Bill Wyman's Blues Odyssey* [Dorling Kindersley (UK) 2001]

Bill Wyman, *Rolling With the Stones* [Dorling Kindersley (UK) 2002]

Material was also consulted from the following publications and web sites: *Billboard, Cash Box, Chicago Defender, Downbeat, fRoots, Life, Melody Maker, New York Times, Record Changer, Record Research, Rolling Stone* www.bluesquotes.com, http://bg.buddyguy.com, www.jasobrecht.com, www.allmusic.com

QUOTE SOURCES

Chapter 1

Page 14: "The blues came from the man farthest down…"
W.C.Handy quoted in Nat Shapiro and Nat Hentoff, *Hear Me Talkin' To Ya* [Dover Publications (US) 1966]

Page 14: "You know there's only one blues though…"
T-Bone Walker quoted in Nat Shapiro and Nat Hentoff, *Hear Me Talkin' To Ya* [Dover Publications (US) 1966]

Page 14: "See, my blues is not as easy to play…"
Muddy Waters quoted in Peter Guralnick, *Feel Like Going Home* [Penguin (UK) 1992]

Page 14: "Maybe our forefathers…'
B.B. King speaking at Lagos University, Nigeria, 1973, quoted in Valerie Wilmer, *Mama Said There'd Be Days Like This* [The Women's Press (UK) 1999]

Page 14: "The Northern honky-tonk blues…"
Lynwood Perry quoted in Taj Mahal / Stephen Foehr, *Taj Mahal: Autobiography of a Bluesman* [Sanctuary Publishing (UK) 2001]

Page 17: " A lean loose-jointed Negro…"
W.C.Handy, *Father of the Blues:An Autobiography* [Macmillan 1941]

Page 18: "Suddenly one raised such a sound…"
Frederick Law Olmstead, *A Journey in the Seaboard Slave States* [US, 1856] quoted in Paul Oliver, *The Story of the Blues* [Penguin (UK) 1972]

Page 22: "The name of this musician was Mamie Desdoumes…"
Jelly Roll Morton, quoted in Alan Lomax *Mister Jelly Roll* [Pantheon Books (US) 1993] and *The Complete Library of Congress Recordings* [Rounder Records, 2005]

Chapter 2

Page 27: "The earliest blues singers…"
Geoffrey C. Ward and Ken Burns, *Jazz: A History of America's Music* [Pimlico (UK) 2001]

Page 31: "We're telling' you there's none finer or grander…"
OKeh Records publicity material, quoted in Paul Oliver, *The Story of the Blues* [Penguin (UK) 1972]

Page 34: "The distinctiveness of the jug…"
Samuel Charters, liner notes *The Jug Bands* [Folkways Records 1963]

Page 36: "These are… classic examples of great blues singing, powerful and haunting expressions of human feeling."
James Lincoln Collier, *The Making of Jazz* [Macmillan (UK)1981]

Page 38: "My Handy Man" (Andy Razav)

Page 38: Organ Grinder Blues (Clarence Williams)

Page 38: "Black Snake Moan" (Blind Lemmon Jefferson) [Copyright Control]

Page 38"All Around Man" (Bo Carter)

Page 38: "Shake Rattle and Roll (Charles Calhoun) [Unichappell Music Inc.]

Page 39: "Ma Rainey's Black Bottom" (Gertrude Rainey) [Universal Music Publishing Group]

Page 41: "She came in, she planted those two flat feet firmly on the floor…"
Robert Paul Smith, *Record Changer*, 1936, quoted in Chris Albertson, *Bessie: Empress of the Blues* [Sphere Books (UK) 1975]

Page 45: "You know, it has been a big thing…"
Jerry Wexler quoted in Mike Evans, *Ray Charles: The Birth of Soul* [Omnibus Press (UK) 2005]

Page 46: "There's fourteen million Negroes in our great country…"
Perry Bradford, quoted in Geoffrey C. Ward and Ken Burns, *Jazz: A History of America's Music* [Pimlico (UK) 2001]

Page 48: "… just this side of voluptuous…"
Mezz Mezzrow, quoted in Francis Davis, *The History of the Blues* [Hyperion (US) 1995]

Page 48: "Nobody Knows You When You're Down and Out" (Jimmy Cox) [B. Feldman & Co. Ltd]

Page 50: "Shave Em' Dry" (Lucille Bogan) [Munka Music, Wabash Music Co.]

Page 50: "Empty Bed Blues" (J.C. Johnson) [EMI Harmonies Ltd]

Page 51: "He came to fame towards the end of the 'classic blues' era…"
John Collis, CD notes *Leroy Carr:American Blues Legend* [Charly Records 1998]

Chapter 3

Page 57: "Right where blues songs were born…"
OKeh Records advertising copy for Ed Andrews' "Time Aint Gonna Make Me Stay," 1924

Page 59: "Blind Lemon was a medium-size…"
Victoria Spivey, *Record Research* 1966

Page 61: "almost certainly born in 1891."
Dr David Evans, CD box set notes *Screamin' and Hollerin' the Blues: The Worlds of Charley Patton* [Revenant Records 2001]

Page 62 "Cross Road Blues" (Robert Johnson) [King of Spades Music]

Page 63: "He [Robert Johnson] told me about going to the crossroads…"
David "Honeyboy" Edwards, quoted in Paul Trynka *Portrait of the Blues* [Hamlyn (UK) 1996]

Page 65: "Charley Patton's appeal to us…"
Dick Spotswood, CD box set notes *Screamin' and Hollerin' the Blues: The Worlds of Charley Patton* [Revenant Records 2001]

Page 69: "Working Man Blues" (Sleepy John Estes) [Copyright Control]

Page 69: "Oh I started out young…"
Muddy Waters quoted in Robert Gordon, *Can't Be Satisfied: the Life and Times of Muddy Waters* [Little, Brown (US) 2002]

Page 69: "You see a white face there…"
Jimmie Rogers talking to Robert Gordon

Page 69: "Robert Johnson was playing with Son House…
Honeyboy Edwards talking to Robert Gordon

Page 69: "I worked there [in Memphis] as an usher…"
John Lee Hooker quoted in Charles Shaar Murray, *Boogie Man* [Canongate (UK) 2011]

Page 69: "…there was a lot of guitar playing in the neighborhood"
Taj Mahal quoted in Taj Mahal / Stephen Foehr, *Taj Mahal: Autobiography of a Bluesman* [Sanctuary Publishing (UK) 2001]

Page 70: "Robert was tall, brown-skin…"
David "Honeyboy" Edwards talking to Pete Welding, quoted in Paul Oliver, *The Story of the Blues* [Penguin (UK) 1972]

Page 73: "I had to face that here were the people…"
Alan Lomax quoted in John Szwed, *Alan Lomax: The Man Who Recorded the World*, [Viking Adult (US) 2010]

Page 76: "Robert Johnson is little, very little…"
Original liner notes, *Robert Johnson: King of the Delta Blues Singers*

Page 81: "one of the great country blues singers…."
Wolfgang Saxon, *New York Times* [February 1, 1982]

Page 83: "There was no leader, there was no one person…"
Isabel Wilkerson, *The Warmth of Other Suns: The Epic Story of America's Great Migration* [Random House (US) 2010]

Page 85: "I were in a place called Marigold Mississippi…"
Big Bill Broonzy quoted in Alan Lomax, *The Land Where the Blues Began* [Methuen (UK) 1993]

Page 86: "Blind Willie Johnson had great dexterity…"
Ry Cooder quoted in Jas Obrecht Music Archive, 2011 [www.jasobrecht.com]

Page 87: "I hate to think of not having a Lightnin' Hopkins…"
B.B. King speaking in *When Lightnin' Strikes* [Fast Cut Films, 2011]

Page 90: "By the late 1940s…."
Francis Davis, *The History of the Blues* [Hyperion (US) 1995]

Chapter 4

Page 96: "The blues are played and sung…"
Whitney Balliett, liner notes *Joe Turner: The Boss of the Blues* [Atlantic Records, 1956]

Page 97: "They didn't have no microphones…"
Joe Turner, quoted in Billy Vera liner notes *The Very Best of Big Joe Turner* [Rhino Entertainment Company, 1998]

Page 102: "Singing the blues is a separate art"
Gene Lees, CD liner notes *Miss Peggy Lee Sings the Blues* [Musicmasters, 1988]

Page 106: "As for Wynonie Harris…"
Florent Mazzoleni (translated from French by Charles Penwarden), *Rock 'n' Roll 39-59* [Fondation Cartier (France) 2007]

Page 107: "Now the Sunset…"
Mary Lou Williams quoted in Nat Shapiro and Nat Hentoff, *Hear Me Talkin' To Ya* [Dover Publications (US) 1966]

Page 107: "Piney Brown ran the Sunset…"
Jo Jones quoted in Nat Shapiro and Nat Hentoff, *Hear Me Talkin' To Ya* [Dover Publications (US) 1966]

Page 107: "Well in the old days…"
Al Reed quoted in John Broven *Walking To New Orleans* [Blues Unlimited (UK) 1974]

Page 109: "Ida Cox—since I was a kid…"
T-Bone Walker, *Record Changer* magazine [October, 1947]

Page 112: "The early boogie-woogie pianists…"
Peter Silvester, *A Left Hand Like God* [Quartet Books (UK) 1988]

Page 116: "I just naturally started to play music…"
T-Bone Walker, *Record Changer* magazine [October, 1947]

Page 118: "There were parallels between the blues…"
Paul Oliver, *The Story of the Blues* [Penguin (UK) 1972]

Chapter 5

Page 125: "Musical tastes had changed…
Pete Welding, CD liner notes *Roy Brown: The Complete Imperial Recordings* [Capitol Records, 1995]

Page 126: "I was a real fan of Louis Jordan…"
Ray Charles, BBC *Omnibus* 1986, quoted in Mike Evans, *Ray Charles: The Birth of Soul* [Omnibus Press (UK) 2005]

Page 128: "We were always looking for guitar players who could play the blues…"
Ahmet Ertegun, *What'd I Say: The Atlantic Story* [Orion Publishing (UK) 2001]

Page 129: "The music we play…"
John Lee Hooker, quoted in Paul Trynka *Portrait of the Blues* [Hamlyn (UK) 1996]

Page 136: "A white Texan who could play the blues…"
Kurt Wolff, *Country Music: The Rough Guide* [Rough Guides (UK) 2000]

Page 138: "John Lee Hooker… was the biggest name in Detroit blues…"
Paul Oliver, *The Story of the Blues* [Penguin (UK) 1972]

Page 142: "I wanted to get out of Mississippi…"
Muddy Waters, quoted in Peter Guralnick, *Feel Like Going Home* [Penguin (UK) 1992]

Page 143: "It's real. Muddy's real…"
Big Bill Broonzy quoted in liner notes *The Best of Muddy Waters* [Chess Records, 1958]

Page 150: "The money from playing in jukes…"
Alan Lomax, *The Land Where the Blues Began* [Methuen (UK) 1993]

Page 153: "When you aint got no money…"
Quoted at http://bg.buddyguy.com/gone-but-not-forgotten-howlin-wolf/

Page 157: "We herewith submit…"
The New Yorker, 1941

Page 157: "It Should've Been Me" (Memphis Curtis) [Warner/Chappell Music, Inc.]

Page 157: "The first clothes that I got attached to..." Bobby Bland talking to Robert Gordon

Page 157: Dick Sherman quoted in Sebastian Danchin, *Earl Hooker, Blues Master* [University Press of Mississippi (US) 2001]

P157: "No 1950s blues guitarist..." Bill Dahl writing at www.allmusic.com

Page 157: "The clothes I remember..." Rufus Thomas quoted in Charles Farley, *Soul of the Man: Bobby "Blue" Bland* [University Press of Mississippi (US) 2011]

Page 158: "Smiley Lewis was..." Doctor John ("Mac" Rebennack), quoted in John Broven *Walking To New Orleans* [Blues Unlimited (UK) 1974]

Chapter 6
Page 168: "High Water Everywhere" (Charley Patton) [EMI Music Publishing]

Page 168: "Trouble" (Josh White)

Page 168: "The Bourgeois Blues" (H. Ledbetter) [T.R.O. Inc]

Page 168: "Vietnam Blues" (J.B. Lenoir) [BMG Platinum Songs obo ARC Music]

Page 168: "Down In Mississippi" (J.B. Lenoir) [BMG Platinum Songs obo ARC Music]

Page 169: "signal event in the history of the music..." Ted Gioia, *The Delta Blues* [W.W. Norton (US) 2008]

Page 171: "The blues is like this.." Lead Belly on radio WNYC, quoted in Charles Wolfe and Kip Lornell *The Life and Legend of Leadbelly* [Secker & Warburg (UK) 1993]

Page 176: "Lonnie used to do a Lead Belly blues..." Chris Barber, quoted in Patrick Humphries *Lonnie Donegan: The Birth of British Rock & Roll* [Robson Press (UK) 2012]

Page 184: "Soul is when you take a song..." Ray Charles quoted in *Life* magazine [July 1966]

Page 186: "The first time I saw him..." Chris Barber, quoted in *fRoots* magazine [UK, August/September 2005]

Chapter 7
Page 195: "We first met Brian Jones....." Keith Richards, *Life* [Weidenfeld & Nicolson (UK) 2010]

Page 199: "Just when it looked like maybe the blues were gone..." Tom Piazza, CD notes *Martin Scorsese Presents The Blues* [Hip-O Records 2003]

Page 201: "I think those shows..." Paul Jones quoted in Rob Bowman, liner notes to *The American Folk Blues Festival 1962-1966 Volume 1* (DVD) [Reelin' In The Years Productions, 2003]

Page 210: "....It was at this time that Brian..." Bill Wyman, *Rolling With the Stones* [Dorling Kindersley (UK) 2002]

Page 210: "I don't even think I'd heard of Robert Johnson..." Eric Clapton quoted in James Miller, *Almost Grown* [Arrow Books (UK) 2000] from Peter Guralnick, *Musician* magazine [February 1990]

Page 210: "And there were the seminal sounds..." Keith Richards, *Life* [Weidenfeld & Nicolson (UK) 2010]

Page 210: "They were playing..." Janis Joplin quoted in Deborah Landau, *Janis Joplin: Her Life And Times* [Paperback Library (US) 1971]

Page 210: "I can imagine how Columbus felt..." B.B. King talking to Robert Gordon

Page 210: "They call it rhythm and blues..." Jimmy Witherspoon talking to Max Jones, *Melody Maker* [September 15, 1964]

Chapter 8
Page 221: "If you do music long enough..." Taj Mahal quoted in Taj Mahal and Stephen Foehr *Taj Mahal: Autobiography of a Bluesman* [Sanctuary Publishing (UK) 2001]

Page 228: "My songs, they have just the one chord...." Junior Kimbrough, quoted in Paul Trynka *Portrait of the Blues* [Hamlyn (UK) 1996]

Page 230: "In 1976, we had just done this run at this one club in Eugene.." Robert Cray talking to Pat Pemberton, *Rolling Stone* [October 2013]

Page 231: "All I knew was I wanted to play the piano..." Ray Charles talking to Robert Gordon

Page 231: "I grew up singing gospel songs..." B.B. King talking to Robert Gordon

Page 231: "I caught a ride to Memphis..." Honeyboy Edwards talking to Robert Gordon

Page 231: "We didn't have electricity outside Memphis..." Koko Taylor talking to Robert Gordon

Page 231: "The blues is true'..." Bobby Bland talking to Robert Gordon

Page 236: "It's not too far a stretch of the imagination..." Rev. Keith A. Gordon, reviewing Chris Thomas King's *21st Century Blues...From da'Hood* at http://www.allmusic.com

PHOTO CREDITS

Every effort has been made to trace the copyright holders of the artworks in this book. In order for any errors or omissions to be corrected in future editions, please contact Elephant Book Company.

Key: t = top; b = bottom; l = left; r = right; c = center

Alamy/Ace Stock Ltd: 158r, 202l; /Alamy Celebrity: 209tr, 218br, 233l, 235bl, 241; /CTK: 218bl; /David Lyons: 230; /Emma Stoner: 199tr; /Everett Collection Historical: 80, 88, 170l, 175l, 178l, 180, 183tl; /Eyebrowz: 189r, 221tr; /Hanan Isachar: 240t; /Heritage Image Partnership Ltd: 131; /i4images: 237; /INTERFOTO: 206, 212, 221tl; /Jeff Morgan: 114l, 192br, 209br, 199l; /Jon Arnold Images Ltd: 54tl; /MARKA: 183tr; /Martin Bond: 120b; /Mixpix: 167l; /Pictorial Press Ltd: 17bl, 20tl, 20tr, 24br, 27bl, 31l, 37bl, 39l, 40r, 42l, 45c, 50, 58l, 74l, 74r, 77r, 79tr, 81, 86l, 91l, 92tl, 92tr, 101l, 101br, 104l, 105, 113, 119tl, 125r, 127, 133tl, 133tr, 133bl, 135br, 137, 139, 140l, 147l, 152, 158l, 159, 160, 162l, 173, 181bl, 181tl, 185, 187l, 188, 190r, 191, 192bl, 195br, 195bl, 203b, 203tr, 207l, 109bl, 212, 216, 217, 235br; /Rodolfo Sassano: 242l; /The Art Archive: 178r; /The Protected Art Archive: 40l; /Tracksimages.com: 199br, 209tl; /White House Photo: 218t, 243; /ZUMA Press, Inc.: 149b, 238l

Alligator Records: 214r

Alan Lomax/Association for Cultural Equity: 73br, 227tl

Beinecke Rare Book and Manuscript Library, Yale University: 67b

Bridgeman Art Library/Private Collection, photo by Christies Images: 204

Chicago Defender: 45r

Corbis/Bettmann Archive: 36, 49; /Michael Ochs Archives: 141r; /Retna Ltd./Erika Goldring: 227tc

David Crosby: 37r, 37tl

David M. Rubenstein Rare Book & Manuscript Library, Duke University: 23, 27br, 84bl

Dick Waterman Music Photography: 140r, 145, 183br, 196, 224l, 224r, 229

Elephant Book Company Ltd./David Julian Leonard: 2, 52, 64, 215

Essential Insanities Photography/ Dennis H. Brigham: 63b

Getty Images/Archive Photos/P.L. Sperr: 28; /David Redfern: 240bl; /Ebet Roberts: 227tr; /Hulton Archive: 19tl, 24inset, 57l, 108; /Jon Sievert: 240br; /LIFE Images Collection/Marvin Lichtner: 203tl; /Michael Ochs Archives: 7, 7 inset, 33b, 53, 60l, 79br, 89l, 91tr, 120tl, 155r, 156, 222r; /Michael Putland: 202r; /Moviepix: 211; /Redferns: 33tr, 58r, 66, 75, 99l, 111r, 114r, 154, 221b; /Redferns/Nigel Osbourne: jacket inset guitar; /Robert Knight Archive: 225l; /The LIFE Picture Collection/William Vandivert: 95tl, 95bl; /Wireimage/Barry Brecheisen: 242tr

Harry Smith Archives/John Palmer: 169l

Courtesy of the Hogan Jazz Archive/Tulane University: 27tl

Hohner Archives: 79l

Jazz Age Editions/Dennis Loren: 95r

Candise Kola: 227br

Courtesy Joe Lauro Collection / Historic Music: 24 inset (x2), 29br, 33tl, 41r, 54 inset, 60r, 63tl, 65r, 68r, 70r, 76r, 77l, 78, 92 inset, 117, 120 inset, 164 inset (x3)

Library of Congress Historic Newspapers Collection: 24tl, 31r; Library of Congress Performing Arts Encyclopedia: 47; Library of Congress Prints and Photographs Division: 13br, 15r, 57r; /Civil War Photographs: 15l, 13tl, 10br; /Farm Security Administration/Office of War Information: 142, 54bl, 83, 84tr, 84br, 149tl, 149tr; /Lomax Collection: 67t, 73tr, 170r, 73l; / Performing Arts Posters: 21; /Detroit Publishing Co.: 19b, 92bl; /National Photo Company Collection: 54br; /Carl Van Vechten Collection: 43l; / William P Gottlieb Collection: 128, 96, 98l, 103, 111l, 120tr

Memphis Public Library and Information Center: 89r

NASA/JPL: 86r

Private Collection: 17r, 20bl, 24tr, 27tr, 30, 45l, 51r, 54 inset, 54tr, 54 inset, 59r, 61, 68l, 71l, 75 inset, 87r, 91br, 92tr, 98r, 101tr, 104r, 106, 115, 118bl, 118r, 123, 124, 126, 130l, 130r, 135tl, 135tr, 144, 147br, 147tr, 161l, 161r, 161 inset, 162r, 163, 167br, 167tr, 175r, 177, 179r, 183bc, 183bl, 186r, 187r, 190l, 192tl, 192 inset (x2), 197r, 198l, 198r, 201tr, 205r, 207r, 218 inset (x3), 222l, 233r, 235t

Shutterstock: jacket background, jacket line illustrations 38r, 70l

Smithsonian Institution Collections/National Museum of American History, Behring Center: 17tl, 172; /Sam DeVincent Collection of Illustrated American Sheet Music: 42r, 43r; / Ralph Rinzler Folklife Archives and Collections: 133br, 164bl, 167tr, 169bl, 181r

Special Collections, University of Houston Libraries: 10tl

State Archives of Florida/Florida Memory: 20bc, 35; /Peggy A Bulger: 13tr; /Woodward: 84tl

Bill Steber: 151

Sylvia Pitcher Photo Library/Sylvia Pitcher: 195t, 201br, 201l, 238r; /Mottram: 225r; The Weston Collection: 10bl, 52, 92 inset, 97, 120 inset (x2), 125l, 129r, 141l, 153r, 155l, 164tl, 164br, 186c, 186l

Topfoto/Granger Collection NY: 24bl

University of Memphis Library: 164tr

UTSA General Photograph collection/Austin Seymour Masterson: 71r

Courtesy of Wellesley College Library, Special Collections, Elbert Collection: 10tr

Wilson Special Collections Library, University of North Carolina at Chapel Hill: 18, 19tr; Courtesy of the William R. Ferris Collection (20367), Southern Folklife Collection, The Wilson Library, University of North Carolina at Chapel Hill: 227bl

Courtesy of the University of Wisconsin—Madison Archives: 13bl

Yorkspace: 20br

INDEX

MIKE EVANS
Author
Rhythm and blues musician Mike Evans began writing about popular music in the 1970s, with a weekly R&B show on local radio in Liverpool. As a freelance writer, his work appeared in a variety of publications, including the UK's leading jazz and rock paper *Melody Maker*. As author his books have included the best-selling *Elvis: A Celebration, Waking Up in New York City*, the 2005 biography *Ray Charles: The Birth of Soul, The Rock 'n' Roll Age* (2007), and *Woodstock: Three Days That Rocked the World* in 2009. He now lives and works in France.

ROBERT GORDON
Consulting Editor
Grammy Award winning writer and filmmaker Robert Gordon has focused on the American south—its music, art, and politics—to create an insider's portrait of his home. His books include the award-winning biography, *Can't Be Satisfied, The Life and Times of Muddy Waters, It Came From Memphis*, and the acclaimed *Respect Yourself: Stax Records and the Soul Explosion*. He has also directed documentaries about Muddy Waters and Stax, and wrote one of Martin Scorsese's episodes for *The Blues*. His writing has appeared in *Rolling Stone, The New York Times, Mojo*, and *The Guardian*. He lives in Memphis, Tennessee.

MARSHALL CHESS
Foreword
The son and nephew of Leonard and Phil Chess, founders of the seminal Chicago rhythm and blues label Chess Records, Marshall Chess experienced the 1950s blues and R&B scene at first hand. After a decade and a half with the label, in 1970 he was hired as founding president of Rolling Stones Records. He went on to produce records for various labels, and began heading Arc Music, a major independent music publisher, in 1992, where he stayed until 2008. He also has hosted the *Chess Records Hour*, featuring the history and music of the legendary label, on satellite radio.

ACKNOWLEDGMENTS

The author and publisher would like to thank the following people for their assistance in producing this book:

Lamar Sorrento, Steve Selvidge, The Highway 61 Blues Museum, Sylvia Pitcher, Dick Waterman, Mark Williams at FMG, Mick Gold.

Many thanks to David Leonard for his assistance with memorabilia photography and to Joe Lauro for access to his wonderful collection of 78s.